The British Party System

The history of British political parties tells of change and continuity. But, how and why?

This textbook continues to provide the best introduction currently available on the British political party system, explaining the history, structure, actors and policies of both the main political parties and the minor parties.

Substantially revised and updated, this fourth edition contains new material on:

- the political party system in post-devolution Scotland and Wales
- the media and political parties
- the emergence of minor parties onto the British political landscape
- the replacement of party ideology with political pragmatism

Stephen Ingle argues that in order to meet formidable national and international challenges the British party system is once more in need of fundamental change, to a less confrontational style of politics. *The British Party System* is the ideal book for students of British politics wanting a topical and accessible text on political parties in the UK.

Stephen Ingle was Head of Politics at the University of Stirling during 1991-2002 having previously been Head of Politics at the University of Hull. He was later awarded an Emeritus Professorship in 2006.

The British Party System
An introduction

Stephen Ingle

Taylor & Francis Group

LONDON AND NEW YORK

First edition published by Basil Blackwell, 1987
Second edition, Basil Blackwell, 1989
Third edition, Pinter, 2000

Fourth edition published 2008
by Routledge
2 Park Square, Milton Park, Abingdon, Oxon OX14 4RN

Simultaneously published in the USA and Canada
by Routledge
270 Madison Avenue, New York, NY 10016

Routledge is an imprint of the Taylor & Francis Group, *an informa business*

© 2008 Stephen Ingle

Typeset in Times New Roman by Saxon Graphics Ltd, Derby
Printed and bound in Great Britain by Antony Rowe Ltd,
Chippenham, Wiltshire

British Library Cataloguing in Publication Data
A catalogue record for this book is available from the
British Library

Library of Congress Cataloging in Publication Data
Ingle, Stephen.
The British party system : an introduction / Stephen Ingle. -- 4th ed.
p. cm.
Includes bibliographical references and index.
ISBN-13: 978-0-415-41234-6 (hardback: alk. paper)
ISBN-10: 0-415-41234-X (hardback: alk. paper)
ISBN-13: 978-0-415-41235-3 (pbk.: alk. paper)
ISBN-10: 0-415-41235-8 (pbk.: alk. paper)
[etc.]
1. Political parties--Great Britain--History. I. Title.
JN1117.I54 2008
324.241--dc22
2007033546

ISBN 10: 0-415-41234-X (hbk)   ISBN 13: 978-0-415-41234-6 (hbk)
ISBN 10: 0-415-41235-8 (pbk)   ISBN 13: 978-0-415-41235-3 (pbk)
ISBN 10: 0-203-93122-X (ebk)   ISBN 13: 978-0-203-93122-6 (ebk)

For Margaret

Contents

Acknowlededgements

It has been my considerable pleasure and good fortune to have researched and written up this book in the Department of Politics at the University of Stirling, where several of my colleagues have discussed its main themes with me over a period of time. It is very helpful to work in such an atmosphere and to have enjoyed the support of Sally Armstrong-Payne in the departmental office in handling the technical and logistic problems that have occurred now and again. I should also like to express my gratitude to Natalja Mortensen of Routledge who has been very supportive during the various stages of the preparation of the manuscript. Whenever I had a query and sent off an email, I always got a reply almost immediately. That has not always been my experience. Tracy Morgan, too, was very helpful at the proof reading stage.

Reading proofs is a misery for me and it is a great relief to call upon my very good friend John Stewart, who has the eye of an eagle, to help me with this crucial task. Finally and most importantly, I have to thank my wife who, as always, had a lot to put up with during the long process of finally producing this book. Or so she tells me. And of course the opportunity costs of undertaking a project like this are substantial and they fall disproportionately on one's partner.

I am truly grateful to all these people but the responsibility for the subject matter and for the particular case that is argued here is, of course, entirely my own.

Stephen Ingle
Stirling, January 2008.

1 Parties and the party system in Britain

'We MUST have a bit of a fight, but I don't much care about going on long,' said Tweedledum. 'What's the time now?' Tweedledee looked at his watch and said 'Half-past four.' 'Let's fight till six, and then have some dinner,' said Tweedledee.

Lewis Carroll, *Through the Looking Glass*, 1872

A schoolboy was taken to the National Gallery in London and, puzzled by a Picasso canvas, asked his father, 'What's this supposed to be?' His father replied, 'Well, it's supposed to be a violin and a fruit dish.' The boy looked again, and then changed his position, examining the picture closely. 'Well, why *isn't* it then?' How should his father have addressed such an important question? With the impact of photography on artistic representation? With the advent of modernism? With the abandonment of perspective? With the new interest among artists in colour and shape signalled by Kandinsky's famous 1911 text *Concerning the Spiritual in Art*? So much in the modern world has changed that it is difficult to know what particular images, concepts or even institutions represent. And yet at the same time there are continuities, traditions, linking Picasso with Fra Angelico, for example. Change and continuity is as much a part of politics as of any other area of human activity. Things are seldom just what they seem – perhaps they never were – and political parties today are certainly not what our Edwardian, Victorian or Georgian forebears would have expected them to be.

In this study we shall try to take as little for granted as we can. We shall explore in detail how political parties in Britain have evolved, what they represent today and how they might be expected to change in the future. We will need to know about the political spaces they inhabit and we will also need to have some understanding of the spaces they don't inhabit. So let us begin with a warning: defining political parties generally – explaining what they are 'supposed to be' as our schoolboy might put it – or even discovering where and when they originated in Britain is no easy task.

In his book *Political Parties and Party Systems* Alan Ware suggests that parties are as easy to recognise but as difficult to define as elephants.[1] This simile seems to suggest either some unhappy experience with large mammals or a rather strange understanding of politics: most of us would surely feel far happier identifying *and* defining elephants than we would political parties. At least we know what elephants are 'supposed to be'! Our first task then, is to get a firm understanding of the nature of the beast that is the subject of this study – British political parties not elephants – and then we might attempt a formal definition.

Parties and how to recognise them

Ware begins his analysis of political parties by pointing out that although they appear to be an essential part of the modern democratic framework, parties are not a feature of all polities. The political philosopher Rousseau saw them not as an emblem of democracy at all but a badge of failed democracy; they represented factions rather than the will of all the people. Some non-democratic political systems are governed by monarchical or dynastic families, some by military or social elites, some by authoritarian or even tyrannical leaders. Often these regimes sustain themselves through the structure of political parties: Stalin's personal rule was exercised through the Soviet Communist Party, which was entirely subservient to him. Saddam Hussein exercised power through the Ba'athist Party. On the other hand, in the British Isles, the self-governing Isle of Man, which possesses one of the oldest democratic parliaments in the world, has no political parties. In a number of US states, laws were introduced at the beginning of the twentieth century banning parties from contesting local elections and when Poland abolished political parties altogether in the late 1920s, the socialist playwright and Fabian polemicist Bernard Shaw welcomed the move: it would set the Polish people truly free.[2] Although we cannot equate the existence of parties with democracy, we shall be dealing here with parties in a democracy, and most democrats would argue that parties bring clear advantages to the running of the democratic system because they fulfil certain essential functions.

Enabling popular involvement in government

Most democratic parties seek to control the executive function of government, what governments do, and in democracies they organise themselves to win elections and form administrations (or at least participate in their formation) in order to control the machinery of government. It is true that some parties seek to destroy and not control the machinery of government. This was the traditional aim of the various Western European communist parties for example,[3] and today in the United Kingdom the Scottish National Party (SNP) and arguably Plaid Cymru (Plaid) seek power in order to dismember, not to run the British state. Sinn Fein has contested British elections while refusing to recognise the legitimacy of Westminster. Its elected representatives do not take their seats in what they regard as an illegitimate institution. Some parties seek not power itself but influence over those who wield power. In the 1997 UK general election the newly formed Referendum Party sought almost exclusively to put pressure on the government-to-be to hold a referendum on the issue of British participation in a single European currency.

Some parties do not seek even to influence but simply to make a statement: the Official Monster Raving Loony Party contested British elections for over twenty years with no intention of forming or influencing a government; so too the Mcgillicuddy Serious Party in New Zealand. In non-democracies, by contrast, either ruling parties do not hold elections at all or they manipulate electoral processes so that the outcome is not really in doubt. Some socialists, including Karl Marx, believed that so-called bourgeois parties stood in the way of real democracy. In a classless society they would simply be unnecessary, hence Bernard Shaw's enthusiasm for the abolition of parties in Poland. Nevertheless all parties claim to seek the involvement of the governed in the processes of their government – they claim to represent the interests of the governed – and this is especially important in a democratic polity.

Emphasising legitimacy

Most parties, we have said, seek power, or at least influence over the holders of power, and in democracies they do so through the electoral process. Most (not all) accept, or at least claim to accept, the legitimacy of that process whatever its outcome. Some may have good grounds to question the legitimacy of the outcome but not the process. (We have already noted that Sinn Fein contests UK elections.) In some countries the United Nations will provide teams of observers to ensure the fairness of elections, so that the outcome is seen to be legitimate. The traditional Irish electoral advice – vote early and vote often – suggests that electoral outcomes even in the British Isles may not always have been completely legitimate. With the advent of postal voting in Britain, an investigating judge declared that irregularities in two Birmingham wards in the local elections of 2004 would have shamed a banana republic.[4] (The government subsequently sought to address these problems by the Electoral Administration Act of 2006.) The Liberal Democrat party has often complained bitterly about the distorting nature of the British first-past-the-post electoral system, which has consistently caused them and their predecessors to be grossly under-represented in the House of Commons. The Westminster electoral system is more generally unfair: it gives more value to some votes than others. In marginal constituencies a handful of voters may be decisive; in many safe seats hundreds, even thousands of voters could participate in a lifetime of elections without ever being able to influence the outcome. These votes are palpably unequal.

Promoting ideology

Ideology is both a crucial and a slippery word. Marx used it pejoratively as representing a kind of distortion of reality, a smokescreen for promoting selfish class interests, though today it is used more neutrally. Ware speaks of parties representing 'organised opinion' and goes on to suggest that it is the range of that opinion which distinguishes even small parties from pressure groups.[5] Heywood talks about parties 'formulating goals', emphasising the dynamics of the relationship between party policy and those they represent.[6] This organised opinion is what is usually understood by the word ideology. We could say it was a party's window on the world. Ware points out, though, that the larger the party the wider the range of opinion it is likely to embrace, and that the need to win the votes of the non-committed has tended to make all major parties to some extent what Kirchheimer called 'catch-all' parties:[7] parties which abandon or minimise ideological commitment in order to gain wide enough support to win elections.[8] There are parties whose primary identification is with a social class or group rather than with an ideology, the former Country (now National) party in Australia for example. The change of name symbolised recognition that to maximise its support, the party had to represent an ideology rather than simply a sectional interest. Class or group-based and even catch-all parties tend to fight elections on the basis of ideology, even if it is mostly symbolic, and that ideology will encourage voters to expect rewards if the party gains power. Some parties may seek to break the mould of traditional ideological confrontation but only to replace it with their own mould. The British Liberal/ Social Democrat (SDP) Alliance of the 1980s sought to bring together disillusioned activists and voters from the left and right of centre so as to 'break the mould' of British party politics; but only to recast it in a more suitable shape.

Leading parties and playing the game

The role of its leader is crucial to the success of any political party and the relationship between leader, party and public is fundamental to the party's success. The powers of leaders vary greatly and the personality of the leader has usually been a key determinant in that relationship. Since the advent of mass democracy charisma, the ability to project a favourable personal image to the public has been seen as a crucial attribute of a leader. In these days of mass communications, leaders are required to personify the values of their party. Now leaders cannot survive for long, whatever their personal qualities, if they are deemed to be uncharismatic, as the fate of Conservative leaders such as William Hague and Ian Duncan Smith ('The Quiet Man') testifies. Conversely the renaissance of the Scottish National party (SNP) at the time of the Holyrood elections of 2007 owed much to the public popularity – charisma – of its leader Alex Salmond.

Parties seek to involve people and groups in the quest for political power legitimately through the electoral process and they claim to represent an organised opinion – an ideology – and often a social or sectional interest too. British parties are committed to the 'rules of the game'. When a party contests an election it accepts that it might lose, if not this time then perhaps next time. Thus it accepts the right of its opponent to govern and as a consequence, even if it wins it will agree to be bound or at least constrained by the 'rules of the game' and not simply seek to attain its goals come what may. Hence an important characteristic of British parties is the fact that they have been prepared, like Tweedledum and Tweedledee, to stop fighting 'at dinner time' whoever is winning, rather than to fight on to the death. In Britain even determined parliamentary socialists believed in the right of their Conservative opponents to govern.

Defining parties

In the newly established United States of America, Madison was not well disposed to parties, seeing them, as did Rousseau, as factions 'actuated by some common impulse of passion, or of interest, adverse to the rights of other citizens, or to the permanent and aggregate interests of the community'.[9] It is salutary to remember that party interests may not equate with the common interest. Downs sees parties as 'teams' (coalitions whose members agree on a spectrum of policies),[10] seeking to 'control the government apparatus by gaining office in a duly constitutional election'.[11] Maor too believes that the attempt to influence the public as well as the policy-makers is a defining characteristic of parties.[12] Ware defines a party as 'an institution that (a) seeks influence in a state, often by attempting to occupy positions in government, and (b) usually consists of more than a single interest in society and to some degree attempts to "aggregate interests"'.[13] Ball insists on more: a degree of permanence, a commitment to fighting elections and gaining influence on the legislature, a commitment to gaining executive power (or to influencing those who have done so) through strength in the legislature.[14] Heywood's definition of parties is even more ambitious.[15] In a section entitled 'Types of Party' he distinguishes between cadre (elitist) and mass parties, representative and integrative parties, constitutional and revolutionary parties and finally left-wing and right-wing parties. While this analysis allows important characteristics to emerge, it is misleading to see it as a typology. These characteristics are really ends of several spectra, and most parties will incorporate varying degrees of, for example, cadre and mass party characteristics, even constitutional and revolutionary characteristics. Moreover there is nothing to prevent a party from being, for example, representative, constitutional and left wing. So these characteristics are descriptive not definitional.

Although each of these definitions adds something to our understanding of what political parties are, none captures the compelling simplicity of Burke's classical, encompassing definition: 'A party is a body of men united for promoting by their joint endeavours the national interest upon some particular principle in which they are all agreed'.[16] For Burke, unlike Madison, there is no contradiction between the interests of the party and the state. Yet even Burke does not achieve the economy of Epstein's disingenuous but realistic definition: 'Almost everything that is called a party in any Western democratic nation can be so regarded'.[17] Perhaps he is right, but then, what kinds of groups would be likely to call themselves parties? A working definition culled from the above might be as follows. Parties are principally *groups of people organised to seek to wield or influence political power through agreed constitutional means in the name of some organised opinion or ideology which binds them together and which distinguishes them from other groups*. Organised opinion may represent, for example, religious, ethnic, geographical, ideological or economic opinion, or more likely some combination of these. Parties may seek to wield that influence directly through control of policy but they may also seek to wield influence indirectly through electoral pressure on those who do control policy. Significantly, to be effective in a democracy, parties will need to demonstrate a synergy between their particular ideology and the national interest.

Parties in Britain

Bearing our description and definition in mind, our most likely starting point for an historical account of parties will be the time when political disputes began to be settled by recourse not to violence but to constitutional means; a time when a commitment to the principle that conflict should be confined within mutually accepted rules became common enough to be relied upon (i.e. legitimate). A precondition of such a commitment is the possibility of victory for competing groups either individually or in combination, and on a reasonably regular basis; an expectation somewhat optimistically represented by the well-known 'swing of the pendulum' theory, usually thought of as having been devised in the 1950s but in fact of much older provenance.[18] Because the credentials of a genuine party system tend to be judged largely by the absence of overt violence and intimidation it is taken for granted that such systems will operate optimally in a constitutional framework, best of all in a constitutional democracy. But let us be clear; the essential function of political parties is not to *avoid* conflict but to *canalise* it into constitutional waters.

Party origins

Given what was said above, it seems reasonable to accept the 'Whig interpretation' of history and begin our story of parties at the time of the constitutional settlement of 1688–89.[19] Certainly the two-party myth begins with the Whigs and the Tories of these days, but Samuel Johnson, who ought to have known, insisted that the first Whig was the Devil himself. Going back to the Fall of the Angels for the origins of parties though could be considered excessive. Indications of nascent political parties however, have been discerned as early as the fourteenth century, in the struggle between the king and his supporters – the 'court party'- on the one hand, and the baronial opposition on the other. More specifically, when they were out of power, the Lancastrians sought consistently to limit monarchical power during the period, and even when the Lancastrian Henry IV occupied the throne he felt obliged to institutionalise the influence of the Council.[20] But the ferocity of the Wars of the Roses gave the lie to the notion that anything resembling political parties had emerged. When writing about the seventeenth century, historians commonly refer to the existence of parties. In the great debate in the House of Commons on 8 February 1641, for example, on the continuance of the episcopacy, Gardiner speaks of two parties standing opposed to each other 'not merely on some incidental question, but on a great principle of action which constituted a permanent bond between those who took one side or the other'.[21] Similarly in 1680 the division over the extent of the legitimate powers of the crown was essentially a division between parties, and the bloodless Revolution of 1688 resulted in the permanent decline in the powers of the crown and its supporters (the Tories) and in the triumph of those who sought to restrict royal power (the Whigs). Now parties would contest power *within parliament*, and already the seventeenth century 'had given them a myth and a martyrology and the name of two gangs of ruffians, Whig and Tory'.[22] As David Hume wrote: 'Factions were indeed extremely animated against each other. The very names, by which each party denominated its antagonist (Whig and Tory), disclose the virulence and rancour which prevailed'.[23]

By the end of the seventeenth century, Namier's well-aired misgivings notwithstanding,[24] two major parties had emerged. They did not operate in a structured party system, however, and there was no general recognition of the benefits to be gained by two parties competing for power: simply the Tories desired to dominate the Whigs and the Whigs the Tories. David Judge observed that the decisive development that made party organisation feasible in Britain was 'the permanency of parliament as an institution': he called parliament the incubator of modern British parties.[25] When the Westminster parliament began to meet annually, executive power – the ability to run the country – became a realistic goal for those parties, roughly organised around aristocratic figures and based upon an ideology of sorts in which religion played the largest part.[26] These parties were much more like the modern ones than were the Lancastrian or Elizabethan groups referred to earlier so we shall begin our story here. Nevertheless at the Convention Parliament of 1689–90, when the national unity that had ousted the House of Stuart became fractured by these emergent parties – to the consternation of many – they took on what Lowther called the 'buried names' of Whig and Tory.[27] So the 'new' party dispensation was seen by some as not new at all but an unwelcome reversion to type. But then, nothing in history ever happens for the first time.

Eighteenth-century parties: parliamentary factions

Throughout the eighteenth century the great parliamentary protagonists tended to be powerful aristocratic families and their political dependants, and though they called themselves parties they possessed neither programmes nor ideologies, nor organisational structures beyond the hierarchical ties of patron and client. William III repaid his debts to the Whigs by preferring them in his governments, and this, as Hill says, only exacerbated party rancour. Basing his classification on important votes, Hill goes on to identify 151 members who could be called Tories and 174 whom he classifies as Whigs. There were, additionally, some 200 members, many new to the House, who were uncommitted, though as time passed and 'party strife rendered independence more difficult', they gravitated towards one or the other party.[28] These continuous clashes, Hill concluded, began to build a sense of identity among protagonists.[29] Nevertheless these protagonists were not easy to dragoon. Elections, especially for county seats, were notoriously expensive during the eighteenth and nineteenth centuries. When Wilberforce stood in Yorkshire in 1784, for example, he and his running mate had to put together £18,000, a very substantial sum at that time. Not surprisingly only about 15 per cent of county seats were contested. Borough elections, too, were expensive. Voters in Hull were awarded a token for the promise of their vote, which they would exchange for substantial amounts of ale. For those who could afford it, membership of the House was a sign of social eminence and members were generally wealthy and independent minded. There was, it is true, a number of young ambitious MPs enjoying the patronage of a landed gentleman – the famous radical Charles James Fox was one – but when their patron's interests were not at stake in the House these ambitious young men had the freedom to act much as they chose. They were quite unlike the professional politicians of today.

Party cohesion as a driver of parliamentary business was not always easily achieved in such circumstances. Parties might coalesce to form governments but they lacked both the sanctions and the rewards – the sticks and the carrots – to encourage any permanent loyalty in the Commons. Nothing more formal than an elementary whipping-in of known supporters on particular issues took place,[30] together with informal gatherings at the great houses or clubs and some cursory canvassing. Whig and Tory could usually be identified among the members of George III's Houses of Parliament but what made a man what he was, in Plucknett's words, was 'not what he proposed to do in the future, but what he thought about the past'.[31] He meant that every Tory saw himself as a latter-day Cavalier and every Whig a latter-day Roundhead.[32] The parties to which they belonged were characterised by the historian Feiling as possessing little more than 'a continuous tradition and some elementary framework{...}and a descent of political ideas'.[33] 'The Whig rhetoric', according to one commentator, 'spoke of reform, parliament and the people', though they were divided as to the definitions and implications of these terms, from the radical Wilkes to the Whig Grey. The Tories were for 'King, Church and Constitution', but the variety of interpretations they gave their causes was illustrated by their divisions over Catholic emancipation and the reform of parliament.[34]

National politics at this time, however, did not concern the vast bulk of the population. Prior to the Great Reform Act of 1832 the entire British electorate comprised only approximately 500,000. Moreover, those who contended for power came almost exclusively from the same class. On the eve of the Great Reform Act British politics could be summed up, according to Moisei Ostrogorski, in a single sentence. 'It was the absolute domination of the aristocratic class.'[35] Ostrogorski went on to make the point that the power and social homogeneity of the ruling class were buttressed by the notion of gentlemanly behaviour which was an 'unwritten charter' like the constitution of the realm. According to a table prepared about 1815, the House of Commons contained no fewer than 471 members who owed their seats to the goodwill of peers and landed gentlemen and it was certainly considered ungentlemanly not to support one's patron. In Disraeli's novel *Coningsby*, Lord Monmouth says to his grandson: 'You go along with your family, sir, like a gentleman; you are not to consider your opinions like a philosopher or political adventurer.'

When Burke wrote to his several thousand Bristol constituents explaining that he owed them not his vote but his judgement, most members in the House thought it gentlemanly to follow the instructions of a single patron. Leslie Stephen summed up the aristocratic dominance as follows: 'The country is aristocratic, because the whole upper and middle, and a great part of the lower, classes have still an instinctive liking for the established order of things.'[36] No parliamentary Reform Act, he felt, could shake that dominance. Divisions in the unreformed House, as Ostrogorski pointed out, 'in no way impaired the homogeneousness of the single united ruling class'.[37] G.K. Chesterton caught the tone of aristocratic government:

> even a tyrant must never appear as a tyrant. He may break down everybody's fences and steal everybody's land, but he must do it by Act of Parliament.... And if he meets the people he's dispossessed, he must be very polite to them and enquire after their rheumatism. That's what's kept the British constitution going – enquiry after rheumatism.[38]

Towards the end of the eighteenth century, however, three major issues were to have a profound effect upon the nature of British political debate: the American War of Independence, the French Revolution, and parliamentary reform. Numbers of influential Whigs were favourably disposed to the American colonists in their struggle for political rights, which those Whigs felt to be no more than the birth-right of the British (though the overwhelming majority of the British did not enjoy them). The Tory government was opposed to the colonists' claims and sought to deny them by force. During the eighteenth century Britain had been well enough governed.[39] As Baker points out, wars had been won, major social unrest avoided, the colonies expanded and relative prosperity maintained. The undeniable failures of the American War of Independence, however, marked a 'decisive turning point in both the performance of government and attitudes towards it'.[40] There was some initial support among the more radically minded Whigs for the principles of the French Revolution also, whereas the Tories almost to a man were staunchly opposed, as were many Whig magnates. Finally the Whigs favoured extending the franchise to the middle class (in fact some wished to give all adult males the right to vote) whereas most Tories were staunchly opposed to reform. These were divisive ideological arguments about the very relationship of parliament to the people and they affected the evolution of parties. As a consequence a more coherent party system was beginning to emerge in parliament.[41]

Nineteenth-century parties: the growth of democracy

The early nineteenth century brought that enormous change in Britain's social structure and way of life referred to as the Industrial Revolution. With it came a new social class with wealth and influence and, to some extent, a distinctive ideology, but with no direct political influence. The energy and ambition of this new class are well captured by Sir Thomas Throgmorton about whom the *Quarterly Review* of 1825 reported that he would appear at dinner wearing a suit of cloth, which had been on the backs of his own sheep that very morning. These thrusting radicals, the Gradgrinds and Bounderbys of Charles Dickens' *Hard Times*, did not represent a threat to the social order. As Martin Wiener has demonstrated, the overwhelming ambition of the *nouveaux riches* was, or at any rate became, not to replace the aristocracy but to join it.[42] Their growing influence led not to the immediate decline of aristocratic dominance but to what H.G. Wells called its gradual deliquescence.[43] Nevertheless their economic interests were opposed to those of the large landowners and they were able to use the party system of 'we' and 'they', Whig and Tory, to their own advantage. Championed by the Whigs they were enfranchised in 1832 and later, with Whig support, they were able to forge a party of their own, the Liberal Party, and to challenge the dominance of the landed aristocracy.

What was the radicalism that many of these men supported? According to John Stuart Mill it represented a frontal attack on the 'wretched supposition' that British institutions were models of excellence and hence not to be improved upon. More specifically radicals believed that democratic suffrage constituted the essential foundation of representative government. This belief was one of the driving forces behind the Great Reform Act. For radicals like the Utilitarians James Mill and Jeremy Bentham,[44] 1832 was the first step on the path to full male suffrage; to their Whig allies, whom they regarded as 'squeezable material', the Reform Act represented pretty much the opposite, the perfecting of existing constitutional arrangements: the last step, not the first. To most Tories reform was anathema. All the same, the 1832 Act was far from revolutionary; still only about 7 per cent of the population could vote. Even so, with the obvious decline of royal influence and patronage, party leaders began to seek their authority from 'the people'. This happened most notably in 1834, when Sir Robert Peel beguiled his electors at Tamworth with a platform of policy commitments. These were later incorporated into the famous Tamworth Manifesto, though it was to be another forty years before the party manifesto came to play its modern role.

Nevertheless, for something like half a century, parties would continue to coalesce more around a leadership that could retain allegiance rather than an ideology, set of policy proposals or organisational structure.[45] This continuity, as Gilmour points out, 'was of power and opposition, not of names and parties.'[46] Barker argues that political allegiance means more than ideology. Allegiance satisfies a basic human need for the stimulus of leadership and the warmth of personal contact. Katz and Mair too stressed the importance of individual inter-action, claiming it to be the 'driving force of party life'.[47] Most men (women's feelings on the matter had to wait) have a natural desire for some system of sides or teams to which they can pledge their loyalty. It was natural enough, given the traditional division of 'ins' and 'outs', power and opposition, for the nascent two-party system to develop further. Ideology, while it did not create the parties, added greater cohesion, but the instinctive idea of loyalty gave them continuity.

There are many examples in literature of the emotions evoked, especially at the hustings, by this set of competing traditional allegiances, as Dickens' description of Eatanswill in *The Pickwick Papers* shows:[48]

> It appears then that…every man in Eatanswill, conscious of the weight that attached to his example, felt himself bound to unite heart and soul, with one of the two great parties that divided the town – the Blues and the Buffs…. There were Blue shops and Buff shops. Blue inns and Buff inns – there was a Blue aisle and a Buff aisle in the very church itself.

There are descriptions of the partisanship of nineteenth-century elections in many novels. George Eliot's *Felix Holt* contains an account based upon Miss Eliot's personal experiences of the Nuneaton hustings in 1832 when the Riot Act was read out and a detachment of Scots Greys ordered in. Later in the century Disraeli and George Meredith also gave descriptions of 'robust' election campaigns based upon personal experience. Anthony Trollope, later still, described his fortnight's canvassing in the East Yorkshire borough of Beverley as 'the most wretched fortnight of my manhood'. Fictionalised, his experiences were offered to posterity in the novel *Ralph the Heir*.[49] Most of the participants in the earlier electoral excitement, though, would not even have had the right to vote and virtually none could reasonably have felt that either party represented their interests. Their loyalty and commitment provide evidence for Barker's 'deep human instinct' theory. On the other hand, it is unlikely that these emotions had no ideological substance at all: Dickens' description of a divided society suggests the opposite.

But to return to the plot; if something resembling a modern two-party system was emerging by the late 1830s, it was not destined to last in the same format, for in 1846 the Tory Prime Minister, Sir Robert Peel, repealed the Corn Laws, which his government had been pledged to maintain and which provided the basis of the economic (and hence political) dominance of the landed aristocracy. He thereby smashed the historic Tory party, sending some of the more progressive Conservatives, on his untimely death four years later, into the newly emerging Liberal Party. Corn Law repeal destroyed not only his own party but also that coalition of Whigs and radical and middle-class representatives who had opposed the Tories, for there was no compelling reason for them to stay together any longer. According to Ostrogorski,

> Parliament ceased to exhibit its old consistency because society had lost it. The constant multiplication of degrees in the social scale, the variety of new aspirations, the change of social relations from the concrete to a generalised standard, all found their way into the House, narrow as the entrance to it was at that time.[50]

Ostrogorski's analysis suggests an important caveat to Barker's 'naturalness and inevitability' of two opposed political camps – what we might call tribalism – namely that the 'tribes' themselves will change with time. For Karl Marx this process of change was both social and teleological, leading finally to its own self-destruction in the classless society. As the nineteenth century wore on, the bourgeoisie, Macaulay's 'brave, honest, and stout-hearted class...anxious for the security of society and...hostile to corruption and oppression',[51] was able to challenge aristocratic political eminence by commandeering its own party and helping to create a new two-party system based largely on the opposed class interests of the aristocracy and the bourgeoisie – the Conservatives and the Liberals. The Liberals, though, as befits a left-of-centre party, represented a wide variety of single-issue group activists, campaigning on issues such as temperance and education reform. Such groups were almost invariably associated with Nonconformism and rightly considered themselves to be outsiders.

The nineteenth century: the growth of party organisation

Party realignment was not the only repercussion of the 1832 Act. Previously the duty of preparing electoral lists belonged to the overseers of the poor in every parish and any qualified elector could have his name included in the register (and also object to names already on the list). Shortly after the Act extended the suffrage, registration societies began to be formed with the purpose of ensuring that all known supporters of the party were registered to vote. Sir Robert Peel quickly appreciated the significance of registration, describing it as an element more powerful than king or Commons. 'The registration', he said, 'will govern the disposal of offices, and determine the policy of party attack; and the power of this new element will go on increasing as its secret strength becomes better known and is more fully developed.'[52] Peel prophetically predicted the 'systematic organisation' of registration, because he grasped that in order to win elections candidates would have to gain the votes of a large number of people to whom they were not personally known. They could do this best by outlining what they proposed to do if elected. This is what he himself did in his Tamworth Manifesto, which may be regarded as both the first modern election address and the first party manifesto. It is a nice historical irony that the document was brought out after the election.

Peel's prediction was justified: registration societies multiplied over the next quarter of a century and by 1861 the Liberals had established the Liberal Registration Association which had the principal task of coordinating constituency registration and establishing societies or associations where none existed. The name of this body was later changed to the Liberal Association. Characteristically the registration societies formed after 1832 were not in any sense representative but self-elected and self-perpetuating and it was only with the passage of time that pressures towards greater representativeness made themselves felt. Conservatives in Liverpool, for example, organised originally in 1832, reorganised themselves in 1848 into a representative constitutional association based upon wards with elected officials, each holding positions in the associations. These local Conservative clubs fulfilled a number of social functions, providing reading rooms and educational facilities, sickness benefits, seaside excursions and so on. They helped to integrate into politics a body of men most of whom, until 1867, did not possess the vote.[53] Ostrogorski referred to registration as 'a gap through which the parties...made their way into the constituencies and gradually covered the whole country with their network of organisations'.[54]

The second major electoral reform of the century, however, in 1867, was to transform the franchise much more radically. The electorate more than doubled (to approximately 1,365,000) and organising the party vote was becoming a full-time responsibility. Parties began to appoint agents, to encourage the growth of clubs providing a centre in which the faithful could drink, organise lectures and generally socialise.[55] Within twenty years very few candidates would stand for election without the support of an agent, a constituency association and a number of local clubs.[56]

The 1867 Act also stimulated organisation at the national level. Within a year the National Union of Conservative and Constitutional Associations (NUCCA) had been formed to maximise Conservative support from its workingmen's clubs; local associations were established and annual conferences held. These became important when, at the Crystal Palace in 1872, the party leader Disraeli chose the occasion to make a major speech, signalling in many respects the opening of an epoch of truly national general elections. By 1878 the National Union had grown sufficiently to establish its own provincial bodies. The Conservatives had also established a Central Office in 1870, pretty much under the control of the Chief Whip, to stimulate the growth of new constituency associations and to draw up lists of prospective candidates. The party leadership wished to keep a paternal eye on the activities of NUCCA, but the new arrangement led to both duplication and friction.[57] These problems remained manageable, however, owing to the influence in both bodies of John Gorst, who headed the Central Office and was honorary secretary of NUCCA. Central Office was to grow to the extent that in 1911 the post of party chairman was created to coordinate the organisation and liaise with NUCCA. All in all, Conservative Party organisation was 'in advance of anything the Liberals had and must have greatly helped the Tories towards their first parliamentary majority in thirty years.'[58] Equally important for the future development of the party in the country was Disraeli's Primrose League, founded in 1883 to promote Conservative values. By 1890 membership exceeded one million.[59] As Fisher rightly points out, one of the most important contributions the League made to the development of the Conservative Party was to involve numbers of women, long before they enjoyed the vote, in party organisational affairs.

The Liberals were to respond to the changes ushered in by the Second Reform Act in a spectacularly successful fashion. The 1867 Act created four three-member constituencies, Leeds, Manchester, Liverpool and Birmingham. During the passage of the Bill, the House of Lords had successfully added an amendment, the so-called Minority Clause, to the effect that voters in these cities would be allowed only two votes. Now, the Liberals of Birmingham believed that they could win all three seats and the Birmingham Liberal Association reformed itself on a democratic basis at ward and city level, calculating the number of Liberal voters in each ward and advising them how to use their two votes. Three Liberals were returned for Birmingham. In 1873 the association appointed as its secretary Francis Schnadhorst who, together with Birmingham's favourite-son-to-be, Joseph Chamberlain, sought to gain control of municipal government for the Liberals. That year Chamberlain was elected mayor and the party was massively successful in the council elections. The Birmingham Association was a shining example for municipal political associations throughout the country, an example that the Conservatives would ignore at their peril.

The Conservative electoral success of 1874 was partly attributable to the organisational skills of the National Union and the Central Office, and the lesson was not lost on the Liberals. At a conference held, appropriately, in Birmingham, the National Liberal Federation was formed with Chamberlain as its president and Schnadhorst its secretary. There was an important difference, though, between the

Liberal Federation and the Conservative National Union. The Federation sought, in Chamberlain's words, to take on the mantle, of being a 'Liberal parliament', formulating by open democratic debate the policies to be followed by future Liberal administrations. It was this aspiration that earned for the Federation Disraeli's dismissive description, 'the Birmingham caucus'.[60] If the organisational value of the caucus had been instrumental in the party's 1880 triumph, its radicalism put it at odds both with the parliamentary leadership and with less radical local associations.[61] How this impasse would have been overcome is uncertain, for the Liberal tribe was soon to be riven by the issue of Home Rule for Ireland; in 1886, Chamberlain and the Liberal Unionists left the party to form a separate association. Thereafter, with the fear of Birmingham-inspired radicalism removed, the great majority of local associations affiliated to the National Federation and the leadership reasserted itself.

Another feature of the 1880 election had been the national tour undertaken by the Liberal Party leader, William Gladstone. Hitherto party leaders had satisfied themselves with campaigning in their own constituencies. This new development was said to have filled Queen Victoria with some alarm but it was to become a standard feature of subsequent election campaigns, building on the national role Disraeli had assumed earlier. Equally important for the development of modern parties, especially the Liberals, was the increasing reliance on central funds for constituency campaigning.[62] We have seen already how expensive eighteenth-century campaigns could be but with the growth of the electorate to over five million in 1884, the prospect of 'persuading' electors to support a candidate had become prohibitively expensive.[63] Moreover, the Secret Ballot Act of 1872 made it impossible to judge the effectiveness of persuasion and anyway the Corrupt and Illegal Practices Act of 1883 made it illegal! Pinto-Duschinsky has shown that the percentage of Liberal candidates' expenses provided by central party funds was to grow from 4 per cent in 1880 to 27 per cent by 1906.[64]

Other major changes, too, were taking place in parliamentary procedure in the House of Commons during the 1880s. In order to combat the disruptive tactics of Irish members – sufficiently discomfiting to persuade some country gentlemen to quit parliament altogether[65] – Gladstone began to close debates with a majority vote, thus requiring party cohesion. These changes tended to favour the government and naturally led to a more disciplined opposition. Alpheus Todd, writing in 1887, was moved to declare that the job of the opposition had become to attack 'every measure, act or word, of every member of the ministry, in short to constitute a standard censorship of the government'.[66] Hanham is right to conclude, though, that 'cartoonists who showed Disraeli and Gladstone as two pugilists were nearer to the mark than those who emphasised the overriding importance of ideas and lofty moral aspirations'.[67] In that decisive sense, late nineteenth-century parties, even at their most combative, remained different from modern parties. And we should remember that fewer than 60 per cent of divisions where 'whipped' in the 1860s, whereas by 1906 that figure was nearer 90 per cent. Other developments were afoot. Single-member constituencies were becoming the norm, many entirely working class, and this was having an effect upon tribal representation: in 1886, for the first time, MPs with a commercial or industrial background outnumbered landowners.[68]

Edwardian parties: the emergence of organised labour

Although Victoria would reign for a further twenty years, historians often refer to the period 1880–1910 as the 'Edwardian era'. So shall we. The Edwardian era witnessed one major development in nineteenth-century party history, the displacing of the Liberal Party by Labour. By the 1880s it was becoming clear to an increasing number of labour leaders that the existing party framework was not taking sufficient account of the interests of labour. Working-class males had been enfranchised in 1867 or in 1884 (the Third Reform Act) but only a few were able to become parliamentary candidates because some measure of personal wealth or patronage was still generally necessary to enter politics. For example, the Liberals supported only eleven successful working-class candidates in the 1880s, the so-called Lib-Labs, though miners' candidates also secured election and these too took the Liberal whip. Moreover, the Liberal leader, Gladstone, 'the people's William', was beginning to focus his party's attention more on Ireland and less on domestic reforms.

The Liberal Party took insufficient note of two phenomena related in the modern mind but not in the Edwardian mind: working-class politics and socialism. They came together officially only in 1893 at a conference in Bradford when representatives of trade unions and socialist societies established the Independent Labour Party (ILP) to secure the better representation in parliament of the interests of labour. In 1899 the Trades Union Congress (TUC) called a meeting in London to which representatives of seventy trade unions, the ILP and socialist societies were invited. This conference established a Labour Representation Committee (LRC) with the declared purpose of creating a Labour group in parliament with its own whips and its own policies, ready to cooperate with any party that showed itself interested in promoting legislation in the direct interest of labour. The LRC's first secretary was later to become Britain's first Labour Prime Minister, James Ramsay MacDonald. Shortly the LRC fought its first election, putting forward fifteen candidates of whom two were successfully elected. More important, though, was a decision taken in 1903 that successful parliamentary candidates should sign a pledge restraining them from identifying with any section or interest within the major parties. To be independent, however, required money and the same conference took a decision to make a levy on all members of affiliated bodies to provide MPs with £200 per annum. (In 1911 all MPs were to receive an official salary of £500 per annum.)

Like the bourgeoisie in the first half of the nineteenth century, the working class managed not merely to articulate its own interests within the party framework but also to shape a political party in its own image capable of winning power largely on the back of working-class support. It was, however, entirely fortuitous that Labour's constituency was large enough for the party to aspire to win parliamentary power but not so large that it might drive the owning class to consider extra-constitutional means to hang on to power.

Twentieth-century parties: class politics

The Liberals, severely weakened by the defection of Chamberlain and the Unionists in 1886, exhausted by their attempts to solve 'the Irish problem', failed to secure their hold over the working-class vote. This failure was masked by an amazing paradox: the Liberal Party won the general election of 1906 with a majority over its Conservative opponents of no fewer than 243 seats yet this was to be the last election the Liberal Party would win. Its greatest electoral victory, a reflection not of the party's strength and unity but its opponents' weakness and division, was also to be its last. Even at the moment of triumph, the moles of tribal change were tunnelling away under the edifice of Edwardian Liberalism.[69] It was also very damaging for a Liberal Party to find itself in government when war broke out in 1914, when, by definition, illiberal measures would be essential. Worst of all for the party, though, was the split occasioned by the leadership crisis in 1916 when Lloyd George replaced his party leader Asquith as Prime Minister and head of the wartime coalition.[70] The split between the 'Squiffites' and the Lloyd George Liberals was never to be healed.

When, in 1922, the Conservatives withdrew from the post-war coalition and forced Lloyd George to fight an election, they won easily. Labour overtook the Liberals as the main left-of-centre party and formed a minority government in 1924. Although the party lost seats in the following election (December 1924) Liberal representation collapsed to 40. In 1929 Labour again came to office, this time as the largest single party. The Liberals managed to win only 59 seats. The battle for the centre left was effectively over, at least until the modern era. Coincidentally by this time women had been enfranchised.[71] Contrary to the expectations of some opponents, the party system was not changed in any obvious way at all.

If Liberal decline was long term, Labour success was not; in 1931 Prime Minister MacDonald found it necessary to establish a national coalition government with himself at its head, and as a consequence the bulk of his party left him to his new friends. The depleted Liberals were as divided as Labour: Coalition or National Liberals allied with the Conservatives; independent Liberals managed to win only a handful of seats. Labour's setback proved to be only temporary. When Winston Churchill ended the wartime coalition and declared an election in 1945, the Labour Party achieved an historic success, forming the government with one of the largest majorities of the century. A period of over twenty years of Conservative Party dominance, either independently or as the major partner in a coalition, had come to an abrupt and unexpected end and Liberal representation was down to single figures. A new tribal configuration, apparently along Marxian lines – bourgeoisie and working class – now characterised British politics.

If the distinctive feature of the post-1945 party system was the overwhelming domination of two parties, an equally important if less immediately obvious feature was the considerable amount of agreement that emerged between the parties over a wide variety of policy issues, which was to last for approximately a quarter of a century. The framework of the party system seemed to have acquired a stability not to say rigidity between 1945 and 1959; for example, only 13 out of 168 seats changed hand at by-elections.[72] One of the reasons for the 'me too-ist' character of British politics during these years was the successful attempt made by the Conservative Party to acclimatise itself to the aspirations of a post-war electorate.[73] Although the Labour government contrived to win the 1950 election, it did so with a majority of only six and managed to survive for just eighteen months. In the 1951 election, although gaining more votes than the Conservatives, Labour lost and began thirteen years in opposition.

By the early 1960s Britain's post-war economic boom began to falter and the Conservative government became increasingly unpopular. In 1964 Labour took office under Harold Wilson, though with only a slender majority and so in 1966 Wilson went to the country again. For only the second time in its history the Labour Party came to power with a substantial majority. By this time however, Labour's inability to manage the economy led to a series of confidence-sapping by-election defeats.[74] Soon electorates were routinely turning against governments elected only a year or so before; this was quite new.

In 1970, somewhat against the odds, Edward Heath's Conservatives gained power introducing a legislative programme that moved decisively but temporarily away from consensus politics. Suddenly Heath underwent a mid-term conversion back to interventionism, introducing a statutory incomes policy. In 1974, in the face of a miners' strike that resulted in power cuts and industries working a three-day week, the Conservative leader decided to hold a general election to strengthen his hand. Although the Conservatives polled more votes than Labour, they gained fewer seats. Wilson took office heading the first minority administration since 1929.[75] Eight months later the new Labour government turned to the electorate once again but its position was not greatly improved; it managed a majority of only four.

Beset by a number of economic problems, Labour sought support for its economic and industrial strategies through a concordat with the Trades Union Congress and for a time this approach was successful, but in the winter of 1978–79 the concordat broke down and the so-called 'Winter of Discontent' produced a plethora of damaging strikes that collectively refuted Labour's claim to be the natural party of government precisely because it could work with the unions. In the spring of 1979 the Conservative Party led by its first woman leader, Margaret Thatcher, won a clear victory and once again Labour was banished to the opposition benches, this time for eighteen years.

In many senses 1979 was a traditional British election in which a conservative administration emphasising its managerial skills took on a radical opposition seeking to transform society; in this case, however, the conservative administration was Labour's and the radical would-be transformers were the Conservatives. Committed, like Heath in 1970, to rolling back the state, the new Conservative government initiated a policy designed to cut inflation, limit public expenditure and revitalise British industry. Apparent success with inflation, Labour's internal divisions and the kudos gained from the military successes of the Falklands War enabled the Conservatives to gain a second electoral victory in 1983. The election of that year was also contested by a new political grouping, the Alliance, comprising the Liberals and the new Social Democratic Party fighting together on one manifesto. Alliance intervention helped to produce Labour's worst performance at a general election since 1935, perhaps even 1918.

Britain's party system, based upon two dominant parties since 1945, had once again changed, with the Alliance taking over 25 per cent of votes cast. Labour had lost its hold over its tribe, which was itself in the process of transformation. In 1987 the Alliance was unable to improve upon its position but still managed to secure seven and a half million votes (23 per cent of the total) thereby helping to secure a third successive defeat for Labour. The subsequent demise of the Alliance and the birth of the Liberal Democrats, together with the continuing inability of the Labour Party convincingly to portray itself as a party of government, were to keep Labour out of power until 1997. The Conservative governments of 1979–97 were by no means in the party tradition; the party had transformed its tribal base and abandoned traditional policy positions. Moreover when it finally came to office Labour, too, had transformed itself and become New Labour; it was no longer a tribal party in anything but a symbolic sense. Its subsequent electoral victories in 2001 and 2005, Conservative responses to these victories and the strong performance of the Liberal Democrats have reinforced the notion that the old tribal structures have changed once again, but this time they have not transmogrified into a new pattern of adversarial confrontation. They have simply ceased to be decisive.

Parties and the two-party system

So far we have been talking about parties and not about party systems. Our historical survey indicates that two parties that could be said, at least partly, to have represented two tribes, have dominated the British political system, over the past 300 years or so. Significantly it also shows that the nature of that domination, of the parties themselves and of the tribes, has been subject to constant change. The pattern of party politics, moreover, has changed just as dramatically, with long spells of dominance by one party, with parties breaking up and regrouping, and with third (and fourth) parties playing important parts from time to time. Given the importance of the theme of change it comes as a surprise to find that most prominent writers on British politics tended until recently to underemphasise the nature of change and overemphasise the two-party dominance: Britain, they agree, has always had a two-party system.[76]

Our factual account of the evolution of parties does not support this contention, but what would a more theoretical analysis make of it? Giovanni Sartori uses a widely accepted theoretical framework with four criteria.[77] The first states that the two parties must be in a position to compete for the absolute majority of seats. True or false for Britain? Apart from the obvious exceptions when, at the beginning of our period, party identities were weak, and when for long periods of time, third and fourth parties commanded substantial support, a number of seats in the House were simply uncontested (over 36 per cent in 1900). As late as 1918,

107 candidates were returned unopposed. Only partly true. His second criterion requires one party to win a workable majority. True or false? Jorgen Rasmussen defined a working majority as comprising twenty seats more than its combined opponents.[78] Three-quarters of twentieth-century elections fall into this category – which conversely means that one in four did not. Significantly most commentators regarded John Major's majority of twenty-one in 1992 as insufficient. In 2005 Tony Blair's government, with a majority of sixty-six, had great difficulty in putting key pieces of its legislation onto the statute book. Once again then, only partly true. The third criterion is the willingness of a party with a majority of seats to govern alone and this has certainly been a feature of the British system. So – true. Sartori's fourth criterion is the regular rotation of power between the major parties. A party which has grounds for believing that it has no reasonable possibility of achieving power constitutionally is unlikely to be a strong supporter of a two-party system or indeed the constitution. Until the successes of Tony Blair, rotation has been an illusion. Parties of the left of centre, that is, Liberal and Labour, held power for much shorter periods than the Conservatives and almost always secured smaller parliamentary majorities. Before 1997 there were only three occasions in the twentieth century, totalling thirteen years, when left of centre parties governed with substantial majorities. The Conservatives, in contrast, enjoyed good working majorities on thirteen occasions totalling sixty-three years (including eighteen years when they were the dominant party in national coalitions). Throughout the twentieth century there was no need to ask for whom the pendulum swung; it swung for the Conservatives.[79] So number four is demonstrably false.

Underpinning the notion of two-party politics is an assumption so basic that it goes unquestioned: that the two dominant parties reflect the balance of public opinion. Yet on only four occasions since the mid 1880s has an incoming government actually won a majority of votes. The Conservatives in alliance with the Unionists in 1886 and 1900 won the first two and the second two were won by Conservative-dominated coalitions in 1931 and 1935. Moreover in three of the four the majority was marginal. In short, only once, in 1931, was a substantial majority of public opinion – 61 per cent of those who voted – even nominally behind the incoming government, and that government was a national coalition. Let me put this as plainly as it can be put: only once in more than a hundred years could a British government have claimed to represent 'the people'; only once in over a century could its claim to have a popular mandate be taken seriously.

It has been argued by writers like L.S. Amery that the strongest democracies, the Anglo-Saxon ones, were two-party systems and that the deviant continental multi-party systems were somehow inferior, carrying, in Henry Drucker's words, 'a certain opprobrium'.[80] The evident success of many European multi-party systems and the choice of all the new democracies of Eastern Europe to opt for multi-party systems seem to deal a hammer blow to traditional British *amour propre*, but so does a closer look at the Anglo-Saxon systems themselves. American parties, for example, bear a close resemblance to nineteenth-century British parties; they are organisationally weak and owe their periodic unity almost entirely to the personality of their leader. Canadian government (if we consider Canada to be Anglo-Saxon) has been based on three or more parties and several minority administrations (in fact nearly half of Canada's post-war administrations have been minorities). Moreover, one major party, the Liberals, has been in power over three times as long as its major opponent the Conservatives. As for Australia, a two-and-a-half party system dominated by right-wing coalitions has been the norm.[81] Sartori claimed that only New Zealand, with its four million population, could really be said to have operated a two-party system like the British. In fact Sartori, Lijphart and others claimed that New Zealand had a better claim to two-party status than Britain.[82] Even there however the right-wing National party enjoyed office for twice as long as Labour between 1945 and 1996, when New Zealand exchanged its 'perfect' two-party system for a multi-party system following a national referendum on electoral reform. Finally the new systems in Wales and Scotland, set up by Westminster, are multi-party systems. Even elections to the London Assembly and to the European parliament are proportional and produce a number of parties. In short the entire world seems to be out of step with Westminster.

Why are popular and even informed perceptions of British party history so smug and so mistaken about the British party system? Perhaps the fatal division between the Roundheads and the Cavaliers has shaped our thinking. Perhaps that remarkable early psephologist Sergeant Willis is to blame, for it was he who proclaimed, in Gilbert and Sullivan's popular operetta *Iolanthe*, that, with the contrivance of nature:

> Every little boy and gal that's born into the world alive
> Is either a little Liberal or else a little Conservative.

Probably it owed more to that seminal text of British political science, published in 1955, Robert McKenzie's *British Political Parties*,[83] in which 595 of 597 pages were devoted to the two major parties (after all, the Liberals appeared to be on the point of extinction). McKenzie was especially influential as a result not only of this pioneering work but also of his television journalism. Like Bagehot before him McKenzie seemed to take it for granted that his times were typical whereas they turned out to have been anything but. Yet the advent of radio and more especially television coverage of elections cemented the idea of two-party politics in the public mind. A simple 'for' and 'against' model of presentation has clear advantages for organising and processing material and it scarcely seems to have occurred to producers and presenters that there were usually more than two sides to an argument. What emerged as a consequence was a model of politics that assumed the two-party system of the 1950s and 1960s to be fixed, permanent and rational, the final fruit of 300 years of slow maturation. From this false perspective the Whigs and Tories of the eighteenth century and the Liberals and Conservatives of the nineteenth century simply became part of a teleology leading inexorably to the Labour/Conservative duality of the 1950s and 1960s. It was almost a perfect manifestation of George Orwell's precautionary dictum that to control the present is to control the past.

The truth of the matter is that the British party 'system', in Ian Gilmour's words, is the consequence 'neither of the wishes of the British people nor the foresight of British statesmen. Like Tristram Shandy it was begotten in a fit of absence of mind.'[84] Its subsequent development has been every bit as rhapsodic and undistinguished as that young man's and its future as full of uncertainties. It could be said that the British party system has absorbed vast social and economic changes with a minimum of violence and disruption, though cynics might prefer to describe it as an elaborate game designed to legitimise and thereby sustain the power of the 'political establishment'. However it should be noted that a stable two-party system has never applied with equal force across all of the United Kingdom. Neither should it be forgotten that third parties have frequently played decisive parts in the British parliamentary drama. The truth of the matter is that the social framework that underpinned McKenzie's world, like the changing tribal allegiances that Ostrogorski spoke of, has changed beyond recognition and the major parties are drifting like vessels that have broken from their moorings and are subject to eddies and currents that take them off station.

Conclusions

We have described and then defined parties, discussed their functions in a democracy and considered their historical development in Britain. We have discovered that it is in adapting to changing social patterns, in giving political expression to new social configurations that they fulfil their functions. We have examined the foundations of two-party politics, its strengths and limitations. We have discovered that parties are based as much as anything upon leadership and allegiance, and so for competition between two parties to be effective – that is, for a two-party system to operate – two united parties are required, controlled by two leaders of approximately equal stature, who can command the respect and loyalty of their parties in parliament and the support of approximately equal numbers of voters. There is no reason whatever to regard such a state of affairs as natural, still less inevitable. History seems to suggest that it happens rarely – Gladstone and Disraeli, Churchill and Attlee, perhaps Wilson and Heath – are the exceptions that prove the 'rarity' rule. (At the end of this study we might conclude that such a well-demarcated two-party competition is not only rare but also no longer even desirable.) All this having been said, British politics operates as if it *were* a two-party system and the two main parties perform in an adversarial way, so we too shall use the phrase but with all the caveats in mind.

Having established a framework for the detailed consideration of British parties and the party system, it remains only to set out where we go from here. We shall be examining the two major parties in terms of ideology, performance, membership and structure; we shall be considering the Liberal Democrats and also the minor parties in a more general way and throughout we shall be observing the impact of devolution. In a concluding chapter we shall make some final comments on the relative effectiveness of Britain's party system today and its 'fitness for purpose' – to coin a phrase – for tomorrow's world.

2   Conservative Party ideology

'Conservative belief', wrote Anthony Quinton, 'becomes explicit only in reaction to a positive, innovative attack on the traditional scheme of things. What exists speaks for itself simply by existing.'[1] Conservatism has always been with us then, and is therefore prior to other ideologies. Some Conservative thinkers have denied that Conservatism actually constitutes an ideology at all. R.A. Butler, for example, spoke of Conservatism as an 'abiding attitude of mind, a code of values, a way of life'.[2] Hence the support for the established political order: it entails certain principles and virtues that are worth defending. If we are to understand the nature of Conservatism, we should not be seduced into thinking of it as some essentialist, pre-ideological and almost mystical part of the fabric of social reality; instead we must get our hands dirty digging up and identifying the principles and virtues that would invite support for the established political order.

Before doing so, however, let me make an observation. None of the words that we shall use in our analysis – even Tory and Conservative – have clear edges and they frequently overlap. I will use them carefully but cannot claim precision: in the world of ideologies precision is chimerical. Although the old Tory Party of the Duke of Wellington broke on the back of Catholic Emancipation and the Great Reform Act, it was reconstituted by Peel as a vehicle to oppose further reform, to conserve the constitution and became increasingly known as the Conservative Party. Although Peel then broke his new creation when he repealed the Corn Laws, the pieces were picked up by Disraeli and others and the Conservative Party in more or less its modern form was instituted. So although the concepts that we shall be discussing may be imprecise, they form part of an unbroken tradition that has influenced British politics for at least three centuries.

The fundamental principles of Conservatism

Quinton adduces three chief principles of conservatism, which will provide as good a beginning as any.

Traditionalism

A political system that evolves over a long period of time will come to represent the accumulated wisdom of the community, or at least of that part of the community habituated to making decisions. A fixed and settled constitution should be seen as representing the aggregated outcome of innumerable compromises, struggles and adjustments over the years; it may be regarded as a kind of residuum of practical political experience. Conservatism takes consolation from the longevity of institutions and can rationalise this disposition by arguing that, after all, it is only when we know institutions thoroughly that we can make the fullest use of them, bend them to our purposes, learn how to avoid their pitfalls. Such is the complexity of society that it would be impossible to design institutions to fulfil social purposes; much better and safer to adapt those we know, and which have proved their value over time.

Organicism

Quinton's second major principle is what he calls organicism, which holds that society is analogous to a natural living body and not a machine or other man-made structure. There are three chief characteristics of most organisms: they are extraordinarily complex, interconnected and interdependent. Citizens are social beings connected to each other in a complex pattern of mutually beneficial relationships, which are not amenable to wholesale change. Machines, on the other hand, are designed for a specific purpose and may be adapted to fulfil that purpose optimally. An organism, by contrast, develops to fulfil certain functions and bits cannot be chopped off and replaced without grave repercussions for the whole organism. Moreover the complexity and interconnectedness of organisms is not limited by the skill of a human designer. Even minor social engineering must be considered with the greatest care because of its possible effect upon other parts of the living body of the state. O'Sullivan locates the origins of this organic version of Conservatism in the German Romantic Movement, whose exponents were greatly influenced by Hegel's dialectical view of history. Its influence on British conservatism was mediated by nineteenth-century British Romantic writers like Samuel Taylor Coleridge and Thomas Carlyle.[3]

Other Conservative thinkers have understood the existing social order to represent not so much a natural phenomenon as a reflection of divine intention, a view which they shared with medieval thinkers like Saint Augustine. In the well-known nineteenth-century hymn *All Things Bright and Beautiful* there was a verse reminding us of God's design for the world. It is not usually sung nowadays:

> The rich man in his castle,
> The poor man at his gate.
> He made them high and lowly,
> He numbered their estate.

It makes little practical difference whether society represents a natural development or a supernatural intention, for what follows is that things should not or cannot (or both) be other than they are.[4]

Organicism has had a profound influence upon conservatism, tending to stress the mutuality of duties and obligations. Our verse implies that the poor should

accept the reality of their position but the rich man in his castle has clear obligations to the poor man at his gate, giving a paternalistic dimension to conservatism.
Coleridge spoke of the clerisy, a national church founded by society's 'natural'
leaders and dedicated to the welfare of the poor. Disraeli's 'one nation' philosophy,
Harold Macmillan's interventionist administration, the compassionate conservatism of so-called Tory 'wets',[5] and the inclusiveness of the present Conservative
Party leader, David Cameron, have all been expressions of organicism. For all its
compassion, however, organicism implies the retention of hierarchy. As Dr
Johnson told Boswell: 'You are to consider that it is your duty to maintain the
subordination of civilised society; and where there is gross or shameful deviation
from rank, it should be punished so as to deter others from the same perversion.'[6]
This was the fate of Thomas Hardy's Jude, a man who tried to rise above his situation and suffered accordingly. He came to regard himself as a 'frightful example
of what not to do'. In the novels of the Victorian writer George Gissing the conditions of the poor were painted with great sympathy, yet if they attempted to
improve themselves their fate was frightful. The best hope for the poor is the
conscience of the rich, says Gissing.[7]

Scepticism

Quinton's third major principle is scepticism, which holds that life is simply not
very amenable to 'improvement' by the application of social and political theories.
H.G. Wells once remarked that socialism was based upon the assumption that
'things may be calculated upon, may be foreseen'.[8] The Conservative believes
pretty well the opposite: that things may not always be foreseen; better to put
one's faith in established institutions and customary procedures than in untried
political theories like Wells' socialism.

Underpinning Quinton's principle of scepticism (and traditionalism for that
matter) is the overpowering certainty of human fallibility. As Quinton Hogg
argues, this belief has traditionally been associated with the Christian concept of
original sin.[9] Since the fall of Adam we have been tainted with sin; more prosaically, none of us is capable of moral perfection. There are, in addition, modern
secular theories that stress humankind's moral limitations. Freud's hugely influential psychological theories exposed human beings as severely limited by the
effects of early childhood experiences; more recently some geneticists have
pictured humans as prisoners of their genetic structure, their 'selfish genes'.
Conservatives can feel that they have strong support for their scepticism; no
wonder they are suspicious of utopian schemes. As Kant ruefully remarked,
nothing straight could be built out of the crooked timber of humanity. These are
Quinton's three fundamental principles of Conservatism. I will add a fourth.

Defence of property rights

'The possession of property by the individual is the essential condition of liberty',
wrote Quintin Hogg,[10] and the Conservative Party has been unequivocal in its

defence of property. Existing property rights, although by their very nature enshrining inequalities, are the essential characteristic of 'the established order' which Conservatism seeks to defend. Property ownership is held to be a talisman of a free society for it guarantees the disaggregation of economic power, guarantees to individuals some small castle of which they can be king. Property gives the individual a stake in society, thereby offering an inducement towards social stability. The right to own property has two important concomitants: the right to transfer property, usually to one's children, and the right to use one's property to economic advantage (for example to own a means of production). Belief in the organic nature of society implies that ownership of property brings with it social obligations as well as rights, and a Conservative government might be expected to exercise a custodial function to secure the fulfilment of such obligations, especially where property constituted a means of production. Moreover since property constitutes a social good, giving individuals a stake in society should be extended wherever possible. Since 1945 Conservative governments have consistently sought to extend ownership, to promote what has been called a 'property-owning democracy', a phrase erroneously attributed to Eden.[11]

These are the fundamental principles of Conservatism: they may be summarised, to paraphrase O'Sullivan, as the defence of a limited style of politics based upon the idea of imperfection.[12]

Working principles

If this ideology is to be brought to bear on the business of government, it needs to be operationalised. What might be the working principles of Conservative administrations?

Pragmatism

Pragmatism is the belief that doctrines should be judged by their impact upon human interests. Conservative pragmatism is linked to the amount of time that the party has spent in office for, as Blake reminds us, 'political parties seldom philosophise when they are in office'.[13] Richard Rose thought that the Conservative Party was consumed by holding office and that all other considerations, including ideology, were secondary.[14] His argument was endorsed by Conservatives. Iain Macleod said: 'The Socialists can scheme their schemes and the Liberals can dream their dreams but we, at least, have work to do.'[15] Julian Critchley agreed: 'the object of political activity is power, and…sustained and obvious disunity [the by-products of ideology] would oblige us to relinquish it'.[16] S.H. Beer quoted a Tory magnate saying in 1946 that he did not much mind what the Labour government was doing; what he did mind was that *Labour* was doing it.[17] Disraeli described the Conservative Party as working for 'an avowed political end without annunciating an embarrassing array of principles'.[18] Enoch Powell argued that principles did not define what Conservatives might be expected to do in office;[19] rather they were abstracted from 'the way the Conservative Party…*acts* in politics'.[20] Largely because party leaders were motivated by pragmatic considerations – especially gaining or retaining power – they were traditionally able to count upon the loyalty of the parliamentary party to a degree that their rivals envied. Disraeli's famous advice to Bulwer-Lytton during the debate on Corn Law reform sums up this pragmatism pithily: 'Damn your principles! Stick to your party.'

In the nineteenth century the principal threat to 'the traditional scheme of things' was posed by the individualistic doctrines of radical liberalism. In the twentieth century, the threat to the established order came from collectivist socialism which, in order to achieve its objectives, invariably sought to aggregate substantial state power. So in the modern era conservatism has had to defend the paternalist state against the individual and then the individual against the paternalist state. That it managed to do so while remaining predominantly in government is due in no small measure to its native pragmatism.

Limited government

The second working principle we shall consider is limited government and it follows naturally from the fundamental principles of conservatism. Those who are convinced of human frailties, of the benefits of tradition and order, of property-owning rights, and of the difficulty of making large-scale social and political change, are hardly likely to favour placing great power in the hands of governments. Governments are always a potential threat to individual liberty and the more powerful the government, the greater the threat. Governments should be constrained by constitutional, political and social checks and balances. But a limited government is not a weak government and Conservatives have traditionally argued for strong government in the areas of defence and law and order. Neither is it no government, and Conservatives have equally traditionally shown a willingness to act against perceived abuses of power in society through government legislation.

The rule of law

Closely associated with the idea of limited government is that of the rule of law. The law is the chief expression of the accumulated wisdom and experience of society and as such is a far safer guide to proper political action than the programme of any party that happens to be in government. The rule of law constrains governed and governors; it is the rock on which a stable society is set. Its concomitant, equality before the law, provides a framework for social transactions and, in the process, enshrines that fundamental Conservative principle, the right to private property. 'The rule of law', as Norton and Aughey conclude, 'provides that essential breathing space of predictability and security of redress which is at the heart of liberty'.[21]

The national interest

Norton draws our attention to the word 'nation' in Disraeli's 'one-nation' conservatism. It was Disraeli who first associated conservatism with one specific embodiment of the national interest – empire – and he managed this so success-fully that they seem to form a natural association. It is not generally remembered that the main thrust of Conservative thought in the nineteenth century had been anti-imperialist; Disraeli himself once referred to the colonies as 'millstones around our necks'. The idea of an imperial 'mission' cut very little ice with Conservative politicians until well into the second half of the century and Disraeli was one of the first to recognise its electoral value; he extolled the virtues of empire in his famous 1872 Crystal Palace speech. As S.H. Beer wrote, 'in impe-rialism the party had found a cause with a mighty appeal to the voter.'[22] But imperialism was not the only aspect of the national interest that the Conservative Party championed. The Conservatives have always been the party of the Union: they opposed Irish Home Rule, thereby attracting substantial Protestant working-class support in Lancashire and the West of Scotland. In Scotland, Conservatives were referred to as 'the Unionists'.

In emphatically championing the assertion of national interest, the Conservatives 'most successfully exploited the patriotic theme, reinforcing claims to stand above narrow class interests and for the nation as a whole'.[23] Particularly appropriate for the last quarter of the nineteenth and the first half of the twentieth centuries the politics of national interest continues to feature among Conservative working principles, though as the bitter battles over European unity and the party's complete disappearance as an electoral force in Scotland and Wales in 1997 were to show, the consequences nowadays are hardly as electorally beneficial as they were in the heyday of empire.

Tensions within Conservative ideology

As always in the imperfect world of political parties, principles often rub against each other, causing at best friction and often disunity. There are two major areas of tension within Conservatism.

Stability versus change

We began this investigation with Quinton's notion of conservatism as the defence of the established order. When not under threat, Quinton tells us, the 'traditional scheme of things' speaks for itself. Clearly a dialogue is implied here, but what is being said and to whom? The 'traditional scheme of things' seems to suggest something unchanging and unchallenged, but it involves a continuing dialogue about the nature and desirability of change to preserve stability.

Conservatives do not, *cannot* always oppose change. Under what circum-stances should they support the 'traditional scheme of things'? The Conservative writer T.E. Uttley believed that a Conservative government must embody the social disciplines of capitalism necessary to that discipline.[24] But is the social order based upon capital accumulation to have no regard for social harmony as well as order? Peter Walker, a long-serving minister in Mrs Thatcher's govern-ments, suggested a utility test for capitalist inequalities. They should, he declared, finessing John Rawls, contribute to the general welfare.[25] If wealth and opportunity do not 'trickle down', then a Conservative government might have to contemplate 'drastic and radical reforms to secure a *socially responsible capitalism*'.[26] Walker's test does not address the argument of writers like George Santayana whose concern was chiefly cultural: hierarchy must be defended in all circumstances because it has provided 'the source from which all culture has hitherto followed'.[27] It is hard not to see a conflict here, to be played out in times of tension. Norton and Aughey, aware of this tension, declare: 'This is the essence of the Conservative Party's role – to formulate policy that conserves a hierarchy of wealth and power and to make this intelligible and reasonable to a democracy.'[28] Yet when the authors go on to discuss the kinds of policies likely to make inequalities seem reasonable to the less favoured they come exactly upon Walker's problem; when should Conservatives support the 'settled order of things' and when should they not?

Paternalism versus libertarianism

From its earliest days many leading Tories were motivated by a sense of obligation to the disadvantaged summed up by the concept of *noblesse oblige* – obligations that went with the ownership of property. As Disraeli told the House of Commons, the 'proper leaders of the people are the gentlemen of England. If they are not the leaders of the people I do not see why there should be gentlemen'.[29] In fact these nineteen-century radical humanitarians and paternalists were sometimes so wholeheartedly prepared to embrace the state that Carlyle referred to them as the 'prophetic precursors of modern collectivism'.[30]

Disraeli preferred to refer to his version of Conservative ideology as 'one-nation conservatism' and claimed it to be as old as the Tory Party. 'Let me see property acknowledging', he wrote in *Coningsby*, 'as in the old days of faith, that labour is its twin brother, and that the essence of all tenure is the performance of duty'. If paternalistic humanitarianism was as old as the party itself, so was the belief that such power should be limited to what Cobden called truly and properly public, by which he meant peace, safety, order and prosperity.[31] Auberon Herbert became convinced of the arrogance of thinking that

> the handful of us – however well intentioned we might be – spending our nights in the House, could manufacture the life of the nation, could endow it out of hand with happiness, wisdom and prosperity, and endow it with all virtues.[32]

The historian F.C.J. Hearnshaw, writing in the 1930s, advocated an unfettered capitalist system as the only guarantee of individual liberty and saw no gain in creating a proletariat dependent upon state welfare.[33] This libertarian strand of Conservatism influenced the policies of the 1951–55 Conservative government, which denationalised iron and steel, road haulage and land development, the early years of the Heath government, which sought to 'clear away the detritus of half a century', and the Thatcher governments, which sought to roll back the state. These latter-day libertarians declared war on the paternalists. 'We have reached a parting of the ways in terms of attitudes to society and economic management', Blake and Patten declared, going on to argue for nothing less than 'a major reversal of the trends which ever since 1945 Labour has promoted and the Conservatives have accepted'.[34] Paternalism, they concluded, is out, along with welfare consensus.[35]

The guiding principles for changing and preserving, or for paternalistic intervention in the economy or libertarian paring of the state's activities, will vary but in the real world of politics the actual decision will be 'which interests to defend and which expectations to disappoint.'[36] Historians of the Conservative Party have recognised these tensions. Maude referred to them as 'archaeological strata, specimens from all its historic stages';[37] they are indeed inherent within Conservative ideology and they are pivotal to its operation. Change if delayed, timely economic intervention if withheld (or stultifying intervention if imposed) might involve Conservatives in precisely the kind of radical, transformative actions to which they are temperamentally opposed. It was the timidity and paternalism of Macmillan and latter-day Heath that brought forth Thatcherite radical libertarianisms.[38]

Conservatism in action

Let us now see how these tensions have played out in party history.

Toryism and Conservatism

The history of the modern party opens with a resounding defeat for the Tories: the Great Reform Act of 1832. The unreformed constitution had embodied each of the four dominant Conservative values – traditionalism, organicism, scepticism and the defence of property rights – and the working principles of limited government and the rule of law. The party leader whose task was to accommodate the party to the new world was Sir Robert Peel, who is usually credited with founding the modern Conservative Party. For Peel the tension between change and stability was intensified by the emergence of a new wealthy class whose economic interests were opposed to those of the landed aristocracy. The focal point of this opposition was the Corn Law question. The Corn Laws had been enacted to protect British agriculture from cheap foreign wheat, and many Tories had come to see them as representative of the traditional, organic, hierarchical society that needed to be preserved. For the bourgeoisie, moral arguments about cheap bread apart, the availability of cheaper food would prove a disincentive for their workforce to press for higher wages. In the 1840s the Irish potato harvests failed, resulting in mass starvation. The availability of cheap bread in England might release other foodstuffs such as potatoes for Irish consumption. It is not clear how logistically convincing these arguments were, but it was important not to leave undone anything which might ease the suffering across the Irish Sea: paternalistic organicism demanded no less. Peel became convinced of the need for reform.

Here was the classical problem for a Conservative leader: how to 'sell' necessary intervention and change to the landed interest without arousing what Norton and

Aughey called a 'blind emotional reaction' that would damage their cause even further.[39] Peel was unable to carry his party with him: the Corn Laws were repealed with Whig support but in the process Peel's newly created Conservative Party was shattered. Though he failed his party the judgement of historians has been kinder to him than of many of his contemporaries, especially Lord George Bentinck and the waspish Mr Disraeli.

Embracing democracy

It would be difficult to overestimate the importance of Benjamin Disraeli to the history of the Conservative Party – the only party leader, says Gash, to whom the Conservative young of successive generations have turned for inspiration.[40] Disraeli was one of the few Conservative leaders able to 'bring warmth to conservatism and to add to its basic common sense a degree of romance, generosity and excitement'.[41] This was certainly not the judgement of his contemporaries, however, many of whom viewed him with deep distrust.[42] Disraeli's great achievement was to secure an electoral base for future Conservative governments in Britain's expanding democracy through, particularly, the Second Reform Act of 1867. Ward argues that the case for reform had to be pressed upon a reluctant Disraeli, and because he needed the support of the radicals in the House the Act went further than Disraeli had wanted.[43] Norton and Aughey conclude that 'as an act of long-term political strategy the passage of the Reform Bill proved that the Conservatives were no longer bent upon reaction but could accommodate the demands of the day and do so competently'.[44] In fact Disraeli operated not so much a strategy as a stratagem, a piece of political opportunism, which he believed could only benefit the party in the long run.

Disraeli had persuaded his party to take a 'leap in the dark'; not a reluctant acceptance of change but an enthusiastic if opportunistic welcoming of a change that took the ideology of the aristocratic class and made it attractive to significant numbers of the industrial proletariat. Disraeli incorporated the traditional support for property and hierarchy (extended after the defection of the Whigs to include the owners of industrial wealth) with a paternalistic concern for the well-being of the industrial poor. The thrust of Disraelian conservatism, set out imaginatively in his novel *Sybil*,[45] sought to establish a new sense of organicism: 'one nation', a true community, based upon hierarchy, but with the wealthy taking a compassionate concern over the conditions of the poor. Moreover, the Conservatives would also protect the interests of the national organic community overseas by building up the empire and calling into being an imperial community of kith and kin. If Disraelian paternalism secured a future for the party in the democratic age it also earned him the disdain of many of his contemporary Conservatives.

New friends: the impact of the Whigs and the Unionists

The next two decades of Conservative dominance were the consequence more of Liberal disunity than Conservative strength. One important outcome of this disunity, primarily the result of Gladstone's growing preoccupation with Ireland and of the strength of radicalism within the Liberal Party, was the inexorable transfer, charted by James Cornford, of middle-class support from the Liberals to the Conservatives.[46] Equally important was the defection of Chamberlain's radical Unionists who saw only danger in Gladstone's Irish policy. These defections constituted a major event in British party history, adding another dimension to the Conservatives' claim to be a truly national party. There is no doubt that the Whigs reinforced the libertarian strand of conservatism.

Around the turn of the century a policy issue was to emerge as injurious in its consequences for the party, at least in the short term, as Corn Law Repeal had been: imperial preference.[47] Imperial preference entailed the creation of an empire-wide tariff barrier behind which a common defence strategy would develop, leading finally to imperial federation. Although pursued principally by Chamberlain the Unionist, imperial preference fitted well with the Disraelian concept of an empire-wide community of kith and kin. At the same time it was at odds with the laissez-faire stance of libertarian Conservatives and the only palpable consequence of this fiercely contested battle, between change and intervention on the one hand and stability and laissez-faire libertarianism on the other, was to 'cast the Conservative Party into confusion and internecine strife and help to achieve [in 1906] what had seemed inconceivable in 1900 – a Liberal government'.[48]

In those early years of the new century the party's attention was seized by another issue of change versus stability: Home Rule for Ireland. True, the passage of the bill to grant Dublin Home Rule had been made possible only because the Irish held the balance of power; true the House of Lords' constitutional powers of restraint had recently been severely clipped by the Liberal government – again with Irish support – so there were genuine grounds for complaint. With the advent to the leadership of Bonar Law, of Ulster Presbyterian stock, the party's natural reluctance to see the Union weakened intensified to the extent that it offered support to Ulstermen prepared to take up arms to oppose Home Rule. 'Ulster will fight and Ulster will be right' was an unequivocal message whose implication was support for the gun against the ballot box and the dispatch box. Conservative thinkers have always been clear about the primacy of the constitution and the rule of law; to pick and choose which laws an individual will and will not obey is not compatible with Conservatism. Winston Churchill, a minister in the Liberal government but an erstwhile and future Conservative, remarked that Bonar Law's motion of censure on the government's Irish policy constituted support for an attack by the criminal classes upon the police. Events on the continent of Europe in 1914 took precedence over Irish affairs but the issue illustrates the Conservatives' difficulty in adapting to change. Their obduracy could have led to a vicious civil war in the whole of Ireland.

New enemies: Socialists come to power

In the inter-war period Conservatives had to come to terms with a new political order, the chief features of which were the apparently terminal decline of the

Liberal Party and the inexorable rise of Labour. Nevertheless alone or in coalition the party ran the nation's affairs for almost the entire period. When, following the Second World War, Labour was strong enough to provide a coherent challenge; the Conservative Party was swept from power in a comprehensive electoral defeat almost as great as 1906. So stunning was this defeat that it provoked a major reappraisal of Conservative ideology and policy. Once again the party had been wrong-footed by change: it had given the impression of seeking to recreate the conditions of a laissez-faire pre-war world, which most citizens rejected.

The party was fortunate to possess men like Butler and Macmillan, who were committed to transforming the party so that it might convince the electorate, in Butler's words, that 'we had an alternative policy to socialism which was viable, efficient and humane, which could release and reward enterprise and initiative but without abandoning social justice or reverting to mass unemployment'.[49] Under Butler's guidance, a new Industrial Charter, committing the party to a policy of full employment and Keynesian demand-led economic management, was promulgated. This Charter and the others that followed provided the party with modern, more inclusive policies, while at the same time restoring confidence among the shell-shocked party faithful that socialism could be defeated. Butler, who saw his task as being similar to Peel's one hundred or so years earlier, did not create something out of nothing: a group of influential younger Conservatives had laid the foundations in the 1930s and early 1940s.[50]

The public proved ready to respond to a modern non-socialist party, since the austerities of the late 1940s were beginning to sap morale. So in 1951, after Labour had found it impossible to sustain itself in government following a very narrow electoral victory of 1950, the Conservatives came into power for thirteen years. The early years saw deregistration, the burning of ration books, the spread of material benefits among all classes in a way never seen before. The British people became convinced, in a phrase attributed (erroneously) to Prime Minister Harold Macmillan, that they had 'never had it so good'. If at first its policies had been libertarian, they became increasingly more paternalistic under Macmillan.

Macmillan's government probably represented the fullest expression of Conservative organicism or paternalism – his opponents would say collectivism – since Disraeli.[51] The policies of his government sustained the privileges of the wealthy and yet improved the lot of ordinary people: prosperity trickled down. Moreover, Macmillan saw the necessity of fundamental changes in British foreign policy and managed to make many of them. He won his party over to the dismantling of the British Empire, although his failure to gain British membership of the European Economic Community (EEC) as a result of a French veto proved humiliating.

Managerialism and the eclipse of the Tory paternalist tradition

Edward Heath had his own ideas on the proper balance between stability and change. In many respects Heath represented a departure for the Conservatives. Although he was not the first non-patrician to lead the party (Macmillan had been a patrician by marriage) he was the first lower-middle-class leader, the first 'man of the people'. In *The Making of Conservative Party Policy*, Ramsden quotes a letter from a middle-aged industrial manager and lifelong Conservative that sums up the expectations that Heath aroused among Whiggite Conservatives. He writes:

> We were sick of seeing old men dressed in flat caps and bedraggled tweeds strolling about with 12 bores....The nearest approach to our man is Heath.... He is our age, he is capable, he looks like a director [of the country].[52]

That phrase 'he looks like a director' sums up the new balance in Conservatism that Heath sought to build in response to the electoral successes of Harold Wilson in the 1960s. If he had a picture of an ideal Britain when he came to office, it was of a meritocratic society built upon the success of the technological revolution. Not only this, but also his whole approach to politics, the ethos of his cabinet, was radical, libertarian and 'managerial' rather than sceptical, organicist or paternalist; above all, it rejected traditionalism and intervention.

Heath was nothing if not a pro-European and he it was who piloted Britain through the dangerous waters towards membership of the EEC. Not for him the nostalgia for empire nor Powell's belief in national sovereignty, both more traditional Conservative attitudes.[53] Heath's overriding concern was for the efficiency and competitiveness of British industry. His approach, nicknamed the politics of 'Selsdon Man' (after a conference at Selsdon Park in 1970 from which this general approach emerged), was to oppose macro-economic planning and statutory incomes policies and to favour intervention only to limit trade union powers by statute. What Britain needed was resolute business management and the discipline of the market to bring it out of economic stagnation.

By mid-term the centrepiece of Heathite policy, the Industrial Relations Act of 1972, which sought to constrain the power of the unions, was acknowledged to have failed. The Industry Act of 1972 which replaced it constituted a complete rejection of the politics of Selsdon Man. Heath may be accused of reneging, Peel-like, on party commitments; alternatively he may be applauded for having learned from his mistakes. Within the space of a year he was transmogrified from Selsdon Man into Neo-Corporatist Man, a change as complete as that from Jekyll to Hyde (or vice versa). The phase two Heath government, however, proved no more successful than phase one and the party was defeated in 1974;[54] it did not return to office until 1979 under the leadership of Margaret Thatcher. Another attempt to manage change and, in this case, to opt for libertarian detachment as against paternalistic intervention had failed.

New horizons? Thatcherite Conservatism

From the outset Margaret Thatcher described herself as a 'conviction politician', which immediately set her apart from the Conservative pragmatic tradition. The nub of her conviction was that the social democratic state of the post-war consensus had failed at all levels. 'The Thatcher leadership', said Andrew Gamble, in one of the best accounts of her governments, 'united the Conservative Party around the claims that the country had become overtaxed, over-governed and undisciplined'.[55] A Conservative government under Thatcher would 'impose, nurture and stimulate the business values, attitudes and practices necessary to relaunch Britain as a successful capitalist economy'.[56]

Gamble attempted to unravel the interwoven strands of Thatcherite conservatism, though he warned 'her right wing views always appeared to be much more of a matter of instinct than rational argument'.[57] He discerned two tendencies. The first was the neo-liberal belief in the efficacy of markets and 'sound money' (absence of inflation), and the Friedmanite faith in deregulation and privatisation, with its concomitant reduction in taxation and public expenditure.[58] Gamble concluded that, generally speaking, 'the intellectual case for markets appeared overwhelming, much as the intellectual case for planning had appeared overwhelming to an earlier generation of intellectuals'.[59]

Gamble's second tendency was the traditionally Conservative belief in strong government. 'Never let it be said that I am laissez-faire,' Thatcher insisted.

> We are a very strong government. We are strong enough to do these things that government must do and only governments can do. We are strong enough to say 'over to the people' because we believe in their fundamental dignity and freedom.[60]

The Heath government, she believed, had been jostled into a form of corporatism sustained later by Callaghan, but both had been undermined by militant trade unionism. Thatcher made no secret of her ambition to break this particular mould.[61] In the 'truly public' areas of defence, law and order and industrial relations, Thatcher sought a strong government willing and able to force people to be free, so that they could exhibit those values of enterprise, initiative, robust independence and patriotism which were seen to be the foundations of a successful libertarian state. While in opposition she set up two commissions to report on how a future Conservative government might take on militant unions. Their reports were to prove very useful when Thatcher took on and defeated the striking miners in 1984. Were these the marks of a Conservative society? The interventionist Macmillan and the traditional paternalists might not have recognised them as such but a nineteenth-century Whig and a traditional libertarian would have applauded them.

Thatcher's governments did more than any before or since to extend property ownership, through the sale of council houses, to people who could not normally have even aspired to own their own homes. On the other hand Thatcher had nothing but scorn for those traditional institutions that helped to run the despised social democratic consensus. The Church of England, the BBC, the House of Lords, the Civil Service, the army, the navy, the universities, the National Health Service (NHS), even the Football League, all came under threat from the infamous handbag. She was no traditionalist. Her whole philosophy rested upon the assumption of the demonstrable superiority of the market and she was prepared to legislate to create the right domestic framework for market economics. No sceptic she. Thatcher infamously declared that there was no such thing as 'society',[62] to which Gilmour responded: 'there is nothing Tory about a powerful government presiding over a country of atomised individuals, with its intermediate institutions emasculated or abolished'.[63] David Levy seemed to agree: the autonomous individual, free of the 'encrustation of cultural formation', was a Liberal rather than a Conservative, and patently self-destructive.[64] No organicist then.

But Thatcher's governments intervened in matters that libertarians would not have considered 'truly public'. David Marquand pointed out that the Education Reform Act of 1988, one example among many, was highly dirigiste in method and centralist in intent.[65] Thatcher used the state to attempt to reshape society; precisely the kind of enterprise that libertarian Conservatives have traditionally considered both inappropriate and obnoxious. The Education Reform Act of 1988 conferred no fewer than 240 new powers upon the Secretary of State, more than 60 of which were the direct result of government amendments during the passage of the Bill. Moreover, in July 1988 over 500 government-inspired House of Lords amendments to the Education Bill (and over 400 to the Local Government Bill) were driven through the House of Commons in three days.[66] So much for the rule of law, limited government and libertarianism.

Any claim that Thatcher was a pragmatist must be weighed against her government's policy regarding a replacement for domestic rates. That the rating system had all but broken down, especially in Scotland, is generally accepted; that the community charge (the soon-to-be notorious Poll Tax) was a suitable replacement is doubtful. What cannot be accepted or even argued is that a pragmatist would have persevered with the Poll Tax when it received such intense universal opprobrium. The lady was not for turning, even by colleagues offering sound advice.

Margaret Thatcher had not that temperament that marks the traditional Conservative who, according to the Earl of Derby, has no confidence in regenerating his fellow beings and believes instead in gradual, steady, step-by-step amelioration. Not for her the modesty that comes from Burke's mistrust of humankind's 'fallible and feeble' reason.

Picking up the pieces: Conservatism after Thatcher

John Major, Thatcher's successor, was to prove that though pragmatism might be a necessary attribute of a Conservative leader, it was by no means a sufficient one. Major's complete lack of any apparent ideological ballast received critical comment from foes and, significantly, from friends too. Major managed to win the 1992 general election against all expectations (including his own) with a majority of twenty-one – small by Conservative standards – but Britain was forced out of the European Exchange Rate Mechanism within six months of this victory. Growing opposition to his European policies placed severe constraints on Major's position. He continued with Thatcher's policies of privatisation and civil service reform, delivering what many had looked for – Thatcherism without Thatcher. His Citizens' Charters were intended to give the public guaranteed rights in respect of both public and privatised service provision, and his Back to Basics campaign was an ill-fated attempt to promote family values. More in the

Conservative mainstream than his predecessor, Major's room for manoeuvre was limited by his small and diminishing majority but even more by the accelerated programme of European integration, which impaled the government time and again on issues of sovereignty. If all this were not enough, the government was engulfed by a torrent of sleaze that destroyed its credibility, especially with its own voters. Above all else, though, the Conservative Party after Thatcher became a battleground on which ferocious battles were fought in her name between the pro- and anti-Europeans, a battle largely responsible for the party's defeat at the polls in 1997.

Major's resignation immediately after that defeat catapulted the party into a leadership election at a time of maximum confusion when one of the foremost contenders, Michael Portillo, had just lost his seat. In the event the parliamentary party, reduced to 165, elected 35-year-old William Hague, an ex-Secretary of State for Wales, as its leader. Hague earned the enmity of senior pro-Europeans such as Clarke and Heseltine by pursuing Eurosceptic policies. At conference Hague declared a belief in community, in a Conservatism that had 'compassion at its core'. He reached out to the young, to women, to ethnic minorities and to the homosexual community.[67] In 1999 Hague outlined his vision of a Conservatism that would define and champion British values, a rebuke to those within his party who sought to exploit the growing mood of English nationalism, which Hague described as a 'sinister, uncontrollable force'.[68] He emphasised the need to accept change and inclusiveness, in short to anchor the party in the modern world. Yet in the election of 2001 the party reverted to the kind of anti-European, anti-immigrant programme that might gain favour with its core support, and that was all it did.

Following the defeat of 2001 Hague resigned. Iain Duncan Smith, whose main credential was that he was solidly Eurosceptic, began a brief period in office that was eminently forgettable and he was soon ousted to general acclaim by Thatcher's former Home Secretary Michael Howard. Although Howard brought experience and a certain gravitas to the leadership, he was as unable to redefine Conservatism as were his two predecessors and his electoral campaign in 2005 was undistin-guished and unsuccessful. After this third consecutive defeat the party elected the youthful David Cameron as its new leader.

Like his predecessors Cameron has to deal with the Thatcher legacy, less divisive as time passes but still potent. Though he is not a part of that legacy, he does still need to define his Conservatism in response to Thatcherism. Cameron has abstemiously avoided identifying specific policy commitments; instead he has sought to articulate his view of Conservatism's fundamental and working prin-ciples. 'There is a *we* as well as a *me* in politics,' he claims, stressing organicism and its values, and the perceived enemies of this organicism are the all-powerful state and the large corporations. Organicism is to operate in political life via the rebuilding of local communities. Cameron sees New Labour as the enemy of community because it has espoused 'the steady encroachment of the state into the private sphere of voluntarism'. Hybrid organisations, nominally independent but in reality parasitic appendages of the state such as public–private partnership ventures, Network Rail, foundation hospitals, university funding councils and so on, have mushroomed since 1997. Cameron wishes to reinvigorate the sense of community via what is being called localism. In giving control back to local communities Cameron is stressing that, contrary to Thatcher's dictum, there *is* such a thing as society and it, not the individual or the state, is the motor of well-being. Again in marked contrast to Thatcherism, the goal is not wealth and the primacy of the individual but well-being and the primacy of local communities. It is too early to make any judgement on how seriously to take what appears to be a genuine reappraisal of modern conservatism, but at least Cameron and his advisers appear to have cast aside the post-Thatcher laager mentality of xenophobia.[69] If Cameron's approach is not collectivist in tone, neither was Disraeli's one nation Conservatism. Disraeli told electors at Buckingham once that collectivism if unchecked posed a threat to the national character and concluded with an aphorism that, suitably amended, Cameron could take to heart: 'England should be governed by England, not by London'.[70] In 2006 Cameron produced a document, *Built to Last*, which formed a general statement of where he thought conservatism should move.[71] In general terms he sought to infiltrate and take over traditional Labour policy areas, much as Blair had done in respect of traditional Conservative areas of strength in the 1990s, assuring us for example that the NHS would be safer in Conservative hands.

Conclusions

Having established the chief characteristics of Conservatism and viewed them in operation, we might conclude that the actual policies pursued by Conservative leaders frequently show little more than a symbolic relationship to party ideology and tradition: about as related as Picasso's violin and dish were to the real thing. Conservatives were opposed to parliamentary reform and then became its champion; opposed to Corn Law reform and then became its agent; opposed to the development of the empire, then became its enthusiastic supporter, only finally to become the dismantler of empire; in favour of state intervention to the extent of setting up the frame of a neo-corporatist state, only to become an unrelenting critic of such a state. We have portrayed the history of the Conservative Party as a constant struggle between stability and change, paternalism and libertarianism; although this provides a perspective it does not offer a consistent pattern. If Conservatism (defined as what Conservative governments 'do', not what Conservative thinkers say) has any consistency, then perhaps it resides in some other general principle that we have not uncovered so far. Perhaps Namier was right: the party's true identity must be sought elsewhere than in its ideology.

Suppose we were to take Conservatism to represent – substantially though by no means entirely – a rationalisation of the interests of the advantaged, political actions consciously taken by the socially privileged classes to protect their own status. Conservatism defined in these terms would develop as the interests of that class developed.[72] What then of fundamental principles? Traditionalism, as the historian Eric Hobsbawm has argued, is an invention favouring the retention of institutions and customs that allow the advantaged to dominate the polity.[73] Organicism, too, favours the advantaged; it is easier to believe that the hierarchical society is natural when one is nearer the top than the bottom. Again, we should be more inclined to be dismissive of large-scale plans for human betterment, more inclined, that is, to be sceptical, if our own interests were already favoured. Finally, it is safer to argue for limited government when, because of good fortune or wealthy forebears, we are capable of safeguarding our own interests. For the 'poor man at the gate' whose family is hungry, any injury to individual liberty produced by government intervention to feed them would only be welcomed; indeed he might consider the freedom to go hungry a right he was willing to forgo.[74] All in all, while we must recognise the long and distinguished history of benevolent paternalism – humanitarian radicalism Greenleaf called it – we might also give some thought to Bernard Shaw's typically waspish conclusion that the rich had shown themselves prepared to give anything up for the poor except the principle and practice of robbing them.[75] Joseph Chamberlain, while he was still a Liberal, told his lover Beatrice Webb that the rich had always ruled in their own interests – and that they had made a very good job of it.

The twin tensions of Conservatism could be described as attempting to optimise and manage social and economic privilege when the pressures completely to resist change become too great. A Marxist would argue that in sustaining the interests of the capitalist class as a whole, the Conservative Party found it expedient from time to time to sacrifice a fraction of capital. Well, Conservatives have never been as clear-sighted or logical as Marx implied and they were seldom of one mind, but the evidence suggests a relationship between the interests of capital and Conservative ideology and policy. Social cohesion linked to a degree of political change is important to the well-being of modern capitalism and the ability to provide that link through the balance of its fundamental and working principles has traditionally guaranteed the Conservative Party the alliance of wealthy capitalists and the support of the middle class (and sections of the working class).

Let us put this theory briefly to the test. How did Thatcherism for example safeguard the interests of the wealthy? Gamble argues that the apparent disadvantages, such as high interest rates, were short term and limited, and were more than balanced by long-term general advantages; short-term bankruptcies were outweighed by the longer-term improvements in the environment for expansion. 'The essential requirement for this', says Gamble, 'was a government prepared to confront and permanently weaken the organised power of labour.'[76] That surely was Thatcher's lasting legacy.

And yet Thatcherism was surely more than a front for the interests of capital. Some of Thatcher's policies struck such an obvious chord with popular sentiment that Stuart Hall called Thatcherism 'authoritarian populism'.[77] Moreover, as John Gray noted,[78] in its scorn for the identity and continuity of long-established institutions such as the civil service, local government and the NHS, the Tories under Thatcher wrought havoc among many of their natural supporters. Her government's policies weakened, even destroyed, the natural trust of the British for their institutions. Job insecurity and shrinking equity, Gray continues, pauperised sections of the middle class – the reversal of 'bourgeoisification'. Thatcherism was partly concerned to modernise Britain's *ancien régime*; its success was predominantly at the expense of its own supporters especially in Scotland and Wales. In short, if Thatcher is any guide, defence of the interests of the wealthy is not the only motivation of Conservatives.

The one issue that could be said to have defined the party since Thatcher, Euroscepticism, is still its defining characteristic, and it still does not chime with the interests of conservatism's traditional commercial and industrial support.[79] With the routing of the Europhiles more or less complete though, Cameron has the opportunity to claim new ideological ground (or more accurately reclaim old ground) by championing communities through 'localism'.[80] In attempting to modernise his party Cameron has met increasing resistance.[81] His policy to build no new grammar schools, which he misguidedly turned into a test of his authority, was opposed by many within the party and he was obliged to modify his stance. Later the Shadow Chancellor of the Exchequer George Osborne boldly referred to the Tories as the 'heirs to Blair',[82] prompting David Davis, in a statement that caused some alarm, to declare that he and William Hague would act as 'guarantors' of traditional policy.[83] On the other hand, others thought that Cameron's changes were insubstantial; disappointed, one senior colleague jumped ship.[84] Cameron must stake out this ground carefully but firmly if the party is to remain ideologically distinctive and not to drift in a direction some would say that Thatcher had already begun to chart, towards a narrow-minded English nationalism.[85] Towards the end of 2007 he made an audacious bid to do exactly that. He launched a campaign to persuade the Liberal Democrats and the Greens to forge a 'new progressive alliance' to challenge Brown. It was a call for the new Liberal Democrat leader to make a stand against the over-powerful state in favour of true decentralisation and 'empowering individuals and communities'. In a party pamphlet the Conservatives spelled out their new belief that not only was there such a thing as society but that it, not the state, would prove the appropriate means to tackle the country's problems.[86] Sceptics might see this call as a partisan attempt to destabilise the new Liberal Democrat leader – and it might be – but it might also be part of a broad strategy truly to establish the Conservatives as a progressive, decentralising force. Perhaps Cameron's campaign is largely rhetorical but as I shall try to show later, rhetoric and reality are often close cousins.

3   Labour Party ideology

Although dating the origins of British socialism is not difficult, it would be reasonable to ask what the point was: what has socialism got to do with today's Labour Party? The Labour Party has officially turned its back upon what it somewhat dismissively calls Old Labour and socialism. In fact throughout its history many felt that the connection between the Labour Party and socialism was rather tenuous. Nevertheless it would be impossible to write a sensible account of the Labour Party without rooting it in traditional socialism.

The word 'socialist' was used for the first time in November 1827, when Robert Owen's *Co-operative Magazine* advanced the principle that cooperation was superior to competition and that consequently capital should be 'socially' owned.[1] Owen's argument encompasses two related themes, ethical and economic. The ethical theme suggests that people should be far more equal than they were in Owen's time, and that only socially owned industries and enterprises could bring this about. In doing so – in fact as a direct result of doing so – these industries would become more economically efficient.

The basic principles of socialism

Conservatism was plausibly described as an attitude of mind: the word has a meaning outside of politics. The word socialism, in contrast, has no meaning outside politics. It can be used only to describe a political organisation or party that is dedicated to bringing about a socialist state or society. Socialism was the motive for founding the Labour Party so when we look for the basic principles of socialism we will not find them through an historical analysis of parliamentarians but among the thoughts, words and deeds of social activists and thinkers.

Owen had been right to establish equality as the *sine qua non* of socialism: it was the one feature about which nearly all socialists agreed.[2] The trouble was, it became increasingly clear that they were not agreed as to what equality actually meant. These differences were sufficiently profound to prompt Dennis and Halsey to note: 'Divisions within socialism have been as bitter and crucial as conflicts between socialism and its competing ideologies.'[3]

Christian socialism

Christian socialism draws its inspiration from the Judaeo-Christian tradition, more especially from the teachings of Christ, who declared that all were equal in the eyes of God. Christ himself was a manual worker, and when he said that it would be easier for a camel to pass through the eye of a needle than it would be for a rich man to enter into Heaven,[4] when he told the pious young man who sought to follow him to give his wealth up to the poor,[5] he appeared to be advocating a society of economic equality. More specifically he said: 'Blessed are you poor, for yours is the Kingdom of God'.[6] In the community dedicated to Christ's teaching, we are told that those who owned property sold it and the proceeds were redistributed 'unto every man according as he had need'.[7] It would be naive to imagine that other political ideologies could not commandeer aspects of Christian teaching to suit their own ideological purposes, but the Christian socialists' case is a strong one; it was often said that British socialism owed more to Methodism than to Marxism.[8]

At the time of the People's Charter (1848), a group of Christian apologists, including the theologian F.D. Maurice,[9] and the writers Charles Kingsley,[10] and Thomas Hughes,[11] discussed how best the Church could support the just grievances of the workers. In *The Kingdom of Christ* Maurice championed Owenite cooperative ideas of profit sharing as a way to ameliorate poverty. Two short-lived journals were published, *Politics of the People* and *The Christian Socialist*, as were a number of pamphlets. As social tensions diminished so the movement lost its way and became influential again only as working-class agitation grew through the 1870s and early 1880s. A variety of new groups emerged, among which the most important were the Christian Social Union and Stewart Headlam's Guild of St Matthew. Their influence was wide and enduring.[12]

Ethical socialism

Though often mistaken for Christian socialists, ethical socialists are not the same animals. What is distinctive about ethical socialism, say Dennis and Halsey,[13] is its faith in 'the good sense of ordinary people',[14] who exhibit the commitment to 'fraternity across the board' that shaped the Labour Party.[15] Among early socialists William Morris could be said to represent this tradition as well as anyone;[16] his utopian novel *News from Nowhere* offered a clear vision of the kind of free, equal community of 'ordinary people' that ethical socialists cherished.[17] If we sought a motto for ethical socialism, we need look no further than Morris's character Father John Ball, who claimed: 'Fellowship is heaven and the lack of fellowship is hell'.[18]

Ethical socialist institutions included the Socialist Sunday School Movement founded in Glasgow in the 1890s. Often these Sunday Schools were not specifically Christian in character and met in premises owned by a trade union. They thrived in the West of Scotland and in the West Riding of Yorkshire but were also to be found in most big cities. The Labour Church movement began in Manchester in 1891. Although the founder was a Christian,[19] many of his followers were not, though they would have sympathised with the aim of establishing the 'Kingdom of God upon Earth'. Many leading figures in the Labour movement were active in the Labour Church, for example Keir Hardie, Ben Tillett, Tom Mann, Fred Jowett and Philip Snowden. The first meeting of the Independent Labour Party in 1893 was held in the Bradford Labour Church.

Scientific socialism

Unlike ethical socialists, scientific socialists did not believe in empowering ordinary people but in the efficient running of the economy and of society, and in the equitable distribution of goods and services. For the scientific socialists, equality had to be built and building was the work of experts. Power should not be dispersed because ordinary people would not know what to do with it. It should be aggregated and used for the benefit of all. Early exemplars of scientific socialism in Britain were the Marxist Social Democratic Federation (SDF) and the Fabians, of whom Bernard Shaw was a founder member. The Fabians held that the state had to be controlled in the interests of all by a scientifically trained elite – such as themselves.

In the early years of its existence the Fabian Society opposed the setting up of a socialist party, preferring instead to act as a pressure group influencing governments of either party. Nevertheless they reluctantly played a part in establishing Labour and were influential in setting the party's policy agenda and later writing its constitution. Moreover it was Fabian influence and largely Fabian money (Beatrice Webb came from a wealthy family) that helped establish the London School of Economics and Political Science precisely to train the kind of elite needed to run a socialist state. After the Russian Revolution of 1917 they drew inspiration from the new Soviet state and several of their leading figures visited Moscow and met Lenin.[20] Fabians have played a major role over the years in the affairs of the Labour Party, in the world both of theory and practice. The Fabian Society remains a Labour 'think tank', publishing papers that have influenced the parliamentary party and providing influential leaders from within its ranks.

Popular socialism

Although I have described socialism as a specifically political and more precisely ideological phenomenon, one of its manifestations was the largely working-class Clarion Movement, which forsook ideology and attempted to live out socialist values. The movement was founded by a journalist, Robert Blatchford, who established a socialist weekly, *The Clarion*. Blatchford's first leading article declared: 'The policy of *The Clarion* is a policy of humanity, a policy not of party, sect or creed; but of justice reason and mercy.' The paper's primary aim was to 'make socialists' by explaining the aims of socialism in simple language. With a weekly circulation of 80,000 the movement bore fruit in a variety of working-class activities: Clarion cycle clubs, vocal unions, choirs, dramatic societies (whose stated aim was to develop dramatic art and to propagate socialist ideas), camera clubs, handicraft groups, swimming clubs, ramblers' clubs and a number of sports groups. In short the Clarion Movement was the embodiment of fellowship, of the effort to build socialism into the lives of ordinary people, and it found a major role in all these things for women. Blatchford produced a book, *Merrie England*, illustrating his socialist ideas, which sold over two million copies.

Trade unions and labourism

Another of the guiding principles of British socialism was provided by the trade union movement.[21] During the 1880s unions representing unskilled workers such as the matchmakers, gas workers and the dockers undertook successful strike action for better pay and working conditions, thereby increasing the self-confidence of the labour movement generally. Union representatives were standing successfully for parliament, and the miners (who at the time took the Liberal parliamentary whip) were especially successful. In 1893 a meeting was called at Bradford by trade unionists, who invited representatives of various socialist societies specifically to advance the parliamentary representation and political visibility of labour. The result was the establishment of the Independent Labour Party (ILP), whose task would be to coordinate support for labour parliamentary candidates (the word 'socialism' was not actually used in documents emerging from Bradford). The next step was the creation in 1900 of the Labour Representation Committee (LRC), which sought to establish a cohesive unit in parliament to advance the cause of labour financed by the unions.[22]

There were always socialists, William Morris for example, who argued against taking the parliamentary path, fearing that socialism would lose both its radical edge and its working-class character. For the unions parliamentary representation made good sense: by the turn of the century the working-class man had the vote and some working-class men sat in the House of Commons. Keir Hardie had won West Ham South in 1892 as an independent socialist but the interests of organised labour (labourism) rather than the ideology of socialism had won Hardie his seat.[23] Keir Hardie's definition of 'labourism' was:

> The theory and practice which accepted the possibility of social change within the existing framework of society; which rejected the revolutionary violence and which increasingly recognised the working of parliamentary democracy as the practical means of achieving its own aims and objectives.[24]

The pre-1914 Labour Party represented, in Coates' words, an 'expression of trade union aspirations which involved no coherent programme and no officially accepted socialist commitment'.[25]

Marxist socialism

Marx's influence on British socialism has been far less direct than on continental socialism, but it has affected the thinking of British socialists greatly.[26] One concept that Marx made common currency among socialists was alienation. Humans, says Marx, are consciously species beings and have a species activity, labour. To find fulfilment individuals must 'objectify' their labour in an end product. But under capitalism the workers have no control over the product of their labour. What people help to *make* becomes more important than what they *are*. Under capitalism workers become alienated from the fruit of their labour, from the activity of labour and from their fellow beings, especially from the exploiters of their labour.

Why not throw off the capitalist yoke? Here we come to Marx's second major contribution to the fundamental principles of socialism: the concept of false consciousness.[27] It is not their consciousness that determines people's social existence, but their social existence that determines their consciousness. And what determines people's social existence? The 'relations of production' (that is, the way economic life is organised). Now, since the relations of production are dominated by the capitalist class, it follows that all the institutions that help to shape people's attitudes, such as the education system, the health system, the churches, the mass media, sport and so on, are also dominated by the values of capitalism, thus shaping people's ideas and attitudes (their consciousness).[28] We see the result of this in Robert Tressell's working-class novel written in 1911, *The Ragged Trousered Philanthropists*, whose characters argue that the world 'can't never be altered...There's always been rich and poor in the world, and there always will be'.[29] The philanthropists of the title are the workers themselves who, cocooned in their false consciousness, donate their birthright to the owners of capital.

But this state of affairs would not continue forever, because a proletarian revolution (Marx's third contribution to fundamental socialist principles) would inevitably occur. Why inevitably? Because all history hitherto had been driven by revolution, and capitalism's internal contradictions would lead the capitalists increasingly to restrict the worker to a subsistence wage so as to make a profit. Competition would intensify, leading to falling profits and hence the growing emiseration of the proletariat, until finally a 'true' consciousness of their position will be forced upon workers, leading inevitably to the final, proletarian revolution and a classless society.

But who would lead the revolution? The proletariat could hardly manage such a grandiose objective without leadership, and here Marx's final contribution to fundamentalist principles emerges, the concept of the 'dictatorship of the proletariat'.[30] There would have to be a transitional stage between the overthrow of capitalism and the establishment of communism when strong leadership would be required and socialist intellectuals would play the leading role. Eventually the state would wither away allowing socialist communism to emerge. Many British socialists subscribed to some or all of Marx's theories.

These are the basic principles of British socialism.[31] We should remember that they were powerful enough to motivate men and women not only to participate in the political system but also to attempt to *change* that system, through persuasion not revolution.

Working principles

When we come to examine how they sought to change the system, we discover a number of working principles of socialism.

Democratic collectivism

This principle was endorsed chiefly by those we have described as scientific socialists. There were two principal groups who could be said to have sponsored the goal of a strong central state. First was the SDF, which had begun in 1881 as the Democratic Federation.[32] It developed as a Marxist group and was dominated by H.M. Hyndman, the best known of the early British Marxists. It was intent upon establishing a Marxist state, and though it was prepared to 'use' parliament,[33] it regularly drilled its members and preached revolution. Second was the avowedly elitist Fabian Society, founded in 1884. Fabian collectivism favoured the creation of the public ownership of the means of production by a strong state, which would act on behalf of citizens. For the Fabians socialism was not about giving power to the people; Bernard Shaw claimed that they had never advanced any pretension even to represent the working man,[34] and when challenged on the obvious lack of democracy implied by this claim – or disclaimer – he countered that the only useful definition of democracy was a political system that aimed for 'the greatest available welfare for the whole population'.[35] Intellectually the Fabians were, and remain, the most influential of the socialist groups, but the Fabian Society always abstemiously avoided a large membership, preferring to see itself as an intellectual vanguard.[36]

Democratic localism

There were other socialists whose aim was a decentralised society of small self-governing communities, as envisaged by Marx's 'withering away' theory. The Socialist League (SL), founded in 1886 by William Morris, Marx's son-in-law Aveling, and Belfort Bax, was revolutionary, anti-parliamentarian and anti-authoritarian, and quickly acquired a reputation for anarchism. In 1891 however, Morris, fearing just such a drift towards anarchism, withdrew to form the Hammersmith Socialist Society; the SL disintegrated into factions and eventually disappeared. Morris's personal influence was always substantial. (One of his 'converts' was the journalist Robert Blatchford, whose socialism was also distinctly localist.) Two other varieties of localism were influential among socialists. The first was the municipal movement that sought to advance socialism through the powerful local authorities that were established during the 1880s. A number who were active in local politics were collectivists at heart but saw localism as a second best. Bernard Shaw, for example, was a vestryman for St Pancras in London.[37] The second was a strand of socialist thought that was more influential in both European and American socialism, syndicalism. Syndicalists believed that to empower a strong central state *à la* Fabian Society would create not socialism but only state capitalism. Far better to give workers a part in the management of the industries in which they worked, so that they might control their own lives. This brand of localism had little to say, however, to non-industrial workers or to the majority of women. A characteristically less abrasive British form of syndicalism, which flourished before 1914, was guild socialism.[38]

Social democratic gradualism

There were considerable numbers of socialists, including the majority of trade unionists, who were not anxious to reconstruct the state but wanted simply to make it work more efficiently for the good of all. They wished to increase working-class representation in parliament so that they could use the constitution to establish broader rights for workers. Many had no fundamental animosity to capitalism but wished to amend the rules under which it worked, to constrain capitalism for the common good. These socialists were pragmatists rather than ideologists and they have remained influential throughout the history of the movement. Foremost among Labour's most influential gradualist (and ethical socialist) thinkers was R.H. Tawney.[39]

Internationalism

The final working principle is internationalism. Socialism was an international movement and it preached unity among all workers. 'Workers of the world unite, and throw off your chains', Marx and Engels exhorted. What a Lanarkshire miner had in common with a Silesian miner was more important than what he had in common with a Fife mine owner. When the nations went to war in 1914 however, socialists forsook their beliefs and fought fellow socialists.[40] In 1939 the socialist writer George Orwell was certain that British workers would not take up arms to defend British capitalism against German capitalism, even in its virulent form of Nazism. But they did, and so did he.[41] Internationalism formed an important strand of socialism in its early days but it proved unable to prevent war in Europe. After the Russian Revolution of 1917, the 'Soviet Sixth' of the world came to constitute the great hope for socialists everywhere. Marx had taught that socialism in one country was not truly viable. In Britain a number of highly placed supporters of the Soviet Union ('fellow travellers') betrayed their country by spying for the Soviets.

Tensions within socialism

From its inception British socialism was at best an uneasy alliance. According to R.N. Berki, socialism was never and nowhere a 'single thing, but a range, an area, an open texture, a self-contradiction'.[42] Like the Conservatives, Labour has had to manage internal tensions in the course of its history.

Ethical socialism versus scientific socialism

The simplest way of expressing this tension is to portray it as contrasting the notions of building socialism up from the bottom and setting it in place from above. When we consider ethical and popular socialism, we can see commonalities. They wanted to use the instinctive common sense and natural propensity towards equality and social justice among ordinary people. They tended to support a system of government that favoured the local community over the strong central state and they had an instinctive distaste for bureaucracy. One of the best known statements of this tradition is George Orwell's *The Road to Wigan Pier* (1937), in which the values of ordinary working people are used as an example of the values that a socialist state should embody.

For the scientific socialists, on the other hand, good government was a science, a thing for specialists and not for ordinary people. They stressed the bureaucratic nature of their enterprise. Home Secretary Herbert Morrison wanted to 'build a new way of life…for one of our purposes is to make men and women better than they are, and to promote "sweetness and light"'.[43] This aim was stated even more forcibly by a Labour local councillor, who said of working people: 'They can't go greyhound racing or do the pools or smoke twenty cigarettes a day or buy monster comics.…We're building a new race of people who won't want to do these things'.[44] Scientific socialists want to *make* men and women better than they were, to *build* a new race of people who would be above simple traditional pleasures. To paraphrase George Orwell, scientific socialists believe that the clever ones should tell the rest of us what to do.[45]

Trade unionism and the wider interest

There is no inevitable conflict between trade union interests and the wider interest but Labour governments might be torn between acting in the national interest while damaging the trade union interests, or vice versa. In 1969, for example, Wilson shied away from implementing reform of the unions, which he considered to be in the public interest because of union pressures from *within* his party. This is an obvious tension for a party that is said to have grown out of the bowels of the trade union movement.

Fundamentalism versus gradualism

For the fundamentalist socialists (scientific or ethical) the way to achieve socialism is through transformation, maybe through revolution. During the 1880s and 1890s many leading socialists championed revolutionary change. Marx, we know, thought revolution pretty well inevitable. In his utopian socialist novel *News from Nowhere*, William Morris devoted one-third of the book to an account of the revolution that brought his utopia into being. Gradualists too had a clear agenda of general social reform to be achieved but they favoured separate small steps rather than great leaps. For the fundamentalists society had to cross a wide chasm to reach socialism: small steps were not a good idea. These were the tensions that made socialism into Berki's 'self-contradiction'; the tensions that prompted H.G. Wells to comment: 'To understand socialism…is to gain a new breadth in outlook: to join a socialist organisation is to join a narrow cult'.[46]

Before concluding this section I should like to draw attention to the part played by women in these early socialist debates and organisations.[47] Not only were there great names such as Beatrice Webb, Eleanor Marx, Annie Besant, Katherine Glazier and Isabella Ford, who would warrant a place in any pantheon of early socialism by virtue of their contribution to the development of ideology as well by their activism, but also mention should be made of the many local activists, such as the women Clarion cyclists who rode about preaching socialism, or the women who travelled in the Clarion vans that covered the English countryside in the twenty years before the First World War, spreading the message and helping to fight elections.

Socialism in action

The Labour Party became a force in 1906, following an electoral pact with the Liberals. Prior to the pact only two Labour candidates had been successful, in the general election of 1900, though three by-electoral successes had followed in the next two years. But in 1906 all of the LRC's leading figures were elected – Hardie, Ramsay MacDonald, Henderson, Snowden and Clynes. The decision of the Miners' Federation in 1909 to take the Labour rather than the Liberal whip, and join what in 1906 had become the Labour Party, was decisive. In the two elections of 1910 the party returned forty and then forty-two members. It would be a mistake to believe that Labour had established itself. The size of the Liberal majority made Labour a parliamentary irrelevance and between 1910 and the First World War it lost five seats in by-elections and seriously considered joining the Liberals. And yet, astonishingly, within ten years a Labour government came into office. Coates ascribed this advance to the party taking on the mantle of a militant class party appropriate to the post-1918 world. More important perhaps the party survived the war intact whereas the Liberals, despite (or perhaps because of) Lloyd George's dominance, survived it in tatters.

The emergence of Labour as a major party

If the new position was to be built on, it was important for Labour to establish itself as an independent force with an identity separate from the Liberals. Reforms undertaken by the party in 1918 saw the gradualist trade union movement, and not the fundamentalist socialist societies, becoming the dominant force in party affairs. The party's agenda was set out in a document *Labour and the New Social Order* in which, says Coates, Labour 'appealed to the working class electorate for the first time in its history as a socialist party'.[48] This document, with its grand claims, may have been little more than totemic, yet perhaps totems were what the emerging party needed.

In the general election of December 1923 Baldwin's Conservative government was returned with 259 seats compared with 159 for the briefly reunited Liberals and 191 for Labour. Asquith let it be known that the Liberals would neither keep Baldwin in office nor deny Labour the right to govern. The prospect of a socialist administration filled many with alarm: red revolution, according to the conservative press, would destroy the army and the civil service. The Duke of Northumberland prophesied the introduction of free love. To others a Labour government offered nothing less than a new way of life.

Baldwin's government was soon defeated and on 22 January 1924 Ramsay MacDonald kissed hands as Britain's first Labour Prime Minister. To many people's surprise, the sky did not fall in. Minority governments have little opportunity to bring the skies down, even if they wished to. But in any case, Labour had already painted itself into a gradualist corner: the Cabinet may have contained two old-guard 'scientific' Fabians but it also contained a former Liberal minister, a former Viceroy of India and several middle-class and aristocratic recruits from the older parties.[49] There were, to be sure, seven trade unionists (including three ex-miners) but these men were gradualists. Small wonder that the great institutions of the state (and the institution of marriage) remained unravaged.

MacDonald was aware that making a good fist of administering the country was not enough: he had to convince his own fundamentalists that the government was at least attempting to implement some of the party's socialist programme. Labour was defeated when it went to the people in 1924 after losing on a motion of censure but it was the Liberals who were routed. Moreover the fundamentalists (especially the militant Clydesiders) had been appeased. The Cabinet had established public works schemes, and Wheatley's Housing Act, providing housing for the poor through the local authorities, was generally popular. The government's major piece of legislation, its budget, was described as a political masterstroke.[50]

In 1929 Labour formed a minority government again, though now it was the largest single party. Significantly the world was about to be engulfed by a slump and a collapse of the international money market. Here was the opportunity, surely, for a fundamentalist response. But Labour had already tied gradualism to the masthead when it offered no support to the General Strike of 1926, calling it an industrial dispute and not a political opportunity.[51] Not surprisingly then, the government's response to the slump was conventional deflationary economic policies. It rejected the Keynesian public works programme of the Liberals and the radical interventionist strategy of Oswald Mosley, one of its junior ministers. To paraphrase Keynes, the government promised nothing and kept its word. Anticipating the necessity of a foreign loan, the government sought to agree on a substantial deflationary package. Riven by tensions between trade union interests and the perceived national interest and between fundamentalism and gradualism, the government failed to agree. MacDonald, inclined to resign, was persuaded by King George V to head a national coalition government.[52] He was subsequently expelled from the Labour Party and found himself fighting a general election against most of his former colleagues. His government had died not from a surfeit of fundamentalist socialism but from anaemic gradualism.

MacDonald remained Prime Minister for a time but the party he had helped to build was reduced to only fifty-two MPs in the general election of 1931. The fundamentalists had their revenge.

Labour and the collectivist state

In how different a mood did the Labour Party next come into office in 1945? It had an overall majority of 146 seats; the leadership was known to the public but was not tainted by the failures of the 1930s; the Cabinet was dominated by men with solid ministerial experience, like Attlee himself, Bevin and Morrison. It contained imaginative appointments too, none more so than the Minister of Health, the mercurial radical socialist Aneurin Bevan. The machinery established during the war to plan and control all major aspects of the nation's economic life was still in existence and people had grown accustomed to it. Investment was controlled by licence, consumer spending severely restrained by rationing and the balance of payments shored up by import controls. The coalition government had planned major programmes of social reform in health, education and housing. They were there ready for Labour to amend, implement and claim. Overall the degree of central management was something that scientific socialists could only have dreamed about earlier.

Soon the Bank of England, coal, electricity, gas and much of inland transport were nationalised. A comprehensive system of insurance based upon the wartime Beveridge report was established, the provisions of Butler's wartime Education Act implemented and the minimum school-leaving age raised to 15. New controls were established over the development of land, a programme of council house building was initiated and finally – and most important – a comprehensive National Health Service, free to all at the point of use was created in 1948. In foreign policy the government had taken the first steps towards dismantling the empire by granting independence to India, Burma and Ceylon. On the face of it, Labour had managed, in this magisterial legislative sweep, both to resolve its tensions by securing many of its fundamental principles and to pursue an ethical international foreign policy.[53] However ethical socialists would have pointed out that the government had acted *on behalf of* ordinary people; this socialism, as Orwell would have said, was what 'we', the clever ones, impose upon 'them', the people.[54] In foreign affairs the first steps towards dismantling the empire and the strong support for the United Nations were balanced by membership of the anti-Soviet North Atlantic Treaty Organisation (NATO) and by participation in the Korean War, which required the most costly peacetime rearmament programme in history. Labour fought and very narrowly won the 1950 general election but was soon facing many other problems.

To counter the deteriorating economic climate and to finance the rearmament programme, Labour increased taxation and introduced charges for spectacles under the supposedly free NHS. The general public had become tired of scarcity and regimentation, and the government, some of whose leading lights had retired or died, was being harassed by the opposition in such a way as to make life intolerable. Attlee went to the people and in 1951 Labour's great period of office came to an end.

The desert years: 1951–64

Although they actually polled more votes than the Conservatives, Labour leaders must have left office somewhat disheartened. If Labour could not establish itself as the natural party of government in the world of 1945, could it ever? Ethical socialists could not have been satisfied with the government's programme; it had not basically shifted the balance of power in society. Equally disillusioned fundamentalists called for new and more radical forms of socialisation. Scientific socialists were dismayed that their planning had not been more effective and argued that it had not gone far enough. More nationalisation, more control, was the answer. Internationalists despaired of Labour's Cold War stance. Defeat in 1951 was followed by heavier defeats in 1955 and 1959: thirteen years of recriminations, division and bitterness.

Basing his argument on the writings of Anthony Crosland,[55] Richard Crossman,[56] and John Strachey,[57] the new party leader Hugh Gaitskell began to argue for a revision of the aims and objectives of socialism. Modern industry had produced a new breed of potential enemies of socialism: managers who did not own the businesses they managed. This new enemy might be found as easily in state-run industries as in private industry, so nationalisation offered no direct road to socialism. Socialist revision was the answer, said the gradualists (some of whom were beginning to think of themselves as social democrats); more full-blooded socialism was the answer, said the fundamentalists; empower ordinary people instead of state bureaucrats, insisted the ethical socialists. Matters came to a head after Labour's third defeat in 1959. At the following party conference, Gaitskell argued that not to amend the traditional policy on nationalisation (embodied in Clause Four of the constitution) would condemn the party to permanent opposition.[58] He inaugurated one of the most acrimonious conference debates since the 1930s, which ended in defeat for the revisionist social democrats. Riven on major issues, indecisively led and pursuing unpopular and outmoded policies, Labour appeared to be a spent force, all but destroyed by its conflicting tensions.

Within two years the situation had been transformed, not because these tensions had been resolved but because opposition to two government policies brought the party together: Britain's proposed entry into the European Economic Community and the Commonwealth Immigration Act of 1962, which terminated the traditional rights of Her Majesty's Commonwealth subjects to settle in Britain. Almost to a person the party was opposed to both. Party unity was aided further by the untimely death of Hugh Gaitskell and his replacement by Harold Wilson.

Technology and managerialism: 1964–79

With considerable acumen, Wilson managed to circumvent the whole debate concerning the future of socialism by revamping Robert Owen's faith in science and technology. The 'white heat of the technological revolution' would be harnessed; science and technology would be used to create the conditions for the burgeoning of a modern socialism that would incorporate the best features of ethical and scientific and fundamentalist and gradualist socialism, and be implemented with help from the trade unions. By superior economic management a Labour government would transform the lives of all citizens. Labour won the 1964 general election, though by the slenderest of margins.

Wilson established a new Department of Economic Affairs that would take on macro-economic management, drawing up a five-year plan with the help of the unions, and a National Board for Prices and Incomes that would manage price increases and wage demands. I have called this approach managerialist. In 1966 Labour sought to strengthen its hand by appealing to the electorate again; it was rewarded with an overall majority just short of a hundred and returned to its task with new vigour. However, within two months a seven-week seamen's strike led to a dramatic collapse in the value of sterling. Once again a Labour government felt itself obliged to follow a policy of deflation, including a wage and dividend freeze. The five-year plan was effectively torpedoed and the new unity was severely shaken. And things got worse. In November the pound was devalued and drastic cuts in public expenditure were to follow, including reimposition of NHS prescription charges.[59]

The government's strategy had not been completely deflected. An Industrial Reorganisation Corporation was created to encourage the restructuring of industry; iron and steel were renationalised; the government began to dismantle the selective system of secondary education; a range of payments to the disadvantaged was inaugurated. If these policies eased some traditional tensions within the party, the attempted reform of the trade unions, stimulated by the seamen's damaging strike did the opposite.[60] After six months of struggle within the parliamentary party, this failed attempt at modernisation left a legacy of bitterness among fundamentalists and trade unionists because of what it intended, and among social democrats and gradualists because it failed. Labour's unexpected defeat in 1970 led to the customary period of recrimination. What had Wilson's tenure of office amounted to? Was it a failed attempt to adapt socialism to managerialism almost by sleight of hand or was it, as one fundamentalist said, an attempt to replace a middle-class Conservative government by a working-class conservative government?

When the party came back to office in 1974 to take on the mantra of managerialism again, it was just as divided, not only on major issues of policy but also on the general direction in which the party appeared to be moving. Worse, the party came to office – again – in the middle of a state of emergency, with British industry working a three-day week and the population experiencing regular power cuts, both consequences of the dispute between Heath's Conservative government and the miners over pay. If these were not problems enough, Labour's was a minority government again. During the summer of 1974 the government outlined the policies it planned to pursue, including the public ownership of development land and greater government involvement in industrial development and – something to hearten the local democrats – devolution of some government powers to Scotland and Wales. On this platform Labour called for another election in October, which it duly won though with an overall majority of only three. The narrowness of its success did not prevent Labour governments under Wilson and then Callaghan from implementing several of their managerialist policies, though few of these appealed much to fundamentalist sentiment, and the whole ethos of managerialism was anathema to ethical socialists and local socialists.

In 1978 the government's attempt to control wages collapsed and a series of damaging strikes followed involving, among others, ambulance, lorry and petrol-tanker drivers and public service manual workers. This was the infamous 'Winter of Discontent'. The social contract which bound the unions and government together had been shattered, as had Labour's claim to managerial competence (based on its ability to work with the unions). In the general election in the spring of 1979 Labour and the whole managerial project were decisively defeated.

Back to the desert: 1979–97

After the debacle of 1979 the fundamentalists attempted to save the party for socialism. Managerialism, the last refuge of the social democrats and gradualists, had failed, and the fundamentalists began to 'democratise' the party.[61] They planned to control the party policy-making apparatus so that no future Labour government would be able to renege on radical policy commitments. Their successes worried some leading social democrats so much that four of the most prominent, along with twenty-three backbenchers, left the party to found the Social Democratic Party (SDP) in 1980. Labour fought the general election of 1983 on a fundamentalist manifesto, the *Alternative Economic Strategy*, which envisaged sweeping reflation, the extension of public ownership to encompass profitable firms, the introduction of planning agreements with other major companies, price controls, import controls and the introduction of schemes of industrial democracy.[62] The consequence was Labour's most humiliating defeat since 1931; the fundamentalist leader Michael Foot felt obliged to resign. With the subsequent election to the leadership and deputy leadership of the social democrats' 'dream ticket' of Neil Kinnock and Roy Hattersley, the fundamentalist project was firmly put into reverse.

The world in which the Labour Party grew up had changed. The Soviet Union ceased to be either socialist or united and the command economies of Eastern Europe collapsed one after another. Twenty years after Joseph Schumpeter predicted the imminent demise of capitalism,[63] Francis Fukuyama declared the absolute and irreversible triumph of liberalism.[64] In 1985 Labour began to develop a new economic strategy emphasising the creation rather than the redistribution of wealth.[65] The party fought the 1987 election with considerable confidence but despite a widely acclaimed campaign, it was defeated yet again. Reacting to this defeat, David Marquand suggested that to win again Labour would have to abandon its three most distinctive aspects: its opposition to the European Union (EU), its close relationship with the trade unions and its attachment to socialism.

In short, he said, it would have to 'cease to be the Labour Party'.[66] He thought this was whistling down the wind but how wrong he turned out to be.

Kinnock turned his attention to reforming the party structure.[67] By the 1992 election significant progress had been made and victory seemed to be within the party's grasp, especially after Shadow Chancellor John Smith's studied policy of 'cosying up' to the captains of industry – the so-called 'prawn raids'. 'One more push' was the battle cry. But the party lost again and Kinnock, feeling more like Sisyphus than Hercules, stood down.

The post-socialist Labour Party

Kinnock's efforts to modernise the party had been chiefly organisational; the accession of Tony Blair, following the sudden death of John Smith, brought a new dimension to modernisation. Blair could scarcely have signalled his intentions more clearly: within a year of succeeding to the leadership he sought to revise Clause Four. Blair announced his intention to a stunned and silent conference in 1994. At the outset some 90 per cent of constituencies and the great majority of the affiliated unions were against reform but Blair eventually won a surprisingly comfortable victory.[68] Clause Four now reads that the party should work for a 'dynamic economy…the rigour of competition…a just society…an open democracy'.[69] Justin Fisher described his victory as relatively easy, but in fact it was the consequence of consummately skilful campaigning.[70] The symbolic significance of this reform for Blair's modernising project can hardly be overstated.

New Labourism

Blair coined the phrase 'New Labour' to capture the flavour of his project.[71] New Labour can be summarised as: a rejection of the traditional distinction between state and market, public and private; a scepticism towards state enterprise and a supportive attitude towards private ownership and thus towards privatisation; a willingness to experiment with the application of market disciplines in the provision, management and delivery of 'public' services; a rejection of the traditionally close relationship between Labour and the unions; a belief in the virtues of devolved government and of creating a new style of 'inclusive' (as opposed to adversarial) politics involving further constitutional reform, and a general sympathy towards consumer-orientated values rather than the traditional collectivist ones. Some critics have emphasised the continuities between New Labour policy and the aims of both the traditional social democrats and then the revisionists in Old Labour.[72] They are correct to do so, but the discontinuities are greater. Looking back it seems inconceivable that Conservative opponents could still argue that underneath all the verbiage, the beast of fundamentalism still lurked.

The rejection of traditional Labour policies can be seen as responding to changes in the international economy – globalisation – which 'strictly circumscribe the capacity of the nation state to control its own economic destiny'.[73] Almost two decades of Conservative government had produced a 'new conventional wisdom' that saw no room for centralised state ownership.[74] As Eric Shaw says, 'in a new, more individualistic and consumer-orientated world what mattered most to voters was the freedom to dispose of their income as they chose'; this meant, Radice and Pollard concluded, projecting an image of Labour as a party representing individual citizens, not a particular class or group.[75]

Among the groups most affected were the trade unions, Labour's founders, paymasters and allies. Blair told the unions before the 1997 election that they could expect 'fairness and not favours' from a Labour government. Realistically unions were no longer able to mobilise sufficient electoral support to ensure a Labour victory. In fact strong links to the unions were perceived as an electoral liability. The historic link was not severed – the party still needed financial support – but it was weakened beyond recognition. One trade union leader likened the new relationship to that between a teenager and her parents: a parent (the unions) could give her (the party) a lift to the club, pay for her to go in and pick her up again afterwards – but they would have to make sure that none of her friends saw them.

When Blair became leader, journalists noted the influence of Christian socialism within the party,[76] but soon talk was of 'Stakeholding'.[77] Based in part on the writing of the economist Will Hutton,[78] Stakeholding was supposed to be neither collectivist nor individualist but inclusive and cooperative, cohesive and productive.[79] Stakeholding owed little or nothing to socialist principles, nor did its successor, the 'Third Way', associated originally with the political sociologist Anthony Giddens.[80] What distinguished the Third Way from Stakeholding was primarily its emphasis on the notion of economic and personal responsibility. 'Welfare systems', Giddens wrote, 'need to contribute to the entrepreneurial spirit, encourage the resilience to cope with a world of speeded-up change, but provide security when things go wrong.'[81] The Third Way was an ambitious international movement,[82] which claimed to be concerned to promote equality of opportunity, to champion mutual responsibility and to empower citizens to act for themselves.[83] In Britain the Third Way began to resemble classical liberalism, looking to the market because, suitably managed, it offered the best way of securing the welfare of all citizens.[84]

Blair's Third Way is not socialist, perhaps not even social democratic. It looked to some like Thatcherism with its concern for her project, what Marquand calls 'the hollowing out of the public domain',[85] drawing its inspiration not from European social democracy but from the United States. Though he concluded that it was not just Thatcherism, Marquand felt that Labour's social vision was 'closer to Thatcherism than to any other tendency'. Only New Labour's attachment to constitutional reform was distinctive, though it was achieved rather like Britain acquired its empire, in a fit of absence of mind. Constitutional change clearly has its own dynamic; it is already transforming British politics in unimagined ways, and New Labour seems to have no clear idea of what it wishes to achieve.

In general, although New Labourism is not ethical or Christian socialist, it represents the antithesis of radical socialism and abjures most of the aspirations of scientific socialism. New Labour has done what Marquand inadvertently advised it to do in 1987: it has ceased to be Labour.[86] No wonder he rejoined the party. In

June 2007 Labour acquired a new leader, Gordon Brown, whose policies of inclusiveness sound remarkably like the policies with which Blair came to office. If he implements them he might reconnect Labour's traditional concerns with modern methods of delivery more successfully than Wilson did. That was never even part of Blair's agenda.

Conclusions

Because of the debt it owed to the unions, Labour has been more open about the class nature of its ideology than the Conservatives. The decline of that class, partly a measure of the success of Labour's social reforms, has impacted upon party ideology. Socialism developed as an intellectual critique of nineteenth-century capitalist society. It had ethical and popular dimensions which drew heavily upon Judaeo-Christian values, a labourist dimension rooted in its close relationship with the unions, and a scientific dimension, which concentrated on capitalism's alleged inefficiencies and inhumanity. Given the manifestly ideological nature of socialism, these tensions played an important part in its development. The Labour government of 1945–50 represented the apogee of socialist achievement, creating what S.H. Beer referred to as a collectivist state.[87] In the half a century that followed, however, this state was administered mostly by Conservative governments. From the late 1950s onwards Labour leaders sought to reposition the party, to 'modernise' to meet social change and voter aspirations in a generally more affluent society.[88] They enjoyed little success. Only when Labour lost its fourth successive general election in the most propitious circumstances in 1992 did party leaders make the kind of changes that could truly be described as transformative. This did not take the form of a readjustment of the basic principles of socialism: it took the form of a rejection of socialism.

Socialism's decline as an international force, signalled as early as 1956 by the Soviet invasion of Hungary, became incontrovertible by the late 1980s. In Britain the great metaphors of socialist discourse, as Peter Kellner points out,[89] came from the factory and from mechanisation; the lives of working people revolved around these massive units of production. In this world perhaps the most compelling metaphor comes from the 1997 film *The Full Monty*. The film tells a story of industrial dereliction, the decline of manufacture, the eclipse of working men as the dominant force in society, and it ends memorably with the men 'taking their kit off' for money in a Sheffield club, with 'the working class, backbone of the Labour Party...weakened by affluence, broken by neo-liberalism, finally exiting stage left, naked, with a song. A more powerful [metaphor for] the decline of working-class socialism would be difficult to imagine'.[90] This was the world that Blair inherited following Labour's defeat in 1992 and he recognised its ramifications instinctively.[91] In turning its back on the unions, on nationalisation and on the Old Labour public service ethos, and championing instead structural reform and the business ethos, specialist academies and foundation hospitals, New Labour has forsaken the empire of traditional socialism. Stakeholding and the Third Way notwithstanding, it has yet to find a role.

4   Conservative Party organisation

If ideologies are ever to find expression in governmental policies they need party machines to bring unity and direction to the various and sometimes disparate elements that support those ideologies. British parties have to focus on two distinct areas, the parliamentary and the public domains. A key player in the development of both is the party leader, and policy, its formulation and implementation, is the leader's most important instrument. Various institutional relationships within the structure allow the leader to put that instrument to use and we shall examine each, before looking at the structure of the party machine itself.

Leading the party

Many who write about the relationship between Conservative leaders and their party seek to provide analogies to clarify the relationship, presumably because it is not formalised and cannot be understood in strictly constitutional terms. The most common are probably the monarchical analogy, emphasising the relationship between status and power; the baronial analogy, with the emphasis on bargaining and coalition-building;[1] the Hobbesian Leviathan, to whom absolute power is covenanted on the assumption that the interests of the supporters are optimised (by electoral victory).[2] For Norton and Aughey the preferred analogy is that of the traditional family, where power is cemented 'by ties of loyalty, respect and kinship'.[3] But heads of household are neither elected nor easily dismissed and they are bound by no obligations beyond what the law imposes and those they choose to adopt. None of these analogies tells the whole story. There is, however, another, more appropriately modern analogy: managers of soccer clubs, who have great freedom of manoeuvre but cannot succeed without the committed support of their club, fans and players. Whatever their record over the years, managers are only as good as their last dozen or so fixtures. Conservative leaders, like soccer managers, are only as good as the most recent result as portrayed in the nation's media. In Winston Churchill's words:

> The loyalties which centre upon number one are enormous. If he trips he must be sustained. If he makes mistakes they must be covered. If he sleeps he must not be wantonly disturbed. If he is no good, he must be pole-axed.[4]

The status of the leader

No Conservative leader was elected before 1965; previously, Conservative leaders were judged to have 'emerged', minimising open struggles for the succession. But what if no leader emerged? At the resignation of Harold Macmillan in 1963 contenders for the leadership used the party conference to launch a public beauty contest, making the proceedings resemble an American party convention. There was no agreed front-runner and so a compromise candidate was chosen, Lord Home, whose chief qualification was his anonymity. The system had failed and it was decided that leaders should henceforth be chosen by election rather than selection by the 'magic circle' of senior party figures. Election was to be by the parliamentary party, the winner to receive an overall majority plus 15 per cent on the first ballot. Additional candidates could join a subsequent ballot, if needed, and if no overall majority was obtained then, the three top candidates would proceed to a third ballot using the alternative vote method.

This cumbersome system remained unaltered (and unused) for a decade, when an additional refinement was introduced – re-election. Once again this development was not driven by democratic principles but by the need to solve a problem: the growing unpopularity of Edward Heath, the first elected leader. Provision was consequently made for elections at the beginning of every new parliamentary session. At the same time the first-ballot rule was amended: henceforth victory would require 15 per cent above an overall majority of eligible voters. Much to his and most people's surprise, Edward Heath lost the leadership of the party to Margaret Thatcher in the first such challenge. He became both the first elected and the first de-elected leader of the party. Democracy had not solved the selection problem; it had merely relocated the responsibility.

Re-election can both weaken and strengthen the leader's hand. It was the prospect of a close re-election battle that persuaded Margaret Thatcher to resign in 1990. A leader can bank on the instinct to loyalty of the average Conservative backbencher to face a challenger down, but only a decisive victory would strengthen their position. In 1995 Prime Minister John Major resigned as leader. Fed up with frontbench sniping at his leadership style, he sought to strengthen his hand by a decisive victory in a subsequent election. He invited his opponents to 'put up or shut up'. One of his Cabinet critics, John Redwood, stood against him. Major's subsequent victory rid him of Redwood but it was not a convincing win and its fruits were not enjoyed for long. Major's eventual resignation, following defeat in the election of 1997, was damagingly precipitate and a sure indication of his continuing disillusionment with party colleagues.[5]

In 1997 William Hague instituted a major reform of the party, which included the system for leadership elections. The theme of Hague's reforms was to empower the membership. A leadership election would be triggered either by the leader's resignation or by the loss of a vote of no confidence in the parliamentary party.[6] If the leader failed to win a simple majority he/she would be obliged to resign and be deemed ineligible to stand in the ensuing election, which would produce two front-runners. At this stage the party membership would elect the new leader from the two front-runners. Widely endorsed when it was devised, this system was used for the first time following Hague's resignation after the 2001 election defeat. It resulted in the victory of the relatively unknown and widely unadmired Iain Duncan Smith, who was as insecure a leader as any the party has had. Within two years a vote of no confidence among his parliamentary colleagues (lost 75 to 90) forced Duncan Smith's resignation. He was replaced, without an election, by Michael Howard. Another system, another failure.

Following electoral defeat in 2005 Howard in turn resigned and the parliamentary party, overlooking the veteran Kenneth Clarke, chose David Davis and the youthful David Cameron to contest the election. The 2005 party conference witnessed another beauty contest, which Davis, entering as favourite, lost. His conference performance was flat in contrast to Cameron's sparkling speech. Cameron duly went on to a comfortable victory among the party faithful.

Norton has pointed out that each of the first thirteen Conservative Party leaders in the twentieth century became Prime Minister, seven holding office for at least nine years, an eighth (Major) for seven years.[7] Of the remainder, two retired through ill health. Only three could be said to have felt obliged to resign through political failure – the two Chamberlains and Douglas Home – though Eden's Suez failure was responsible for the ill health that obliged him to resign. In the twenty-first century, there have been four leaders, of whom none has been Prime Minister (so far) and none has held office for more than four years. Like the soccer manager the best, indeed the only, insurance against incapacitating criticism is success. When the party feels that its manager is likely to lose the big match, even the most apparently secure, like Margaret Thatcher in 1990, becomes a candidate for the pole-axe.

Leaders and Cabinets

The Conservative Party spent the greater part of the twentieth century in power. Conservative Prime Ministers were expected to achieve a balance when constructing their Cabinets in which the principal ideological strains and sectional interests would be represented. Edward Heath's original Cabinet appointments favoured colleagues personally loyal to him (i.e. pro-European) and Norton and Aughey saw this as a source of weakness because Heath 'deprived himself of any means of communication between the pro- and anti-marketeers. The latter feel dispossessed. They are on the other side of the tracks'.[8] The authors contrast Heath's attitude with Thatcher's, who originally rated parliamentary ability higher than personal loyalty. However, her inability to persuade Cabinet to accept a second round of public expenditure cuts in 1981 convinced Thatcher that balance was not always a good thing. Her subsequent reshuffle produced such a swing to the right that Shirley Williams observed that Thatcher had replaced her Cabinet with an echo chamber.[9]

Unsurprisingly Thatcher's relations with her Cabinet became volatile. In 1985–86 Minister of Defence Michael Heseltine resigned because, he claimed, the Prime Minister had prevented a full discussion in Cabinet of the sale of the Westland helicopter company, a matter that came within his remit.[10] Other senior figures, notably Geoffrey Howe, felt similarly marginalised. In 1988 in Scotland and the following year in England and Wales, the government introduced the detested 'poll tax'.[11] In the autumn of 1989 a backbencher, Sir Anthony Meyer, challenged for the leadership. Although Meyer entertained no hope of success – he saw himself as a 'stalking horse' – some thirty-three Conservatives voted for him. A further number, probably around sixty, let Thatcher's campaign managers know that their continued support was conditional upon a more conciliatory and pragmatic approach to the poll tax and to European issues. Nothing changed. In November 1990, following widespread poll-tax riots and more disastrous by-election defeats, Sir Geoffrey Howe, Leader of the House and Deputy Prime Minister, resigned. His resignation speech could hardly have been more critical of Thatcher's leadership and the following day Michael Heseltine formally challenged for the leadership. Mrs Thatcher headed the first ballot but did not win it outright. Turning to her Cabinet colleagues for support, she found none forthcoming and chose not to participate in a second ballot. John Major, seen as a compromise candidate, won the ensuing election.

In a sense Thatcher's story is paradigmatic: it shows how a Conservative leader can mould a Cabinet to her image. In doing so she inured herself against the kind of criticism that would normally be productive of sensible compromise. Finally, having alienated many senior colleagues, she planned to take the field defiantly against all challengers, rather like Shakespeare's Richard III, only to suffer, as he did, many grave defections on the day of battle. Unlike Richard, she withdrew from the field and was saved from bloody assassination, but not from ritual humiliation.

John Major, her successor, held office for seven years. His leadership style was more naturally collegiate than his predecessor's but it was also more circumscribed by external factors. Major's parliamentary majority was only twenty-one and began soon to diminish further as a result of by-election defeats. He attempted to run a balanced Cabinet and to seek consensus where Thatcher had sought confrontation. His instinctive collegiality led Major to indecision and his government to a lack of momentum. When Norman Lamont, the Chancellor of the Exchequer, felt obliged to resign in 1993, he castigated his leader for 'too much short-termism, too much reacting to events, and not enough shaping of events. We give the impression of being in office but not in power'.[12] Major was opposed in Cabinet and in the parliamentary party over the provisions of the Maastricht Treaty, involving further European integration. Moreover his adoption of a 'Back to Basics' campaign at the 1993 conference, widely seen as encouraging a return to traditional family values, rebounded as a seemingly endless sequence of financial and sexual scandals – the 'sleaze factor' – hit the headlines,[13] leading to the establishment in 1996 of the Nolan Commission on standards in public life. There occurred a veritable cascade of fallen ministers and discredited backbenchers.[14] So much for the Prime Minister's moral crusade.[15] From the dynamic, authoritarian, ideological leadership style of the 'Iron Lady' to the failed collegiality and pragmatism of the anonymous 'Grey Man' could only be characterised as a leap out of the frying pan and into the fridge.

The three leaders who followed Major in quick succession made little impact upon the party or upon British politics generally. For the inexperienced William Hague, leadership came ten years too soon. His Shadow Cabinet was dominated by senior figures from the previous administration, more Thatcherite than balanced. He did not survive defeat in the general election of 2001 and on his resignation the poisoned chalice (for such it had become) passed to Iain Duncan Smith who, as one of the dissidents in the previous Major government, was very much a poacher turned gamekeeper. His Shadow Cabinet was heavily weighted towards Euroscepticism, but at least it contained mostly new blood. The third incumbent Michael Howard imaginatively cut his Shadow Cabinet down to twelve and set up an advisory board comprising his two predecessors and other senior figures. Electoral defeat in 2005 was as unavoidable as it had been in 2001, however, and Howard in turn gave way to the youthful, telegenic David Cameron. Cameron's Shadow Cabinet included former leader Hague and Cameron's opponents in the leadership race. It included four women, of whom one is the Shadow Deputy Prime Minister, and has a rough interventionist/libertarian balance.

Leaders and the parliamentary party

As Conservative ideology developed in response to changing circumstances and events, so did the way the party operated in parliament. By far the most significant development occurred as a reaction against Lloyd George's dominance of the post-1918 coalition government: the founding of 'The 1922'. This committee took its name from the meeting of newly elected Conservative backbenchers at the Carlton Club in that year when opposition to the coalition was strong enough to oblige the compliant Conservative leader, Sir Austen Chamberlain, to resign. Backbenchers in the next government formed a permanent committee to 'enable new members to take a more active interest and part in parliamentary life'.[16] The new committee elected officers and an executive committee. Official recognition followed and a Whip began regularly to attend meetings to give details of business for the following week. Within a few years membership was extended to all back-benchers and as it grew its activities became more institutionalised. Party Whips began to attend the meetings of these committees and by the 1950s a comprehensive structure had developed that still exists today, allowing for the transmission to the leadership of advice and opinion, with the chairman of The 1922 having ready access to the party leader. Chairmen hold office for about four years on average, though the first was in post for nine years and more recently the urbane Edward du Cann for twelve. Although a list of such chairmen comprises some well-known names, none went on to eminence. They were, for the most part, traditional Tory gentlemen, though one, appropriately during the Thatcher years, was a down-to-earth Yorkshireman with a fearsome reputation, Sir Marcus Fox, the 'Shipley Strangler'.

Meetings of The 1922 provide a useful forum for the discussion of general issues, though more detailed policies are the prerogative of the twenty-four subject committees or perhaps the geographical area committees which also usually meet on a weekly (or fortnightly) basis. The 1922 can be a force to be reckoned with especially during elections to its own executive (a good barometer of the strength of ideological groups) and elections to the party leadership, which it organises. Meetings of The 1922 are frequently addressed by Ministers when the party is in office and their reception may affect the Minister's career subsequently. In 1982, for example, the Foreign Secretary, Lord Carrington's rough ride in the face of the government's lack of preparedness for the Argentine invasion of the Falkland Isles helped persuade him to resign from office. Likewise the then Trade and Industry Secretary, Leon Britten, met a hostile reception in 1986 and resigned the next day. Junior ministers, too, have been persuaded to resign by direct and indirect pressure from The 1922, for example David Mellor in 1992 and Michael Mates in 1993. In popular mythology the leaders of The 1922 – the famous 'men in grey suits' – have the power even to remove a party leader.[17] However, they have never actually done so. It is not in the interest of even a powerful minister completely to ignore messages from the troops. For example, in 1985, the Secretary of State for Education Sir Keith Joseph sought to increase university tuition fees. At question time Sir Keith faced one of the most concerted onslaughts ever experienced by a Tory Cabinet minister from his own side. A few hours later he met The 1922 and even greater hostility. Sir Keith gave way to his tormentors.[18]

It used to be argued that a rough balance existed within the ranks of Conservative parliamentarians between the left of centre groups, such as the Bow group, the Reform group, the One Nation Group and the Lollards (who used to meet in the tower of that name in Lambeth Palace), and the right of centre groups such as The 92 (called after the Cheyne Walk address of its founder, the late Sir Patrick Wall), the Selsdon group and the No-Turning Back group, with the Monday Club further to the right. Such groups were more numerous and on the whole less exclusive than their Labour counterparts but under Thatcher the great distinction in the parliamentary party was between 'the drys' (her supporters) and 'the wets' (the old-fashioned Tories). After her departure the real consuming division was between the Eurosceptics and the Europhiles, beside which any other allegiance was irrelevant.

The oil that usually keeps the party machine running smoothly is provided by the Whips of whom there are fourteen. The Chief Whip has a deputy, seven Whips and five assistant Whips. Their tasks are often thought of as being to 'organise' the backbenchers so as to maximise support for the leader. Initially the role of the Whip was to inform backbenchers of government business, since MPs devoted much of their time to other activities. After the Reform Act of 1832, the number of Whips rose from two to five but their function was still basically to provide information.[19] They would underline the weekly document of government business circulated to backbenchers (also confusingly referred to as the whip) to indicate the more important issues. Crucial votes would be underlined three times – a 'three-line whip'. Nowadays, the whip system has as much to do with informing the leadership of the feelings of the backbenchers. Nevertheless, it is an important task of the Whips to attempt to persuade disgruntled backbenchers to support the leadership, though they have few formal sanctions at their disposal,[20] and some 'rebels' are beyond any threat. In the 1970–74 parliament former Cabinet minister Enoch Powell voted against his government on 113 occasions. In the first eighteen months of Thatcher's second term of office (1983–85), Edward Heath supported his government on only 6 out of a possible 129 occasions. For mere mortals, however, the pressures that Whips can apply can be unpleasant. A list of the names of Chief Whips contains few who went on to greater things, though Heath himself (1951–59) and William Whitelaw (1964–70) were exceptions. The Chief Whip's office is said to have a black book listing the indiscretions of their backbenchers, details of which can easily be made available to local party chairmen, or partners. Enough said!

Norton[21] and Cowley[22] have shown that since the 1970s, Conservative MPs voted against their government more often, in greater numbers and with greater effect than ever before. Heath's government was defeated three times on a three-line whip; even the Thatcher administration was defeated on a three-line whip in 1986 on an unsuccessful bill to allow Sunday trading. The Major government with its diminishing majority was more prone to derailment. In 1994 eight backbenchers voted against the government on a motion of confidence following the government's defeat on the European Finance Bill, the ultimate – and previously unthinkable – act of disloyalty. The leadership responded by withdrawing the whip, effectively temporarily expelling them from the parliamentary party. No Conservative MP had had the whip withdrawn for over fifty years. But the eight, joined by a ninth who relinquished the whip voluntarily, acted as a party within a party – and a party that held the balance of parliamentary power: it was 'the tail which wagged the Tory dog'.[23] When, finally, the whip was restored, the rebels gave no undertakings regarding their future conduct. They had won. Europe was corrosive, like almost no other issue since Irish Home Rule and Conservative backbenchers were openly hostile.[24]

Tory leaders cannot take parliamentary loyalty for granted now. Duncan Smith, who had been one of 'the whipless eight', insisted on issuing a three-line whip to colleagues in 2003 to vote against the Children and Adoption Bill, which sought to extend adoption rights to unmarried couples (the government had allowed its backbenchers a free vote). In the event, when it became clear that a number of Conservatives would nevertheless support the bill, the Whips Office declared the whip to be a 'soft' whip. Master of the oxymoron, Duncan Smith was not master of his parliamentary party. The following January a popular greeting among Tory MPs was: 'Happy New Leader!'

Conservative organisation in the Lords is a pale reflection of that in the Commons.[25] The whipping system comprises a Chief and Deputy Whip and five Whips but contact with backbenchers is fairly perfunctory except on major issues. There is an association of independent Unionist peers, which meets weekly with a role similar to that of The 1922 but it possesses no permanent committee structure. Those who wish will attend relevant meetings of the Commons committees, though surprisingly little formal contact exists between the party in the Lords and the Commons. Before Labour's reforms changed the House forever, a Conservative leader, acting *in extremis*, could always summon the so-called 'backwoodsmen' (serial non-attending peers) from the shires to support or defeat a bill. The House of Lords can no longer be described, in Lloyd George's terms, as the Conservative leader's poodle.

In the first direct elections to the European Parliament held in Britain, shortly after the general election of 1979, no fewer than sixty of the eighty-one seats fell to the Conservatives; in 1994 Conservative Party representation was reduced to a mere eighteen seats. In 1993 the group joined the European People's Party (EPP), among whom the German Christian Democrats are the dominant force. Currently there are twenty-seven Conservative Members of the European Parliament (MEPs) and they are at loggerheads with the party leader. Cameron stated his intention of withdrawing the group from the EPP, but the newly re-elected European leader opposed withdrawal. Pro-EPP Conservatives openly challenged Cameron's authority, speaking darkly of a split should he go ahead with his plan, and it was subsequently shelved.

Leaders and party policy

The establishment of the main thrust of policy – agenda setting – bears directly on the leader's role. Conservative leaders provide a context within which priorities may be established and this will affect policy-making at two levels. First, at the level of policy options: under Thatcher, for example, it would have been unthinkable for policies favourable to reflating the economy to have emerged anywhere within the party machine, at least before 1986; under Major no gesture towards devolution was possible, whatever the consequences for the party in Scotland and Wales. Second, at the level of selecting policy priorities, especially when the party is in office: here the powers of Conservative leaders are formidable and they imprint their personality upon party policy in a manner to which past Labour leaders have seldom aspired.[26]

The clearest exposition of party policy is the election manifesto; the leader's influence on this document has always been substantial, though the very comprehensiveness and detail of the modern manifesto require a formal process of preparation. In 1949 a broadly representative advisory committee serviced by the research department of Central Office was established to consider reports from study groups and discussion groups. The committee was wound up by Thatcher, and the groups began to report directly to the leader. A small group, with the research department chiefs and the head of the leader's policy unit, would produce a paper based upon group reports. Senior ministers would be called in for advice, a manifesto committee of trusted advisers would report directly to the leader, and details of the manifesto would be finalised. Major's approach differed little in 1992 but by 1997 senior ministers and their advisers exercised more influence, though still the final word rested with the party leader. As part of his reform measures, William Hague promised members a direct influence (via a referendum) on the chief aspects of the party election manifesto. He actually held a referendum on joining the European Monetary Union (EMU) in 1998, which overwhelmingly confirmed Hague's anti-EMU position. This was and remains a unique event in

British party politics. Coincidentally it helped Hague to wrong-foot the pro-EMU faction headed by Heseltine and Clarke.[27] Under Cameron the members were also called upon to endorse *Built to Last*, his statement of broad aims. Although the document was approved by almost 97 per cent of those who voted, fewer than 27 per cent bothered to do so.

In government party leaders cannot control all the policies of their ministers, but they can control some of them. Norton offers two examples from 1995 when Major exerted influence on the Secretary of State for Education in respect of competitive sport in schools and the nursery education voucher system.[28] Ten years earlier Thatcher had personally prevented the reform of the English A-level examination despite departmental support for change and the report of a government-sponsored committee, the Higginson Report, which also recommended change.[29] These are small beer though in comparison to Heath's about-turn on economic policy or Thatcher's unremitting support for the poll tax, unpopular with Cabinet, parliamentary party, membership and voters. Not being heads of governments, Messrs Hague, Duncan Smith and Howard were in no position to exert such personal influence on policy, though each spoke about the need to 'modernise' party policy. Cameron, by contrast, seems intent on a major policy initiative: his own modernisation project. Many of the party faithful are bemused by his apparent intention completely to reorientate the party, and some commentators doubt his sincerity or his capacity to deliver such change.

Leaders and the party bureaucracy

'Constitutionally the Conservative Party, my party, is no better than the old Soviet Communist party and it stinks.' So said the Tory 'dissident' Eric Chalker.[30] He went on to complain that absolute control of party headquarters – and of party funds – was passed from the old leader to the new like personal property. Formally the relationship between Conservative leaders and the party bureaucracy is unambiguous: party chairmen are appointed by the Prime Minister, and party headquarters has been referred to as the leader's personal machine. Few chairmen have seen it as their responsibility to act as tribunes for the broader movement. Accordingly when party chairmen are chosen they will ideally be well-known party figures, preferably on the frontbench, with proven administrative skills and a good ability to mix with and inspire the party faithful, and above all a loyal supporter of the party leader. Pinto-Duschinsky has pointed out that it is by no means always easy to find people with the requisite skills or to persuade them to take on the job.[31] Thatcher's appointment of Cecil Parkinson and then Norman Tebbit indicates the importance that the party leader attaches to the post.[32] But such men are often reluctant to forsake a ministerial post and leaders have sometimes been obliged to make appointments they would probably have preferred not to have made.[33] Between 1979 and 1993 eight chairmen were appointed, none of whom lasted two years and only one of whom, Cecil Parkinson – later to be reappointed by William Hague – could be considered to have enhanced their reputation in the post.[34] Since 1993 a further nine have held office, including David

Davis and Liam Fox (in tandem with Maurice Saatchi), Theresa May, the first woman chairman, and Francis Maude. The leader will also influence other appointments, for example the director of the research department, or the deputy chairmen. However, the leader traditionally had no direct authority over the voluntary wing of the party; the former National Union had to be persuaded not cajoled,[35] though its instinct was for loyalty.

Managing the party

Traditionally the Conservative Party comprised three separate entities: the parliamentary party, the National Union of Conservative and Unionist Associations together with the constituency organisations, and Central Office. In Conservative history and mythology, there was no doubt which was the dominant body: the parliamentary party was 'the party'. It was the task of the other bodies to support and sustain the party and its leader.

The movement

The National Union of Conservative and Constitutional Associations was set up in 1867 to orchestrate the activities of existing local associations and to help create new ones. In 1912 it exchanged 'Constitutional' for 'Unionist' to take account of the arrival of the Liberal Unionists. One of its chief activities was the dissemination of information, and from the beginning, its role was entirely supportive of the party at Westminster; it was never considered to be a means to assure accountability of the party to its supporters.[36] Robert McKenzie quoted the chairman at the inaugural meeting as declaring that members had not met to discuss Conservative principles because they were in agreement about these; their task was 'to consider by what particular organisation we may make these Conservative principles effective among the masses'.[37] From its inception the National Union jealously guarded its autonomy against the party bureaucrats, and the relationship was often fractious. Two inquiries addressed these problems. The first created a Board of Management, bringing together the voluntary, the elected and the professional wings of the party. Tether pointedly referred to this process as the 'colonisation' of the National Union,[38] though the Union and the local associations, jealously independent, defied domination. Until 1997 that is, when William Hague established a committee to create a 'mass volunteer party equipped to spread the Conservative message to all parts of the nation'. The ensuing reforms represented 'the biggest reorganisation of the party since Disraeli's time'.[39]

The two wings of the movement were amalgamated into the National Conservative Convention (NCC). At the apex of the movement is the Board, consisting of the party chairman, two deputy chairmen (one elected by the NCC, one appointed by the leader), four members elected by the NCC, the leader in the Lords, the chairman of The 1922, a representative of the Scottish Conservative and Unionist party, the chairman for Wales, the chairman of the Conservative Councillors Association, the party treasurer, a senior member of the professional staff and one potential further member nominated by the party leader. The Board can establish any committees it wishes, though it is required to have standing subcommittees on candidate recruitment, conference (preparation and management) and membership. The Board's formal duties are: the development of policy, campaigning, membership and fund raising, and maintaining the party organisation. It approves and monitors the Central Office budget, appoints most senior staff, manages the membership and candidate lists, oversees constituency association matters, ensures that women and young people are properly involved and represented, resolves internal disputes, and oversees leadership elections. Under the Board comes the 900 strong NCC itself, meeting twice yearly, and representative of the party structure throughout the UK, including recognised groups such as Conservative Future and the Conservative Women's Organisation (which claims to be the largest women's political organisation in the western world).[40] NCC provides a focus for the views of party members and links membership and leaders. The party leader, officers and Board members are invited to attend.

Hague sought to cement these reforms through the endorsement of the membership and some 400,000 ballot papers were distributed, though in the absence of a centralised membership list (one of the reasons for reform) this was probably wishful thinking. In the event 81 per cent of 176,391 voters endorsed the reform.

The movement in England

At the grass roots of the party are the constituency associations, with four main responsibilities. The first is to 'sustain and promote the object and values of the Conservative Party'. The others are to provide an effective campaigning organisation, to secure the return of Conservative candidates and to contribute to party funds. The constitution sets out a core management structure, through which annual objectives are set and planned for. Each association is represented on the area committees and at the annual party conference. The party's area structure comprises forty-four areas, based on county and metropolitan boundaries, and they sit within a structure of eleven regions.

In addition to the formal structure of the NCC a number of recognised organisations exist, for example the Conservative Women's Organisation (with its own regional structure, which offers training and mentoring to women and holds an annual conference), the Conservative Muslim Forum, the Ethnic Diversity Council, the Conservative Christian Fellowship, the Conservative Medical Society and the Countryside Forum, each of which seeks to influence policy development through their activities. In the 1980s its youth wing presented the leadership with problems: Young Conservatives experienced a dramatic decline in their membership and the Confederation of Conservative Students came under the influence of right-wing libertarian groups and was disaffiliated.[41] The reformers established an umbrella youth organisation, Conservative Future, for members under 30 years of age. Conservative Future, which is run nationally by an executive, with a dedicated full-time official from headquarters, claims a membership of 15,000, and is represented at conference and in the NCC.

This machine in the country is oiled by the work of the party agents, who have responsibilities for groups of constituencies. Agents are responsible not to the constituencies but to the Board, which has assumed responsibility for training and career development. Regional directors (or equivalent) have a key strategic role to play in the deployment of party agents. Outside of elections their main responsibilities are handling the media and fund-raising.

One of the principal tasks of the party organisation is to select parliamentary candidates. A permanent subcommittee of the Board has responsibility for maintaining a list of approved candidates. Not only has this broadly representative subcommittee excluded 'unsuitable' candidates but also it has actively sought out suitable ones. A more specialist list of candidates considered suitable for by-elections existed and constituency associations were strongly encouraged to select candidates from this list.[42] A standardised candidates' *curriculum vitae* was developed, and all candidates on the approved list were trained in campaigning and in handling the media. The candidates' association, to which all belong, also provided public speaking opportunities and mentoring by sitting MPs. Constituency associations, in reality, retained a considerable influence in MP and MEP candidate selection,[43] and had complete control over selecting candidates for local elections. More recently David Cameron has taken steps to reconstruct the specialist list, the 'A' list, to ensure the greater representation of women among candidates for winnable seats.[44] Of fifty winnable constituencies where new candidates were selected in 2005, only six chose women candidates and overall only seventeen women were elected. Cameron has substantially enhanced the prospects for women candidates. His aim is to secure 50 per cent of winnable seats for women candidates. The 'A' list is being referred to as the 'W' list by opponents resentful at de facto discrimination and 'undue' pressure from the group Women2Win. Cameron is also actively seeking advice on how to attract ethnic minority candidates and candidates with disabilities.[45]

Celtic Conservatism

Conservatives north of the border traditionally reacted to poor electoral performances by organisational reform.[46] In 1992 the Scottish Tories lost all representation at Westminster, though currently there is one Scottish Tory MP, and the party has two Members of the European Parliament. In 1998, following another dismal general election and the prospect of fighting a Scottish election, the autonomous Scottish Conservative and Unionist Association set up a review under Lord Strathclyde, most of whose recommendations were accepted at a special conference. Nowadays the Scottish Tories are focused chiefly on the Scottish Parliament at Holyrood. In the 2007 Scottish elections the party returned seventeen Members of the Scottish Parliament (MSPs). The Scottish leadership, formerly the gift of the national party leader, is now elected by a college comprising party members (30 per cent) and MSPs (70 per cent). Annabel Goldie's title is Leader of the Scottish Conservatives in the Scottish Parliament. Party policy in Scotland is the responsibility of the Executive and is formulated in much the same way as in the national party, and it is not bound by national party policy at Westminster.[47] The party holds an annual conference in spring. Although for the most part staunchly unionist, some of the party's estimated 16,500 members favour fiscal independence for Scotland and others even stronger forms of autonomy, feeling that the cause of Conservatism in Scotland would be better served if it were not seen as irretrievably bound to the Union.[48]

The situation of the Conservative Party in Wales is rather different. At its head is the board of management, presided over by the party chairman, and including MPs (there are four) and MEPs (one) as well as representatives of the five areas. There are ten Conservative Assembly Members (AMs) elected regionally and one constituency AM. Welsh Conservatism is not as stirred as its Scottish counterpart by thoughts of autonomy. The party meets annually in June. Northern Ireland for its part – the Conservatives are the only major party to operate in Northern Ireland – has the status of an area of the national party, so its leader is David Cameron. However, it seldom commands more than 1 per cent support in the elections that it fights.

That element of state funding which the party receives for campaigning comes to the devolved parties through the national party. Traditionally constituency associations had attached little importance to ideology and a lot to fund-raising, seeing themselves, and being seen by many in the party at Westminster, as election machines. The model rules set up to guide constituency associations listed eleven functions of which only one was not expressly directed towards optimal electoral efficiency, and that was to spread the knowledge of Conservative principles and policy. Ideological debate was the responsibility of the Conservative Political Centre (CPC), which operated a contact programme in which issues were regularly selected at national level for local debate. Norton and Aughey considered that this provided 'a reinforcement to a sense of belonging',[49] rather than any substantial influence on policy. It may well be that nothing more substantial existed because there was no wide demand for it. There were always, and still are, 'revolutionaries' within the party who seek genuine participation: the Charter movement, for example, with its own newsletter, regularly campaigned for greater democracy within the party. '"Traditional party democracy" is not democracy. It is a substitute for the real thing, intended to divert the unwary into believing that no further scrutiny is necessary. Nothing could be further from the truth.'[50] Yet most members appear to be largely unconcerned, a point made much earlier by McKenzie,[51] and reiterated twenty-five years later by Gamble, who spoke of a 'largely sleeping membership' as far as policy-making was concerned.[52]

Among the Hague reforms was the establishment of the Conservative Policy Forum (CPF), whose task was to encourage a genuine 'two-way movement' of ideas between leaders and members. The CPF, which came into being in 2002, replacing the Conservative Political Centre,[53] seeks to coordinate the work of constituency deputy chairmen responsible for setting up discussion groups. A range of issues was suggested for local discussion, including health, transport, youth crime, education, the environment and so on, and the results are sent to the research department, summarised and passed on to the chairs of the various policy groups. Whatever the structures though, Conservative policy-making is still the outcome of discussion between the policy group chairs and the leadership, and as these groups began to report in 2006, it became clear that some found greater favour with the leadership and were promoted accordingly. The policy group on social justice, for example, under Duncan Smith, reported in December and was generally well received. The contribution of the party membership remains marginal to the process, though CPF runs a lively fringe programme at the party conference.

The annual conference

Following the Hague reforms, organising the conference has become the business of the Board, through a committee comprising the president of the NCC (who chairs conference) and the director of the Policy Forum. The committee will set the agenda based upon motions submitted by the various organs within the new structure. Although there is no formal process through which conference decisions become binding on the party, an innovation – the spring assembly in which the Policy Forum plays a leading role – ensures that issues of policy are aired not only through full debate but also through workshop sessions.

The essence of the Conservative Party conference has traditionally been consolidation, rallying the troops and inspiring them to greater efforts; in the words of one Conservative backbencher, 'to repay party workers for the tedious business of selling endless raffle tickets'. The constitutional status of the annual conference was formally acknowledged by the 1948 Maxwell Fyfe committee on the party organisation to be 'primarily deliberative and advisory' and not surprisingly, given its size. At around 9000 it is one of the largest political gatherings in Western democracies.[54] Balfour's much-quoted comment that he would as soon take advice on policy matters from his valet as from conference might have been hyperbole but it is true that, before Heath, party leaders did not actually attend any of the debates but simply addressed conference before it broke up. From Heath onwards all have been regular attenders. Nevertheless, in the eyes of some, conference has no policy-influencing role. Sir Ian Gilmour claimed: 'The conference now has to cheer the faithful and to impress the infidel…and much of the proceedings are more of an exercise in revivalist enthusiasm than a serious discussion of issues and policies'.[55] Kelly quotes thirty-three critical resolutions to the 1996 conference, one of which urged the organisers 'not to manipulate proceedings or stage-manage debates'.[56] None was selected for debate. Since the 1990s the speeches of major party figures have been vetted by party headquarters and distributed in advance, a form of stage management. Stage management can take bizarre Orwellian forms. The official 1994 video showed a large, enthusiastic conference warmly cheering the loyal words of party chairman Brian Mawhinney and a much smaller, more restrained conference politely applauding the right-wing, anti-European onslaught on his own government of Defence Secretary Michael Portillo. The party had to admit later, however, that owing to unfortunate 'editing errors' (no doubt in the Ministry of Truth) the two speeches had been spliced onto the wrong audience responses; the rebellious Portillo had really got the cheers.

It would be a mistake to imagine that conference has no effect on policy.[57] Whiteley et al. argue that the members themselves felt able to influence the leadership,[58] and numerous commentators agreed.[59] Influence must be exercised through some kind of political osmosis by which the leadership leaves the conference with a clear idea of the mood of the party. Later this mood may come to determine the general thrust of policy, as over issues like immigration and law and order in the late 1970s and early 1980s, or, nearly a decade later, poll tax reform.[60] And from time to time conference has taken the leadership on: Balfour over protectionism, Baldwin over India,[61] and more recently Major over Europe (party conferences between 1992 and 1997 could best be described as bilious).

Frontbenchers take conference seriously: their contributions to debates can be crucial to their standing in the party, and a number of very able ministers have progressed less far and less quickly than expected because of lacklustre conference performances. Hence Quintin Hogg's failure to impress as a potential leader in 1963, and Reginald Maudling's failure to achieve the leadership in 1965. Virginia Bottomley, Minister of Health, chose to sing to conference in 1995, blighting her future both as Cabinet Minister and as music hall diva. David Davis' lacklustre performance in 2005 more or less lost him the leadership. Others have greatly enhanced their standing in the party, none more so than the former Ministers of Defence, Michael Heseltine, a perennial 'darling' of conference, and Michael Portillo. Conference is a living organism, not only in the way it responds to speeches but also in the way it responds to stage management. The disaffected members develop flourishing fringe meetings in which the leadership is regularly pummelled. These meetings have taken on a role as vibrant as that of the Fringe at the Edinburgh Festival. Conference, in short, is like a sausage-shaped balloon: if the leadership squeezes in one place (the formal debates), the balloon bubbles out somewhere else (fringe meetings).

Conservative campaign headquarters

The machine that had been established under Disraeli in 1870 was soon fully committed to all the professional supportive work required by the party both nationally and locally and, despite some lean periods, its position became stronger over the years. Initially Central Office was run by the Chief Whip but by the early twentieth century it was necessary for the party leader to appoint a chairman. Andrew Gamble described the machine as 'antique and ramshackle';[62] Norton and Aughey coyly found its eccentricities 'understandable' to Conservatives. Its basic role was to give advice on how to achieve power when the party is in opposition and to provide loyal support for the leadership when in office. Whatever its shortcomings, Central Office was usually considered superior to its Labour and Liberal counterparts. The three general elections since Thatcher's demise, however, exposed serious deficiencies in presentation and in services to candidates and local parties. John Major's off-the-record description of his bureaucracy was scathing: 'hopeless'.

In 1998 Archie Norman, the new chief executive at Central Office, and future chairman Michael Ancram were given the task of modernising Central Office and of saving money.[63] 'People in different departments don't speak to each other,' claimed one party worker, 'they scribble away in dark corners...we are out of date and out of touch'.[64] Norman trimmed the workforce, forcing out the campaign director because he had resisted the spending cuts.[65] Norman made an immediate and lasting impact on management practices, but Central Office still had a long way to go to recapture its former prestige.

The research section, established in 1929 and reorganised in 1948, was traditionally headed by a senior politician, the most celebrated being R.A. Butler (1945–1964). Now however it is run by a full-time director. In the past the research department earned a reputation as the party's 'think-tank' in which flourished young men of intellect and promise who were later to make a name for themselves in the House; for example Maudling, Macleod, Powell and, more recently, Letwin, Osborne and Cameron. It also earned a reputation for being somewhat to the left of centre and its influence in policy formulation was challenged in the Thatcher years by the Centre for Policy Studies, an independent body established by Keith Joseph and Thatcher. In the 2005 election Michael Howard used the research department as a 'policy secretariat', but Cameron reduced the department as part of a cost-cutting exercise: it now has a full-time establishment of only six.

In the autumn of 2004 Lynton Crosby, who had managed successful Liberal Party campaigns in Australia, was appointed general election campaign manager for the Conservatives. As part of his regime of sharpening the party's focus and campaign management, he renamed the old Central Office and transformed a 'rusty party machine into the Rolls Royce it was in Margaret Thatcher's heyday'.[66] Central Office in Smith Square, the party's former home, had been a rabbit warren of small rooms, 'well suited to cabals and plots'; the new headquarters in Victoria Street became open plan. Under Crosby's focused discipline, headquarters operated with enough effectiveness in 2005 to worry Labour. Today, headquarters is situated, ironically, in Millbank Towers, Labour's former home. The configuration of the offices indicates the considerable influence exercised by the deputy chairman and party benefactor Lord Ashcroft. Though Cameron and his election manager Shadow Chancellor George Osborne share a room (the Thatcher room), with key personal staff just outside, Ashcroft occupies an office far bigger with a staff substantially more numerous than the party leader. From here he dispenses his own funds to marginal seats and manages party agents. Party chairman Caroline Spellman sees herself as director of operations, though some insiders claim that she has been effectively sidelined. The old Research Department remains, though it is smaller. In addition there is a press team, a treasurer's department, and 'the hub', a response unit similar to Labour's in 1997, headed by the former editor of the *News of the World*. Crosby's gains have been entrenched in this well-oiled, well financed machine.[67]

Party funding

The funding of the Conservative Party has, over recent years, become an issue of major controversy. Pinto-Duschinsky identified three phases in the development of party fund-raising: the aristocratic era when voters were habitually bribed and parliamentary seats bought, the plutocratic era when honours were sold in return for party donations (until the law prevented this) and the modern era of mass membership subscriptions and major corporate donations.[68] Fisher suggests a post-modern era in which personal donations and, more recently, loans dominate.[69] Donations as a percentage of party income have risen to 83 per cent whereas constituency-quota income now comprises 6 per cent. Running a national party is an expensive business and not just at election time, though for the two major parties, modern elections cost in excess of £20 million. The Conservative Party was kept afloat – just – by undeclared donations by individuals often on behalf of major, usually multinational companies.[70] It was revealed after the 1997 election, for example, that the party had accepted a donation of £13 million from a Hong Kong businessman.[71]

As part of his reform measures William Hague sought to address the funding question by requiring all donations of over £5,000 to be declared. No donations from overseas were to be accepted. Hague's reforms were overtaken, however, by the Political Parties, Elections and Referendum Act of 2000 which, for the first time, established a regulatory framework for party finances at the national level. The provisions of that Act were as follows: parties to make regular reports on donations and expenditure; gifts of over £5,000 to be declared; anonymous gifts of over £200 to be disallowed; spending at the national level to be capped (at £30,000 per constituency contested); a new agency, the Electoral Commission, to be set up to oversee the operation of the Act.[72] In the 2001 election the major parties stayed well within their limits, though they had secured large donations before the Act came into force. Fighting elections is not getting cheaper and controlling this 'arms race' proved problematical in 2005 when both parties augmented their funds by securing loans rather than donations. Although the Conservatives have been successful fund-raisers since the election, with numbers of loans being converted into donations, the party was still over-dependent on major donors. Loans taken on commercial terms do not have to be declared, but in 2006 the Commission reported that the Conservative Party would have to repay £20 million of a total debt of £53 million. However, the party had spent £16 million on buying back the freehold of its former headquarters and this could be sold at a profit or used as security against debt.[73] Nevertheless reliance on such large loans must mean that campaigns (and hence perhaps policies) are likely to be influenced by a small number of rich individuals and major interests. Conservative party funding has been transformed by the contribution of deputy chairman Lord Ashcroft. When the latter was nominated for a peerage by William Hague in 2000, it was on the understanding that he would become a UK tax payer – at the time he was resident in Belize. Some years after taking his place in the House of Lords however, his residence was still listed as Belize. His tax status remains unclear but even assuming that he pays UK tax and is therefore entitled to payroll marginal constituency work, it might still be considered inappropriate for the party to be so dependent upon wealthy individuals. [74]

Conclusions

At the end of our inquiry into who runs the Conservative Party, we would surely accept that McKenzie's answer – that it is the party leader – is still basically accurate. While we have to acknowledge the personal status and prestige of the leader first brought to our notice fifty years ago by McKenzie, we can say that this has been largely a reflection of the perception of the Conservatives as a party of government rather than ideology. Margaret Thatcher broke that mould. Her status and prestige as leader and Prime Minister were unparalleled, yet even after three consecutive electoral victories her Cabinet brought her down. Since Thatcher, the leader can no longer simply assume the support of Cabinet (or Shadow Cabinet) or the effectiveness and solvency of the party apparatus. So long as Conservative leaders act pragmatically to safeguard the general interests of capital and the growing middle class, convincingly dressed up as the national interest, only electoral failure will prompt a challenge to their leadership. It is true that Hague's changes to the rules of leadership election actually structured the possibility of division into the party at large, but there is still an instinct towards loyalty among Conservatives at all levels, and Hague's institutional reform of the National Union makes that loyalty even more readily available to a successful leader.

5 Labour Party organisation

In terms of both of its style and structure of leadership and its organisation the Labour Party has always been quite a different animal from the Conservative Party. However, as we shall see, the reshaping of the party organisation under the leadership of Kinnock (and briefly Smith) but especially Blair has created what is in effect a new party and this new party has come increasingly to resemble the Conservative Party.

Leading the party

The Labour Party has traditionally expected far more of its leader than has the Conservative Party. While the latter has always been seen as the leader of a party seeking to run the country successfully, the Labour leader has also been seen as the leader of a moral crusade to make the world, or at least this part of it, a better place. No small task! Moreover the structure of the party, traditionally federal in nature, has always made any kind of leadership more problematical.

The status of the leader

Although historically the Conservative Party comprised three disparate elements, the party leader was undisputed head of each. For Labour leaders, however, the party's federal structure comprised a parliamentary party that prided itself on being its own master rather than an instrument of the leader (until 1922 the leader was formally described as chairman of the parliamentary party); an autonomous party organisation whose efficiency was less than legendary but which saw itself as a genuine institutional check on the leader; an ideologically active party membership that expected to have an influence on policy and a number of major affiliated trade unions that paid the piper and often liked to call the tune.

However, there was always more to it than structure. Loyalty has played a great part in Labour Party politics, but not loyalty to the leader. Loyalty has traditionally been owed to a concept, or more accurately two concepts. First, to socialism, even if there was never universal agreement as to what that was. Second, to the interests of the working class, perhaps even more chimerical. Some might see these concepts as two sides of the same coin, and from time to time they were but not always. Moreover the interests of the working class might not coincide with the ambitions of organised unionism. These real differences have pulled the party in different directions and Labour leaders have always had to counter a tendency to sectarian division. None has been entirely successful in this and so none has been entirely secure as leader. Nobody ever sought to describe Labour leaders as monarchs, barons, leviathans or soccer managers, or at least not before 1997.

Leaders and Cabinets

Until 1922 the leader of the Labour Party was designated as chairman of the parliamentary party, an elected post. Between 1906 and 1922 there were no fewer than eight chairmen and the position commanded little of the loyalty owed to the leaders of the other parties. Thereafter he was referred to as chairman *and leader*. Two years later, when MacDonald became Labour's first Prime Minister, he formed his own Cabinet without official party consultations, thereby rejecting the radical precedent set by the party's significantly more successful sister, the Australian Labor Party and conforming instead to the practice of the other British parties.[1] Not only did MacDonald face the standard problem of creating ideological balance in his Cabinet, but also he had to optimise the services of experienced defectors from the Liberals. In 1931, however, following his Cabinet's inability to agree an effective economic strategy, MacDonald formed a national coalition, thereby appearing, to most of his former colleagues, to have sold his party out, leaving what Francis Williams referred to as a permanent scar on the party's psyche.[2] The so-called cult of individualism remained an emotive and powerful charge levelled at any party leader who sought to assert his own authority until Blair's early years as leader turned the notion upside down. To criticise Blair's leadership as being tainted with the cult of the individual would be like criticising Genghis Khan for mood swings. In 1997 Blair's allies warned senior civil servants that his leadership style was 'Napoleonic'.[3]

Before Blair even the most successful Labour leader, Clement Attlee (1945–51), was frequently under threat from within his Cabinet.[4] Labour came into office with unusual advantages, not the least the national spirit that had helped to win the war, but the tensions inherent within the Cabinet soon came to the fore and Attlee's personal position was challenged, especially by his deputy Herbert Morrison. The latter was widely expected to take over the party leadership from Attlee after the defeat of 1951 but Attlee obdurately retained the leadership until 1955, by which time Morrison, at 67, was deemed to be too old to take over.

Harold Wilson, Labour's next Prime Minister (1964–70 and 1974–76) sought to make socialism and working-class interests synonymous with technological change and the ethos of managerialism, and in wholeheartedly promoting the latter, to appear to be promoting the former. In reality he was attempting to reconcile the fundamentalists and the social democrats within the Cabinet. For a while he appeared to succeed but in major policy areas decisions were taken which offended the fundamentalists, for example the attempt to join the European

Economic Community (EEC), the retention of Polaris submarines and the acceptance of the Immigration Act of 1962.[5]

In his second administration Wilson's managerialism was largely negated in Cabinet by fundamentalists like Tony Benn, and by traditionalists opposed to Wilson's attempt at trade union reform, like James Callaghan. When Wilson returned in 1974 for a third term, Britain had joined the EEC but party policy, dismissive of any move towards European integration as a conspiracy against traditional values, was to withdraw. Wilson and several senior ministers thought this inimical to the nation's interest. Half of the Cabinet was opposed to continued membership of the EEC and it was simply impossible for Wilson to enforce collective responsibility in his Cabinet. What was the Prime Minister to do?

Wilson called for a renegotiation of Britain's terms of entry, held a national referendum on the outcome and allowed his Cabinet colleagues to campaign as they saw fit. Was this skilfully manoeuvring to secure the nation's interest? Was it an extraordinary dereliction of national leadership, abandoning Cabinet collective responsibility? Was it a sell-out of party policy and principles? Perhaps something of each. At any rate, Britain remained within the EEC, the Labour Cabinet remained in office with no major resignations and Wilson remained party leader and Prime Minister. Wilson's third administration also pursued traditional values. Its fiscal policies narrowed material inequalities a little, especially through the Child Benefit scheme, and its assault on selective secondary education attempted to create greater equality of opportunity. Nevertheless Wilson failed to modernise Britain or his own party and, in the eyes of his traditionalist opponents, abandoned socialism.[6]

Wilson left the party in the hands of the experienced James Callaghan. The success of the Scottish and Welsh nationalist parties through the 1970s obliged Callaghan actively to pursue plans to devolve powers to Scotland and Wales, although this was not generally popular with the many within Cabinet or the parliamentary party. Even less popular with fundamentalists were his government's deflationary economic policies and its attempt to control wages through statute, both seen as an affront to traditional values.[7] The trade unions opposed government policies, primarily through widespread industrial action: the infamous Winter of Discontent that brought Britain to its knees. When he resigned after electoral defeat in 1979, Callaghan left the party defeated, demoralised and in disarray. Opposition to his policies from within the Cabinet had been both continuous and public. His fundamentalist critics thought that the party had lost contact with its roots. Following the Winter of Discontent it had certainly lost contact with the majority of the British electorate.[8]

Although as a backbencher Blair could speak the language of traditional Labour,[9] from the beginning of his leadership challenge he made no bones about his mission: it was not simply to modernise but to transform the party. The reform of Clause Four marked the starting point not the culmination of Blair's crusade of transformation. Blair ran his Shadow Cabinet, then his Cabinet, with a firm control that critics have described as autocratic. Under Blair, Cabinet met less frequently and for shorter periods than under any previous Prime Minister and Cabinet's ability to make policy collectively was surgically removed like some growth that might prove dangerous to the body politic. He made it clear that he did not expect to meet opposition to his government's policy proposals in Cabinet. If ministers had problems with the policies, they were expected to come to see him personally.[10] One of the Blair government's first measures in 1997 was to give the Bank of England control to manage inflation, hugely significant but never discussed in Cabinet.[11] Blair ran his governments via a tightly controlled small group of ministers and advisers around himself.[12]

To complete this picture of the Blair Cabinet, we have to paint in the brooding figure of the Chancellor, Gordon Brown, who exercised personal power over economic policy following an agreement with the Prime Minister. Brown's autonomy in the economic sphere was unique in Cabinet history. For example the decision not to enter the European Single Currency (Euro) was finally Brown's and not Blair's. Blair asked Development Secretary Clare Short to sound Brown out about supporting Britain's entry into the Euro in return for a promise that he, Blair, would then stand down in favour of the Chancellor. According to Short, Brown's response was that this was no way to make policy and that he couldn't trust the Prime Minister to deliver his part of the bargain.[13]

As Prime Minister, Blair introduced another innovation which we can call outreach. He portrayed himself as the listening Prime Minister and initiated a number of public 'listening' campaigns so that his government's policy could be informed by public opinion, or so he said. The *reductio ad absurdum* of this approach was the establishment of an e-petition website through which individuals could actually petition the Prime Minister. Over 1.5 million signed a petition against the government's intention to introduce road pricing and vehicle tracking. The Transport Secretary is reported to have commented pithily: 'Whoever came up with this idea must be a prat'.[14] More generally it was perceived, as was Blair's whole approach to outreach, to be a publicity exercise rather than an extension of public participation.

So far we have been talking about Labour Prime Ministers but four post-war party leaders never reached that office. Hugh Gaitskell was the first. He could be called the first modernising leader, as he attempted to steer the party away from its commitment to nationalisation. In the ensuing conference debate on the party's 'mission' in 1960, Clause Four became 'The Tablets of Stone' or 'The Thirty-Nine Articles', and poor Gaitskell wistfully reflected that he would sooner have led a 'political party and not a religious movement'.[15] Within a few months he had abandoned any attempt to change the party constitution.[16] He died suddenly in 1963.

Michael Foot, a modern Robespierre when young,[17] came to the leadership in 1979 following Callaghan's resignation. Foot's accession to the leadership stalled an open confrontation between the fundamentalists (led by Tony Benn) and social democrats (led by Denis Healey); it owed much to his ability 'to obscure issues', as backbencher Austin Mitchell indiscreetly put it.[18] According to Peter Shore, Foot's inheritance represented a more 'disastrous and bankrupt estate' than that bequeathed to any other Labour leader.[19] Ken Livingstone added that it was Foot's 'basic humanity and compassion' that saved the party from 'destruction…by our enemies'.[20] Foot was less successful in saving it from its friends,[21] and the 1983 election was fought on the clearest statement of fundamentalist values since 1945. Labour was annihilated, its manifesto famously dismissed by former minister Gerald Kaufman as the longest suicide note in history.

On becoming leader, Foot's successor Neil Kinnock had the advantage of popularity. He was the candidate most preferred by Labour supporters (56 per cent); Foot, by contrast, had been only fourth choice of Labour supporters.[22] Kinnock's difficult task was made worse by the outbreak of a miners' strike in spring 1984, led from Yorkshire by Arthur Scargill. Should Kinnock side with Scargill in the name of traditional values and suffer general public opprobrium or denounce Scargill and be accused of class treachery by the fundamentalists? Kinnock did not support the strike and managed to ride out these storms. With the help of a more united Shadow Cabinet, he set in train a revamping of traditional Labour policies, deftly substituting 'social ownership' for nationalisation as the major objective. Other important changes included a moderation of the party's proposals for reforming the Conservatives' trade union legislation, a muted acceptance of council house sales, no pledge to leave the European Community, and a strong commitment to conventional defence spending. The 1987 campaign, though unsuccessful, was a personal triumph for Kinnock. Over the next five years he strengthened his hold over the party, pushing it decisively towards social democracy and away from fundamentalism, towards modernisation and away from traditional values.[23]

Kinnock's resignation after the unexpected election defeat of 1992 brought his erstwhile Shadow Chancellor John Smith to the leadership. In the short time that he held the post before his sudden death in 1994, Smith reduced the union's voting strength at conference, removed their block vote for candidate selection and pressed for the principle of 'one member one vote' (OMOV) in all party elections. These steps together, it has been said, 'effectively broke the power of the unions in the party'.[24] With the help of a younger and more united Shadow Cabinet, Smith accomplished much, but he died before being put to the test at the polls.

Leaders and the parliamentary party

Strictly speaking there is no Labour equivalent to the Conservative backbench 1922 Committee. The whole Parliamentary Labour Party (PLP), including the frontbench, meets twice weekly; once very briefly to set out forthcoming business and once for more general debate on issues and policy. Brand is right, though, to argue that such meetings do not provide 'a satisfactory forum to explore policy'.[25] In addition to the full PLP meetings, the party is organised into regional and departmental committees. From the earliest days fundamentalists in the PLP sought to pressurise the leadership into adopting policies to transform the economic and social structure. After all, wasn't this what socialism was about?[26] Even after the apparently triumphant administration of 1945–50, a number of left-wing MPs formed themselves into a group called Keep Left, under the chairmanship ironically of Harold Wilson. By 1958 a larger and better-organised group, Victory for Socialism, was formed which coordinated the struggle against Gaitskell's revisionism. Traditionally the largest of the left-wing parliamentary groups was Tribune, named after the famous house journal of the Labour left (founded in 1937 – George Orwell was once its literary editor). The group was established in 1964 and for some thirty years was the most important of the factions within the parliamentary party, with two future leaders, Foot and Kinnock, within its ranks. During the 1970s the left was generally dominant on issues such as Europe, trade union reform and constitutional change. In 1974 the left-winger Ian Mikardo became party chairman, though he was soon to be ousted by the right. In the 1979–83 parliament Tribune was particularly influential, achieving a membership of more than seventy, though twenty members eventually left the group, feeling it to be insufficiently radical. When Kinnock became leader he effectively drew Tribune into an anti-fundamentalist alliance and it lost the political idealism that had been its hallmark. It disappeared in the 1990s, only to re-emerge in 2005 'by invitation'.

Tribune's mantle of the champion of fundamentalism was picked up by the Campaign Group, founded in 1982 by MPs leaving Tribune. Campaign was strong enough to put up its own slate for elections to the National Executive Committee (NEC), though with decreasing success as the 1980s wore on. After 1987, Kinnock attempted, with increasing confidence, to take on the fundamentalists in parliament, in the NEC and in the movement at large, and build an alliance against them.[27] By the late 1990s the diminishing Campaign Group (with thirty-one MPs claiming allegiance), in fact the left at large, had become chiefly of only symbolic importance. Its charismatic champion Tony Benn finally left the House in 2005 – to devote more time to politics, he said.

Social democrat gradualists were represented by the Manifesto Group, established in 1974. The group, open only to backbenchers, always kept its membership secret but it was considered influential despite the defection in 1981 of some leading social democrats to become Social Democrats. Labour First, formed in 1980, took up the cudgels for the gradualists. Numbering approximately thirty, they campaigned for 'one member one vote' elections (OMOV) but they were unequal to forces that were pushing the party inexorably to the left. Historically speaking, though, the right has never had the same need to organise as the left, simply because it has usually dominated the party leadership through compliant trade union bosses.

A significant number of Labour MPs have traditionally been sponsored by trade unions, under the financial arrangements set down in the Hastings Agreement (1933), which allowed for the subsidising of up to 80 per cent of election expenses (though usually less was given). Currently eighteen unions affiliate to the Labour Party and they form an umbrella organisation known as the Trade Union and Labour Party Liaison Organisation (TULO). In 2004 TULO came to an agreement at Warwick in which the government made certain specific pledges to promote union interests. The long-term implications of this agreement might be even more significant. Union support has not been as financially important to the party in recent years as it was,[28] but the future of party donations is currently in doubt and the leadership, fearing something much worse, might find itself once again grabbing the hand of nurse.[29] Of the 180 or so candidates who are regularly sponsored, over two-thirds are usually elected. It would be unconstitutional for unions to attempt to exercise direct influence over sponsored MPs, and sponsored MPs have frequently voted in a way contrary to union policy, though few have had their sponsorship withdrawn.[30]

The PLP also includes the Co-operative Party, the political arm of the Co-operative Movement, which is officially the electoral partner of the Labour Party. The party holds an annual conference but seeks to advance its agenda through the PLP and the Scottish and Welsh parties. In 2005 there were twenty-nine Co-operative MPs at Westminster, eight MSPs at Holyrood and four AMs in Cardiff. There are also eleven Co-operative peers and an informal party group in the European Parliament.[31]

It was some time before the Labour group in the European Parliament made any impact in Brussels, hardly surprising given the party's official opposition to membership. In the elections of 1984 thirty-two were successful and their frequently disruptive tactics led to comparisons with English soccer hooligans.[32] But the Labour presence in Brussels grew largely as a reflection of growing Conservative unpopularity, and with the left-of-centre grouping at Brussels firmly in control of the European Parliament, Prime Minister Major could even speak, hyperbolically at least, of a 'socialist super state'. Although MEPs now have recognised status within the party structure, they are not an influential group. In 1999 Labour introduced a closed party list system for election to Brussels, allowing it to keep a firmer control over its representatives. Two sitting Labour MEPs opposed the move; they were expelled from the party.[33]

There are currently 212 Labour peers in the semi-reformed House of Lords, forming the largest party. But there are 201 crossbenchers, 208 Conservative peers and 79 taking the Liberal Democrat whip (along with 26 bishops and 1 Green). As a whole their lordships have been a constant thorn in the flesh of Blair's government, and whereas in previous parliaments the upper chamber tended to give up on amendments that the Commons rejected, from 2001 to 2005 the Lords reinserted no fewer than fifteen rejected amendments (previously the highest number had been four).[34] Russell and Sciara talk about a 'kind of partnership' emerging between the Lords and the Commons backbenches. Labour peers provide the one sector of the parliamentary party not to have withered under Blair; quite the reverse.

Just as the Cabinet has been transformed under Blair, so too has the PLP. Some, like Matthew Taylor, believe that the leadership has been broadly right to limit the influence of the parliamentary party, since the latter was not representative of Labour voters.[35] Smith, on the other hand, speaks of Blair's 'command and control' party management ('parliamentary Leninism' as some call it),[36] 'hollowing out the democratic process'.[37] What they agree on is that the days of subgroups representing fundamentalists and social democrats fighting for control of the parliamentary party are gone, just as the influence of the parliamentary party has gone.

After the 2001 election the government created a new tier of MPs, 100-strong, who would act as aides, supporting ministerial lines among their backbench colleagues. One MP described this as a 'crude and patronising attempt to extend the Whips' control'.[38] The parliamentary committee, half-elected and half-appointed, which meets the Prime Minister each week to liaise, has itself found its influence waning, complaining of a 'well-organised loyalist majority'.[39]

Nevertheless in January 2004 the PLP came very close to defeating the government (with its 146 majority) on a major bill introducing university top-up fees, when 71 Labour MPs voted against their government. The bill was carried by 5 votes.[40] Within six months of the new parliament sitting in 2005, the government had been defeated twice. One of these defeats was on a whipped vote, on the Terrorism Bill, the first since Labour came to power, and the largest majority against a government since 1978. Rebellions have become commonplace; so much so that even the larger are sometimes unreported by the major media.[41]

Leaders and party policy

In comparison with the Conservative Party, Labour's policy-making machine has not traditionally been the creature of the party leader. It has always represented that notion of federalism, which has provided the backdrop to Labour's history. And the linchpin of federalism has been the NEC, described in the party constitution as 'the administrative authority of the party', subject to the control and directions of the conference.[42] But the constitution also gave the NEC a duty to confer with representatives of a Labour government 'prior to the formulation of legislative proposals'. The NEC was, in fact, the hub of a network of policy advisory committees and so oversaw the development of party policy in the longer term. Nevertheless NEC's influence began to wane when Kinnock established the strategic Shadow Communications Agency in 1986 under the party's first director of campaigns and communications (an NEC appointment) Peter Mandelson, and gave it a key role in election and public relations strategy. As the red rose replaced the red flag as Labour's symbol in the late 1980s, the NEC became less of a barrier to the ambitions of the leadership.[43]

Nowadays party policy is formally the responsibility of the National Policy Forum (NPF). This body, which originated in the policy review set in train by Kinnock's campaign strategy committee, was established by the 1990 conference.[44] The creation of NPF took responsibility for policy largely out of the hands of the NEC and conference and embodied it in a process that was more systematic, broader based and, not by accident, easier for the leadership to control. NPF membership comprises representatives of the CLPs, the regions, Scotland and Wales, the unions, the parliamentarians, the Co-operative Party, the Black Socialist Society, local government and the NEC. Each category is required to include a given proportion of women.

The chief task of this large (currently 184 members) body is to set up and oversee the development of party policy in the so-called rolling programme. It meets two or sometimes three times each year. Between these meetings policy is generated and processed via policy commissions in the following areas: Britain in the world; creating sustainable communities; crime, justice, citizenship and equalities; education and skills, and finally prosperity and work. Each commission has between 18 and 22 members, about half of whom are NPF members and the others NEC members plus the relevant ministers. A Joint Policy Committee representing NEC and NPF generally oversees the whole process, agrees policy recommendations and signs off final policy documents. The intention is to have reviewed the whole of party policy within the frame of one parliament. The process is known as *Partnership in Power*. Throughout this process documents, drafted by ministers with the assistance of party staff, are discussed in NPF and sent for comment to regional forums. *Partnership in Power* began in 2006 and was due to be completed by 2008, but already many critics have pointed out the extent to which the process is controlled by the party leadership. It is difficult to achieve a sense of balance in such a process and it is worth remembering that the party was seeking to escape from the ill-disciplined, block-vote-dominated procedures for deciding on party policy at conference that had gone before.

Brief mention must also be made of the existence of a plethora of socialist intellectual groups, the largest and most formidable of which is the Fabian Society. Nowadays the Fabian has an active branch in most cities and publishes a substantial number of books and policy documents. Its influence on Labour policies over the years has been considerable and it has no real counterpart in the Conservative Party, or anywhere in the world. In August 1988 a left-wing 'think-tank', the Institute for Policy Research, was established. Modelled on the Thatcherite Centre for Policy Studies, the Institute is funded partly through the Labour Party and is sympathetic to its aspirations. Other 'think-tanks' such as Demos and, earlier, Charter 88 have also been influential in shaping Labour thinking. On becoming Prime Minister, Blair surrounded himself with policy advisers drawn from these and other groups.

Leaders and the party bureaucracy

Back now to the NEC, which Kavanagh described as defying 'any coherent theory of representation.'[45] When the constitution was drawn up in 1918, NEC comprised sixteen members, representing the unions, the socialist societies and local trades councils. As women's sections and individual constituency parties developed, so the NEC grew to reflect this new structure. NEC positions were elected by the whole conference (thus effectively decided by the union block votes) and it was not until 1937 that constituency parties (CLPs) gained the power freely to elect their own representatives, although in reality the constituencies would choose MPs. For half a century after 1945 MPs provided more than half of the membership of the NEC, including nearly all constituency and women's representatives. Cabinet ministers frequently sat on the NEC and used it as a forum within which to attack the policies of their own government (for example Callaghan attacked Prime Minister Wilson's trade union reforms, Benn attacked Prime Minister Callaghan's economic policies).

The NEC currently comprises thirty-two members and like the NPF is broadly representative of the party's federal nature. The leader, deputy leader and leader of the European party sit ex officio. The Prime Minister chairs a pivotal Joint Policy Committee including equal membership from the government and the NEC, with responsibility for the 'strategic oversight of policy development...and the rolling programme'.[46] The NEC is also represented on a Joint Campaign and Elections Committee, with strategic responsibility for 'campaigns and message delivery', though its influence is no longer crucial. However, the NEC's responsibilities for candidate selection and re-election have been devolved to a senior committee. Significantly, with their own sections on NEC now, MPs and MEPs may no longer stand for other sections; henceforth parliamentary fundamentalists and their allies will find it far more difficult (and less worthwhile) to control the NEC.

Despite focusing of its responsibilities,[47] representation on the NEC – and particularly the constituency section – remains an important target for competing groups. There was much rejoicing among fundamentalists when Ken Livingstone defeated Peter Mandelson in the 1997 elections.[48] In 1998 the leadership ran a campaign to ensure the defeat of a slate put up by the fundamentalist (or more generally anti-Blair) Grass Roots Alliance.[49] But four of the six grass-roots candidates were elected all the same.[50] In 2006 the anti-Blair camp cocked another snook at the leadership when Walter Wolfgang was elected. (At the 2005 conference Wolfgang had been forcibly ejected from the hall for shouting 'nonsense' during a speech by the Foreign Secretary. He was later prevented by the police from re-entering the hall under the Terrorism Act.) The 82-year-old Wolfgang was adopted as a mascot by those opposed to Blair's 'command and control' party management.

If the NEC has been transformed in recent years, so has party headquarters. Originally NEC operated through ninety subcommittees overseeing all aspects of party affairs. When he was leader, Kinnock and the general secretary of the day managed to reduce this number to fewer than twenty. One of the new committees, the campaign strategy committee, set up a review in 1984 to consider the structure of the party organisation, and its recommendations were acted upon (including the establishment of NPF). What was needed was to change the profile of headquarters by shifting resources into campaigning. Headquarters was to give more attention to recruiting and training than to 'serving the constitutional bodies of the party', said the committee. The committee spoke of the organisation as being less efficient, less adventurous and less flexible than that of the Conservatives. The party's new general secretary Larry Whitty was concerned to change the atmosphere of headquarters from neighbourly anarchy to task-oriented professionalism. It is not certain that the NEC knew just what it was doing when it appointed Whitty and Mandelson, but Kinnock knew. The committee suggested a strategic management structure, which was put into effect in 1986. The resulting structure proved far more efficient if less cosy than its predecessors. As Mandelson said, the days when a general secretary could declare that Labour would not 'sell' politicians 'as if they were a breakfast food or baked beans' were long over.[51] Parties exist to win elections and they do so largely, as Blumler says, through winning a 'competitive struggle to influence and control popular perceptions…through the mass media'.[52] What Keir Hardie would have made of all this scarcely bears thinking about, but it represented the shape of things to come. To put it bluntly, Peter Mandelson was the shape of things to come.

Managing the party

The Labour Party, so it is said, was born out of the bowels of the trade union movement. It represented an attempt by organised Labour to secure the active representation of its interests, and those of the working class in general, in the House of Commons. We have described the party as federal and its relationship with the trade union movement explains why.

The trade union connection

The unions played a leading part in the founding of the party, providing the organisational infrastructure, and social base and finance;[53] they also influenced its ideology, moving Labour decisively away from radical socialism and towards what we called labourism. The unions were frequently decisive in shaping the party's subsequent history. It was primarily the TUC's opposition to cuts in public expenditure which brought down MacDonald's government in 1931, and it was the two union leaders Bevin and Citrine who took control of the Labour rump after the 1935 election and rebuilt it, through the Joint National Council. The Transport and General Workers Union (TGWU) was especially dominant. One commentator argued: 'The historic role of general secretaries of the TGWU has been to make or break Labour Party leaders. To that end they have often acted with brutal decisiveness.'[54]

The unions' ability to influence the party was particularly felt at the annual conference, where party policy was formally decided, through the procedure known as the block vote. Affiliated unions commanded a block of votes that represented the number of members paying the political levy to the party. The block vote originated as a device to thwart the fundamentalists at the TUC conference of 1894,[55] but the practice was carried over into the Labour Representation Committee and hence into the party itself. This procedure cemented union influence, making Labour at all levels what Coates and Topham called 'a confederal organisation'.[56] In 1922 a constituency attempt to abolish the block vote was defeated, the leadership pointing out that it was a small price to pay for the 95 per cent of party funds contributed by the unions. Thereafter the block vote was used to control fundamentalist constituency delegates. For example, the block vote helped to constrain Stafford Cripps and the Socialist League in the late 1930s when they attempted to move the party to the left; it defeated Bevan's left-wing challenge in the 1950s. But when the Campaign for Labour Party Democracy (CLPD) challenged the leadership in the late 1970s, the block was no longer solid. Unions had begun to elect a more left-wing leadership but more important, after 1966 the Labour government had initiated a series of assaults on union autonomy through incomes policies and trade union reform. In 1992 the block vote was reduced to 70 per cent and in 1997 to 50 per cent. Party leaders, however, were reluctant to abolish the block vote altogether. As deputy leader Hattersley once remarked: 'We are not going to get rid of the block vote and find ourselves at the mercies of the constituencies'.[57]

Constrained by Conservative laws but even more by the changing nature of employment, membership of the umbrella organisation, the Trades Union Congress (TUC), has halved since 1979. The relationship with Labour was bound to change. The areas of expanding employment in recent years have been outside the traditional union strongholds of full-time, male, manufacture, and rather in part-time, often female service industries where union recognition was spasmodic. Whereas the traditional relationship between Labour governments and the unions was 'voluntarism' – keeping the government out of industrial relations – any new relationship would need to be based on the creation of a new framework of labour law representing the interests of the 'new' workers. And the best prospect of securing such legislation was via Brussels not Westminster. Thus in 1994 the TUC relaunched itself as a non-partisan pressure group. Several unions began to shift funds away from Labour and into the provision of Brussels offices. The TGWU for example reduced its funding of Labour by 50 per cent.[58]

The rationale for the alliance – one of the decisive ingredients of twentieth-century politics in Britain – is no longer decisive in the twenty-first. 'It is simply not clear', Howell argues, 'that there is anything that trade unions can offer a Labour government that it both wants and cannot achieve in other ways'.[59]

The movement

The transformation of Labour's headquarters after the Whitty-Mandelson reforms was completed when, following Labour's victorious 1997 campaign, the party moved permanently to its campaign headquarters, Millbank Towers, on the banks of the Thames. That campaign was managed by what has been described as 'the most sophisticated, efficient, authoritarian election machine ever used in Britain',[60] and Blair put that machine to the job of cementing the leader's authority upon the party's organisational structure. Millbank was inevitably associated with Labour's perceived passion for spin-doctoring and was proving expensive for the party, which subsequently moved its headquarters to 39 Victoria Street.

The movement in the country

Nowadays CLPs comprise a number of branches, usually based upon local government wards, whose tasks are primarily electoral, together with women's sections and Young Labour groups. Trade unions, socialist and co-operative societies may also affiliate to the constituency party at branch level. The party claims that the principle of affiliation is underpinned by the principle of consent: unions must ballot their members every ten years to retain affiliation and members have the right to claim exemption. The CLP is administered by its general management committee, representing the branches. The committee runs the party locally, appoints a campaign committee to coordinate campaigning activity, chooses its delegates to the annual conference and elects an executive committee which undertakes the day-to-day running of the constituency party. The selection of a parliamentary candidate was traditionally the committee's responsibility, following consultations with the NEC, but constituencies were largely their own masters until the mid-1980s, when some selected Militant tendency supporters. Consequently, NEC reasserted its power to overrule constituency selections. Following the introduction of individual votes for each party member, all candidates were chosen by a postal ballot of all CLP members, a procedure that applied to all party elections, including NEC and leadership elections. It was OMOV that enabled Blair to amend Clause Four. Enfranchising the individual member has so far broken the power of groups. The party, Blair concluded, had 'freed itself from the vanguardism of the eighties'.[61]

Although infiltration, or entryism, especially by Militant tendency, became a cause for concern in the 1980s, it was not new. Neither was militancy among constituency parties generally: in 1930 Sidney Webb said that 'the constituency parties were frequently unrepresentative groups of non-entities dominated by fanatics and cranks'.[62] After the electoral defeat of 1979, Militant tendency became an incubus in the body of the movement and the leadership, fearful of the party being pushed towards direct forms of action by these radical elements, finally decided on the expulsion of Militant supporters.[63] In 1986, the NEC established a new body, the National Constitutional Committee (NCC), entrusted with the task of maintaining party discipline – in effect removing Militant supporters from CLPs. The battle against Militant and entryism was a long tedious battle fought on a wide front, but it was waged vigorously and successfully, and the institution of OMOV reinforced the victory.[64]

The youth organisation too, traditionally fell regular prey to the extreme left. In 1964 the then Young Socialists had been reconstituted because they were controlled by Trotskyists, but by the early 1980s the Labour Party Young Socialists (LPYS) was in similar difficulties.[65] The 1988 annual conference was cancelled and the NEC decided to establish a new youth structure altogether. In 1993 the conference established Young Labour, with an upward age limit of 27. At its inauguration Young Labour had some 23,000 members. Since then membership has grown and Young Labour, keyed into the overall party structure, has so far proved immune to entryism.

Above the CLP are nine English regions (plus Scotland and Wales). Each possesses an executive elected by a regional conference. The executive too mirrors in its composition the conference's 'federal' structure, and is responsible for the day-to-day administration of the regional party between conferences (biannual for the Scottish and Welsh parties, biennial for the English regions).

Because of the party's links with the unions, it was not until 1918 that it became possible under the new constitution to take out direct individual membership. Within ten years there were 215,000 individual party members, and this figure grew to a peak of over one million in 1951, declining thereafter. By the 1980s membership stood at 288,776.[66] Kinnock's attempts to boost party membership failed but Blair's efforts, in contrast, were initially highly successful: from 1994 to 1997 membership rose from 305,000 to 405,000. As Patrick Seyd pointed out, Blair sought to expand party membership because he thought it would counterbalance activist fundamentalism (through OMOV) as well as providing more potential campaigners and fund-raisers.[67] Since these halcyon days membership has all but halved.

One distinctive aspect of Labour constituency politics was its use of women-only shortlists. The 1993 conference agreed that women should fight 50 per cent of the most winnable Labour seats and those where Labour MPs were retiring. This decision caused considerable controversy. It was dismissed as a gimmick by the Conservatives and as an attack on their liberty by some male party members, especially in the North of England.[68] In 1996 an industrial tribunal declared that the policy contravened the Sex Discrimination Act of 1975 and it was discontinued. Nevertheless women-only shortlists had already been drawn up in many strong Labour seats. In 1997, 159 women stood for Labour of whom no fewer than 101 were elected. Whatever misgivings they may have engendered, these shortlists worked.

Celtic heartlands

The Scottish and to a lesser extent the Welsh Labour parties have held a symbolically important position in the history of Labour which finds no echo in Conservatism. Keir Hardie founded the party; its first Prime Minister was Ramsay MacDonald. In good days and in bad, since the mid 1960s Scotland and Wales have continued to return Labour MPs in proportions unmatched in Middle England (in 1997 for example fifty-six of Scotland's seventy-two and thirty-three of Wales' forty were Labour). Even in the disastrous 1983 election, Labour secured forty-two Scottish seats, twice as many as the Conservatives, and twenty Welsh seats, almost 50 per cent more than the Conservatives did. Until the referendum on devolution in 1997, the Scottish party owned no buildings, employed no staff, had no members and no leader – all belonged to the national party. By the time of the first elections to the Scottish parliament, however, the Scottish party had built a framework for autonomy.[69] The Scottish Labour Party (SLP) has the same procedure as the national party for electing its leader and deputy leader. The Scottish party comprises the same components as the national party, with biannual conferences organised by a five-member committee representing conference, the Scottish Policy Forum and the Scottish Executive Committee. The latter comprises MSPs, MPs, MEPs and local councillors, as well as the representatives of the unions, Co-operative Party and Young Labour. Party leader and former First Minister Jack McConnell and his party had to keep half an eye on Westminster while proclaiming Scottish separateness. The party had some 18,800 members in 2007, representing a fall of over 30 per cent from 1997. In 2007 the unthinkable happened. Labour hegemony in Scotland was broken, partly as a consequence of an inept campaign, partly as a result of the unpopularity of the Labour administration at Westminster. The Scottish National Party became the party of (minority) government. Local government elections, held on the same day under the single transferable vote (STV) system, were also disastrous for Labour: 3 May 2007 marked a step change for Scottish Labour.

The Welsh (or Wales) Labour Party has gone down much the same route as the SLP, though Wales' focus will remain as much on Westminster as on the Welsh Assembly because the powers of Cardiff, though being increased, are not comparable to those of Edinburgh. In structural terms the Wales Labour Party follows the Scottish model but its leader Rhodri Morgan has pursued a policy line more at variance with the Westminster government: Wales has turned its back on foundation hospitals and school academies, and prescriptions are free. In the elections of 2007 Labour held on to power by its fingernails. All in all, the recent flourishing of Celtic socialism as a result of the Labour government's devolution legislation has not been unproblematical.

The annual conference

Symbolically conference played a crucial role in Labour politics, especially after MacDonald's 'betrayal', when steps were taken to control the parliamentary party.[70] In 1937, Attlee wrote that conference 'lays down the policy of the party and issues instructions which must be carried out by…its representatives in parliament…the Labour Party conference is in fact a parliament of the movement'.[71] After he became Prime Minister Attlee had a change of heart but conference remained a major force in terms of policy-making. Gaitskell's defeat on unilateral nuclear disarmament at the 1960 conference was reversed in 1961; this caused *The Times* to conclude that the party leader had 'exploded the theory that the party conference is the policy-making body which issues orders to the MPs and their chosen leader'.[72] But this was only half right: Gaitskell had not ignored conference. He worked to overturn the 1960 resolution but only through another conference resolution in 1961. Conference could not be ignored.

We have already discussed the new procedure through which party policy evolves largely outside of conference. Following the electoral defeat of 1987, further sweeping changes affected conference.[73] Most important was the requirement that constituency delegates were to be elected through OMOV, thus weakening fundamentalist influence. As a consequence, in 1991 Gerald Kaufman became the first social democrat MP to be elected in the constituency section of the NEC for sixteen years.[74] In the leadership elections of 1992, moreover, John Smith received 90 per cent of the CLP vote; it is hardly conceivable that in the old days activists would have supported him to anything like this extent.

OMOV and NPF together transformed conference. The dog days of the 1970s and 1980s, when the many-headed beasts of fundamentalist activism and entryism stalked the nation's television screens, were replaced by the autumnal respectability of the 1990s and 2000s. Although Labour leaders would deny any such thing, conference is now more or less 'under control'.

The struggle to recapture conference for the leadership had not, as the fundamentalists had claimed, been about democracy being replaced by oligarchy but about a 'parliamentary elite' taking power from an 'unrepresentative grassroots elite'.[75] Unreformed Labour conferences, for those of the general public who bothered to watch, were not so much a parliament of the party as a pantomime in which party leaders would constantly be warned: 'Behind you!', Faucher's study of Labour conferences, tends to be positive about the reforms, arguing that the new policy-making procedures offer 'genuine possibilities of democratic participation' as ordinary members respond to the opportunities for consultation.[76] But she concedes that the process is a tightly controlled one.

Party funding

We have observed the closeness of the traditional relationship between the Labour Party and the trade union movement and nowhere has this been more important than in party funding. The unions contributed in a number of ways, with affiliation payments, grants and donations, with the sponsorship of parliamentary candidates and with indirect help such as the provision of resources and personnel. In recent years, however, the party has sought successfully to diversify the sources of its funding so as to limit its dependence upon the unions. Labour was impressively successful in garnering donations through, for example, 'high-profile dinners'.[77] Substantial donations were also received from a number of wealthy individuals and celebrities including – famously – Bernie Eccleston of Formula One motor racing.[78] This is not an entirely new phenomenon. Wealthy men have donated to socialism in the past, William Morris being an excellent early example. More recently Oswald Mosley, Sir Stafford Cripps and Robert Maxwell exercised generosity to the party. The offices of both Attlee and Wilson benefited from donations; so too did Blair's,[79] and some of his ministers' offices.[80] Seven donors were, no doubt coincidentally, later made life peers; others were given prestigious jobs.[81] The undisclosed personal loan of over £300,000 from Geoffrey Robinson to Peter Mandelson to assist him in buying a house, which, when made public, brought about the latter's resignation, is not strictly classifiable as a loan to socialism.

By the time Labour came to power in 1997, trade unions' contributions had declined as a percentage of income from some 75 per cent to about 40 per cent, replaced by large corporate and individual donations.[82] However, the party found itself in hot water after the 2005 election, when it was disclosed that Labour had to repay loans totalling some £17 million within two years. What impacted upon Labour's ability to make these repayments was the 'sale of peerages' row that erupted, which choked off new sources of loans. The party's chief fund-raiser, Lord Levy, was twice arrested and later released by the Metropolitan Police as part of their inquiries concerning the alleged promise of peerages in return for loans. While such a 'sale' became strictly illegal in 1925, there is no doubt that both parties have rewarded wealthy donors in the past, in part because such individuals have usually made significant contributions to public life generally. However, in this case it is alleged that private 'understandings' were arrived at between individuals and somebody in the leadership. A 'livid' party treasurer Jack Dromey declared that he knew nothing about the loans and would set in train his own inquiries.[83] In the event, though Blair became the first Prime Minister ever to be questioned as part of a criminal enquiry, the Crown Prosecution Service decided (in July 2007) not to bring charges against any of the individuals concerned. This hardly amounted to an exoneration. Later in the year another founding scandal hit Labour. This time it involved a gift of £650,000 to the party made by a North East businessman David Abrahams. The money was channelled to the party via four different individuals over a period of four years in contravention of funding laws brought in by Labour. Once again the Metropolitan Police have begun an enquiry. What was at issue was how many senior figures in the party were aware that the law was being broken. The party General Secretary was obliged to resign immediately but others may be implicated. The enquiry continues.[84]

For the opposition parties Labour's very real discomfiture was doubly satisfying because they don't have to press the case themselves (and both have skeletons in their own cupboards): they can leave it to police probing and the government's own shifty ineptitude. The *Daily Telegraph* went so far as to suggest that the party was 'on the verge of financial ruin, with only the trade union movement keeping the party afloat',[85] but even this lifeline remains problematical. In 2007 Sir Hayden Phillips' inquiry into party funding reported. It recommended not only strict limits on the amount that parties spent on electioneering, but also a limit of £50,000 on individual and corporate donations. The report prevaricated over union contributions but presumed that they could exceed £50,000 only if individual members 'opted in'; whereas currently individuals have to opt *out* if they do not wish their subscriptions to be donated to Labour.[86]

Conclusions

In 1960 the general secretary of the party identified three centres of decision-making within the movement: the parliamentary party, the NEC and the conference. 'None of these elements can dominate the others', he said.[87] If we made good the disingenuous omission of the party leader and the unions, this picture was accurate for a further twenty-five years. But the moles had begun tunnelling and after 1987 the walls of the federalist citadel began to topple. Two processes, centralisation and the empowerment of ordinary members, two sides of the same coin, were at work: as Peter Mair wrote, 'democratisation on paper may…actually coexist with powerful elite influences in practice'.[88] We have seen how the leadership has sought to control both the PLP and Cabinet;[89] how it controls policy development through the JPC, the NPF and the process of policy review; how the wings of the NEC and of conference have been clipped and the influence of the trade unions curtailed. Tony Benn has concluded that these structural reforms will vest 'all effective power in the party…[resulting] in a new elite around the leadership'.[90] The strengthening of the Policy Unit at 10 Downing Street and the boosting of the Cabinet Office allowed Blair an executive authority and strategic grasp that previous leaders would have envied.[91]

The empowerment of ordinary members is potentially just as revolutionary. It overturns one of the traditions of British working-class politics, delegatory democracy, which allowed ordinary members to participate through mandating delegates to national policy-making bodies. This was how trade unions worked and how the Labour Party was supposed to work.[92] The abandonment of delegatory democracy was a response by the reformers to the 'capture' of the party by fundamentalist activists in the early 1980s when the party machine lurched to the left. According to Mandelson and Liddle, the leadership sought to 'ensure that the party's mass, grass-roots membership, rather than unrepresentative groups of activists, has the greatest say in the agreement of polices and the election of its leaders'.[93] Mair has shown that the empowerment of individual members can often enfranchise those who are 'more likely to endorse the policies (and candidates) proposed by the party leadership'.[94]

After the revolution comes the post-revolution, a period in which the revolution is either firmly established or overthrown. Present-day modernisers have gone much further in transforming the party than the fundamentalists did in the 1970s. The modernisers' strategy, as Faucher-King has written, involved 'rebranding the party...through a strict corporate discipline pervasively and progressively extended to all sections of the party through a mixture of authority and cajoling'.[95] Only electoral success could enshrine the new regime and in delivering three consecutive victories, Blair could make the most persuasive of claims to have established the New Labour revolution.

6   Conservative politicians, activists and supporters

One of the most striking features of the Conservative Party, according to Burch and Moran, has been its ability, over many years, to resolve an apparent paradox and 'combine electoral success with social elitism' in a democratic age.[1] They draw our attention to the fact that a party that made no secret of its belief in privilege has nevertheless been able to persuade enough of the less privileged to support it to achieve greater electoral success over the last one hundred and twenty or so years than its more overtly egalitarian rivals. We shall examine three categories of party activity, namely that of parliamentarians (especially MPs), party activists (those who belong to the party) and party supporters (those who regularly vote Conservative) in order to discover who the Conservatives are, what they think and what motivates them. In the process perhaps we will see this paradox of Conservatism unravel.

The parliamentary party: background

The most noticeable feature of the current parliamentary party is its size – or lack of it, for despite some growth from the mere 165 MPs returned in 1997 (smaller than at any time since 1906), the parliamentary party, currently at 198, is still considerably smaller than usual. It is unlikely that such a transformation in size would not imply changes in character and structure. If we are to measure and make sense of this transformation, we need to establish what was transformed: that is, what the 'traditional' Conservative Party looked like.

The backbenches: social background

The first authoritative modern work on the background of members of the House of Commons, Colin Mellors' *The British MP*,[2] considered each new wave of MPs from 1945 to 1979. The Conservative Party, he concluded, was traditionally resistant to social change. In 1945 the typical Conservative MP came from a privileged background, over 80 per cent having been to public school. More than 25 per cent had been to Eton and almost 50 per cent had gone on to Oxbridge from their public school. Mellors said that the Conservatives, in choosing their parliamentary candidates, 'concern themselves more with rank and achievement than party political experience. Breeding and educational attainment are customarily seen as the two most important qualifications...for recruitment to the political elite'.[3] He went on to say that the 'old school tie' was the single most important qualification for would-be Conservative MPs. 'As a guarantee of success it ranked with sponsorship from the mineworkers' union in the Labour party.' It was not simply that Oxbridge dominated the Conservative Party but that the products of four specific Oxford colleges (Christ Church, Balliol, New and Magdalen) and four Cambridge colleges (Trinity, Trinity Hall, King's and Gonville and Caius) dominated. As far as educational background went, the Conservative parliamentary party was homogeneous to an unparalleled degree.

Education has always tended to be an indicator of social class and it may be stated quite simply that the post-war Conservative parliamentary party was (and remains) overwhelmingly upper-middle class. It has some aristocratic connections (not as strong as they were), but has produced only a handful of MPs who could be classified as working class. It may be true, as Robert Louis Stevenson intimated, that politics is the only profession for which no preparation is thought necessary, but it is clear that Conservative candidate selection committees believed that some professional backgrounds were eminently more suitable for aspiring politicians than others. Mellors characterised the parliamentary Conservative Party as representing 'law, land and business' but acknowledged that it was in fact business, and not the law or the land, which provided the preponderance of MPs – the cornerstone of the parliamentary party. We can be more precise and say that a certain category of business people traditionally provided the overwhelming majority of these MPs: company directors.[4] In the thirty years after the Second World War, 273 company directors were elected to parliament, of whom no fewer than 245 were Conservatives. As Mellors concludes, 'it is by far the largest single occupation group represented at Westminster'.[5] It seems abundantly clear that for a substantial majority of Conservative MPs 'training' traditionally consisted of having succeeded in a previous career, usually business. What also characterised the parliamentary party was a concomitant of their professional backgrounds: wealth – professional, commercial, industrial – and, even more traditionally, landed wealth (in the last parliament before the Second World War, well over one-third of Conservative MPs were aristocrats by birth or by marriage).[6]

The pre-war selection procedures were described as exercises in plutocracy, with those candidates able and willing to meet all their election expenses standing the best chance of being selected as candidates.[7] The Conservatives actively sought to broaden the social base of the parliamentary party. When Lord Woolton became party chairman in 1945, he initiated a review of party organisation under Maxwell-Fyfe, which turned its attention to the party's unrepresentativeness. It recommended, among other things, that the entire election expenses of candidates should be the responsibility of the constituency association and that candidates should be permitted to make no contribution to their own campaign.[8] The aim of the recommendations, which were accepted by the party, was to remove financial considerations that might deter ordinary people from standing as Conservative candidates, or dispose constituencies to prefer wealthier candidates. Butler and

Pinto-Duschinsky point out that these reforms had very little effect upon the social composition of the party, either within or outwith the House of Commons.[9]

The Thatcher 'revolution'

It was only in 1979 that social change in the party began to be felt. For the first time the proportion of those following what Burch and Moran had called the meritocratic route – state education followed by university – outnumbered those who followed the traditional route – public school followed by Oxbridge.[10] In 1979 there were more new members educated in the provincial and London universities than there were from Oxbridge and Etonians counted for only about 6 per cent of the new intake. Burch and Moran argued not only that the wider opportunities of the Butler Education Act of 1944 (a good grammar school education) were making themselves felt but also that the appeal to the privileged of a parliamentary career was diminishing; it could no longer easily be coupled with a long-term career in the law or in industry.

Not only were the 1979 newcomers distinctive socially but also many of them were already, in effect, full-time politicians. By 1983 over half of new Conservative MPs had local government experience, representing, in Burch and Moran's words, 'the most striking index of the change'. They continued: 'They would have been amongst the ablest councillors. As chairmen of committees, they would influence budgets worth millions of pounds. Articulate, experienced and opinionated councillors do not make good lobby fodder in Westminster.'[11] Perhaps, but between 1983 and 1992 the size of the government majority lessened the need for Conservative backbenchers to be tightly disciplined or even actually to be present at the House for much of the time. As the 1980s wore on, the new wave of backbenchers became less amenable to the old-style party discipline than their predecessors.

Selection procedures also changed in 1980 and these had some effect upon the kind of candidates being chosen.[12] Residential selection boards operated a system rather like that of the civil service. Prospective candidates were assessed in groups in a number of different situations over a period of forty-eight hours by a team including an MP, an industrialist and a member of the National Union. About 25 per cent failed at this hurdle; the remainder were scrutinised by the party vice chairman in charge of candidates and about 40 per cent failed here. Competition for places on the resulting approved list increased substantially and this helped to improve the quality of candidates to some degree. These new vetting procedures were denounced by one respected agent as a 'hopelessly haphazard process', especially the vetting by the vice chairman, who 'lets everyone go unless they're a raving monster'.[13] However, no gains are made without losses. Like the Maxwell-Fyfe reforms, these procedures tended to replace men from various backgrounds, interests and ideological persuasions who had chiefly one thing in common, their wealth, by candidates who corresponded most closely to an amalgam of all desirable Conservative qualities – identikit candidates – and selection committees began to use candidate 'profiles' in their task.

It is in the nature of a large majority, however, that many of the new MPs elected in the 1980s represented former Labour seats, with mainly working-class electorates. David Thomas argued that they consequently became more attentive to constituency needs than other Tory backbenchers and to reflect a distinctive new brand of urban Conservatism.[14] Moreover, as Baker and Fountain point out,[15] the party began actively to portray itself as representing the upwardly mobile, or to use Critchley's caustic characterisation, it became the party of the estate agent rather than the estate owner.[16] These changes produced not simply a more independent party but arguably a more intellectually self-confident one. By the mid 1980s, 'the standard of professionalism and intellect among Conservative MPs', as Sir David Price (himself an MP for over thirty years) claimed, had become 'infinitely higher than when I first came here'.[17]

The more traditionally minded Tories strove to fight their corner. In 1983 Francis Pym established a parliamentary ginger group called Centre Forward. Critics attacked Pym's self-confessed group of moderates as 'squirearchs and landed gentry from another era', though the journalist Anthony Howard defended them:

> Backbench knightage and baronetage with its roots in the soil provided the Tory party with its ballast – and some of them at least...were markedly enlightened and modern-minded in their outlook...their successors [the 'estate agents'] have tended to be young, thrusting professional politicians, for whom party, if not faction, means all.[18]

Pym's group sought a more compassionate and less radical approach to government. He represented a paternalistic Tory tradition that Thatcher despised. On behalf of traditionalists Julian Critchley characterised the 1975 leadership campaign that brought Thatcher to power and initiated the transformation as the 'Peasants' Revolt'. Thatcher, he said, changed the Conservative Party into an old-fashioned liberal party, turning a 'non-political political party', eschewing ideology, tempering belief with scepticism, and 'flying by the seat of [its] pants', into a party of conviction and crusade.[19]

The new intake of MPs – the revolting peasants – tended to be 'more aggressively business minded...the sort for whom capitalism doesn't have an unacceptable face'.[20] Butler and Pinto-Duschinsky wrote: 'The relatively dumb knight of the shire is said to be a dying breed, replaced by the thrusting city banker or the advertising man'.[21] One senior backbencher MP declared in interview that these changes had made the party less 'gentlemanly'. He said of the new members: 'Their behaviour is boorish and they don't have any real sympathy for the place [parliament]'. Another added: 'they're mostly hard-nosed businessmen who are here for their own reasons, and that includes quick promotion come what may. But they've no time for party loyalty unless it happens to suit'. A third backbencher felt: 'They're a pretty disaffected lot, by and large, with the whole set up, actually. Their attendance at the House is pretty dismal...one of the disadvantages of such a big majority I suppose'. One final comment from a backbencher of long standing: 'They may be a clever lot –

everybody says they are – but they're not my idea of gentlemen. I think they behave as badly as the other side personally'.

As might be imagined, these 'new' Conservatives had little time for tradition. They claimed to be articulating the interests of the majority of ordinary people, and in some senses they were. Crewe and Sarlvik argued that on issues such as law and order, education and morality (populist-authoritarian issues as they called them), they took a pugnacious stand substantially to the right, which was to prove electorally popular throughout the 1980s.[22] Crewe and Sarlvik concluded: 'In a large number of policy areas – foreign affairs, defence, crime, minority rights, and sexual morality – the majority view aligns with Conservative rather than Labour instincts'. As others recognised it was no electoral disadvantage for the Conservatives to become more like the rest of the nation, for 'the Conservatives [had been] damaged by being seen as a class party'.[23]

On the other hand the picture of a 'new' parliamentary party inexorably becoming lower-middle class and Tebbit-like is not sustained. Baker and Fountain[24] and Whiteley, Seyd and Richardson[25] indicate that, if anything, the decline in what they call social exclusivity of the early 1980s was later reversed. 'The Conservative Party is led in parliament', say the former, 'largely by men and women whose education, particularly in the more exclusive institutions such as private schools, Oxford and Cambridge, indicates a continuation of social exclusivity'. They continue: 'The media image of Major as the leader and creator of a more "classless" Conservative Party...appears largely groundless'. The new intake of forty-one in 1997 contained more than its share of 'identikits', including four former Central Office staff. A half-hearted attempt was made to attract more women candidates but in the event only about a hundred were selected, of whom only thirteen were successful, only five of them new. Another factor affecting selection, or more accurately reselection, in 1997 was sleaze: perhaps it was no worse than previously but certainly more government MPs were found out.

The 1997 parliament contained only thirty members who had been elected before 1979, so if the party had undergone a lasting change as a consequence of a Thatcher or Tebbit 'revolution', it should have been obvious in 1997.[26] In fact with the exception of recruitment from the very top public schools (there were none at all from Harrow), in its social background at least, the post-Thatcher/Tebbit Conservative Party returned more or less to the *status quo ante bellum*: the representatives of business and the older professions dominated. The banner of a new post-Tebbit party was carried among the new intake by one, Julie Kirkbride (Bromsgrove), a journalist, Cambridge-educated, right-wing, the daughter of a lorry driver from Halifax.

Conservatives in the present House of Commons are much the same as their predecessors. Somewhat younger than their principal opponents these days, the party is made up of a comparable proportion of professionals, though the largest category in the Conservative Party comprises lawyers (20 per cent to Labour's 8 per cent), whereas teachers and university teachers comprise 3 per cent of the party compared to 21 per cent for Labour. Finally, although manual workers comprise only 10 per cent of the Parliamentary Labour Party, this is still ten times the number of Conservative manual workers.[27] In terms of education, 60 per cent of the parliamentary Conservative Party was educated privately; 81 per cent went on to university, almost half of whom (43 per cent) went to Oxbridge.

Social background in itself is not as important as the narrow perspective that it frequently instils. There may have always been a wealth of knowledge among members on matters of finance, commerce, agriculture and the law, but this was offset by an absolute dearth of first-hand experience of poverty, unemployment, the sharp end of the welfare state, the problems of living in the inner cities, and so on. Voters' perceptions of the parliamentary party may be inferred from the following extract from a tabloid newspaper. Entitled 'School Report', it tells of the decision of Bob Dunn MP to send his son to a local fee-paying school. Nothing very unusual in that, but Dunn happened to be a junior minister in the Department of Education and Science. 'Perhaps', wrote the journalist, 'if it were his child whose future depended upon how he came through the state system, his child who came home semiliterate, rude and uninterested, he might get off his backside and do something to improve it'.[28] Conservative leaders, it seemed, had little understanding of those who suffered from the limitations of state services because they didn't use them. Norman Tebbit told the story of a Tory grandee who, as preparation for a Cabinet discussion, had to ask his senior civil servants what mortgages were and how they worked.[29]

If the post-Thatcher party was less homogeneous, more factious, more abrasive, and less deferential than its predecessors, this hardly amounted to social transformation. No Thatcherite or Tebbittite social revolution, apparently, but what of ideological changes on the backbenches?

The backbenches: ideological background

Norton, quoting Norman Lamont, commented on the Conservatives under Major that they were in office but not in power.[30] He elucidated four reasons for this state of affairs: incompetence (especially economic), disunity, weak leadership, and the lack of what he calls 'the public service ethic', which is similar to the paternalism that Gilmour associates with traditional Tory values. We are not interested here with incompetence or weak leadership, but the divisions on Europe (a leitmotif of Conservatism in the 1990s) and the decline of the public service ethic do tell us something important about the modern parliamentary party.

The issue of Britain's relationship to the European Union, something of a running sore as its member states became more closely aligned, became a major health scare during the passage of the Maastricht Bill in 1992.[31] Although originally the deal that Major had struck at the Maastricht conference of 1991 had been hailed as a triumph, two events changed the nature of the debate. First was Denmark's refusal, by referendum in June 1992, to endorse the treaty (later reversed), which derailed the legislative process in the House of Commons, and second was the United Kingdom's forced withdrawal (in September) from the Exchange Rate Mechanism (ERM), which caused great and lasting bitterness. An early day motion signed by sixty-nine Conservatives urged the government to make a 'fresh start' to future progress.[32] Signatories sought not greater integration but an enlarged Europe that would offer 'a fully competitive common market'. Major, with a small and diminishing majority, needed the support of Liberal Democrats and Ulster Unionists to secure the tortuous progress of the Maastricht legislation.[33] The most remarkable confrontation followed the government's decision in 1994 to make the vote on the annual contribution to the EU budget an issue of confidence: a constitutional outrage, declared the Eurosceptics. As we have noted, eight of them, whip notwithstanding, failed to support their government. The whip was withdrawn from them immediately and a ninth resigned the whip in protest. These MPs posed as a quasi-independent party.[34] The paymaster-general resigned from the government because of its allegedly pro-European stance; at the party conference the former party treasurer Lord McAlpine defected to the Referendum party and three leading party figures addressed large Eurosceptic fringe meetings.[35]

Norton analysed the parliamentary party along the axis of European policy, finding the 'Eurosceptic right' amounted to 32 per cent. Although Major could count on the loyalty of some 49 per cent of his party, almost half of these were 'Eurosceptic leaning'. The 'pro-European integration left' comprised only the remaining 19 per cent.[36] Norton's analysis shows that for more than half the party Europe was an issue so important that it transcended party loyalty, and two-thirds of these were Eurosceptic and right wing. According to Martin Holmes, Major saw the Eurosceptic leaders as his principal parliamentary enemies. 'They were "bastards" who were "spreading poison"'.[37] For their part these leaders saw Major as a traitor to Thatcherism.[38] Such was the importance of the European fissure that it rendered the old categories of partisanship in the parliamentary party more or less irrelevant. For the next decade almost the only issue that counted was Europe. Moreover, the association of Euroscepticism with the right and pro-Europeanism with the left might have been approximate but it was not inaccurate. The preponderance of Eurosceptics which Norton noted in the 1992–97 parliament was only enhanced in the 1997–2001 parliament. Of the 165 Conservative MPs in the house after 1997, only about 35 were pro-European.[39] Michael Heseltine organised them into a group called Mainstream by its supporters, Slipstream or even Backwater by its far more numerous opponents.[40]

Norton also referred to the decline in the 'public service ethos'. Her reforms of the civil service, moreover, concentrated more on sound management than serving the public. When we add to all this the self-confidence (critics would say arrogance) of such a long period in office and stir in the rich mixture of sex scandals – MPs accepting cash payment for asking parliamentary questions; a minister with responsibilities for arms sales being treated to a stay in a luxury Paris hotel by putative purchasers; tales of over-close relationships between MPs and lobby groups; an independent inquiry announcing that a minister had deliberately misled the House[41] – we have a concoction powerful enough to lull the party into forgetting all about its paternalist roots, or what Norton called the public service ethos. David Willets argued: 'It is because people believe, wrongly, that Conservatism just stands for every man for himself and the devil take the hindmost that they also came to dislike the Conservatives'.[42] But were people so wrong? The chairman of the party's National Union executive, who thirty years earlier had criticised the parliamentary party because 'nowadays too many MPs become [company] directors instead of too many directors becoming MPs',[43] would have been stunned by the number of ministers and senior officials who retired and almost immediately took up key positions in major companies in the 1990s.

All in all, it is plausible to argue that by the general election of 1997 some kind of a revolution had indeed taken place within the ranks of the Conservative parliamentary party. The struggle between new and old, left and right, wet and dry had been perpetual but containable. The new struggle, crystallising by 1997 as the battle over Britain's future in Europe, had become more corrosive and proved to be uncontainable. To some degree it replicated, indeed was the continuation of, the division between Thatcher loyalists and those who had engineered her demise. After all, it was she who, having morphed into a modern Boadicea defending British heritage against continental intrusion, opposed vehemently every small step towards a federal Europe. Most Eurosceptics were Thatcherite. No wonder the battle was so bitterly fought. As the retiring backbencher Julian Critchley observed: 'What is so remarkable about the Conservative Party is the extent to which we hate each other'.[44] If Europe is not now so divisive an issue, and it is not, this is only because of the more or less complete triumph of Euroscepticism within the party.

Party leadership

The most striking social feature of the modern Conservative leadership is the fact that six of the seven most recent Conservative leaders have been meritocrats of modest social origins. Edward Heath, the son of a carpenter, won an organ scholarship at Balliol. Daughter of a Grantham grocer, Margaret Thatcher defended grammar schools by declaring: 'People from my sort of background need good schools to compete with children from privileged homes like [Labour Cabinet Ministers of the day] Shirley Williams and Anthony Wedgwood Benn.'[45] Her successor John Major, who did not go to university but did at one time drive a bus, was the son of a travelling showman. His successor William Hague (who, even more unusually, hailed from the North of England – industrial Yorkshire) was the son of a soft drinks manufacturer. Iain Duncan Smith (one-eighth part Japanese and a distant relation of the socialist playwright Bernard Shaw) was educated in a naval training establishment and Sandhurst. Michael Howard from Gorseinon was the son of a Romanian Jewish shopkeeper and went on to study law at Cambridge, via Llanelli grammar school. Only the present incumbent, old Etonian David Cameron, breaks the mould. With his father a wealthy stockbroker, and his mother the daughter of a baronet, Cameron is married to a descendant of King William IV and one of his mistresses, and so distantly related to the Queen.[46] Although Cameron might appear to be the standard bearer of a new Conservatism, he is also the embodiment of a very old tradition that appeared to have gone forever.

In general, since 1885 the percentage of Conservative Cabinet ministers from an aristocratic background varied from 44 per cent in that year down to 22 per cent in Heath's 1970 cabinet, with the principal fall-off occurring during Churchill's last government in 1955. Over these years aristocrats provided an average of 37 per cent of Conservative Cabinets.[47] Baker and Fountain brought the ministerial statistics up to date in 1996,[48] and their figures showed that in fact the numbers of Cabinet ministers who had been privately educated fell from Heath's government to Thatcher's and from Thatcher's to Major's, but only from 86 per cent to 73 per cent. The number of old Etonians at Cabinet level also fell, more dramatically, from 27 per cent down to 9 per cent. Oxbridge-educated Cabinet ministers also declined from 73 per cent to 55 per cent. Baker and Fountain concluded their study: 'The Conservative Party is led in parliament largely by men and women whose education, particularly in the more elite institutions such as private schools, Oxford and Cambridge, indicates a continuation of social exclusivity.' Major and Tebbit remain unrepresentative: 'If "meritocracy" or "classlessness" is growing in the Conservative Party, there are few clear signs yet visible in its parliamentary elite'.[49]

Yet as John Major frequently reminded all who would listen, the fissure over Europe which transformed the backbenches divided Cabinet too. So while Baker and Fountain's picture shows no Thatcher-inspired social revolution among the leadership, if the camera is pointed at ideology a different image emerges. The seeds of deep division had already been sown. Thatcher had been the opponent of consensus and never regarded the idea of her own party as a coalition ('broad church') with any favour: coalitions do not get difficult things done. Unlike traditional Tory sceptics, she had no instinctive warmth for what Edward Pearce of the *Guardian* once called 'chug-chug government'. Quite the opposite in fact. Thatcher's clarity of purpose helped to achieve three electoral victories but in fact, as Ramsden shows,[50] her party never attained the levels of support that those of traditionalists such as Disraeli, Salisbury, Baldwin and Macmillan had done: her victories owed much to the weakness of the Labour Party. Her departure, engineered by opponents in Cabinet, left a bitterness that solidified into a despising of Major's leadership. Europe became the touchstone of ideological loyalty in Cabinet just as it did in the parliamentary party and the movement, and so corrosive that a Prime Minister would state in public (unintentionally, he claimed) that a number of his Cabinet colleagues were 'bastards' and that he was 'out to get them'.

As far as the party leadership is concerned, then, Thatcher's legacy *was* transformative. Cabinet became divided in a way that it had not been since 1906. When Philip Cowley analysed the 1997 leadership contest, he divided the party into three: Eurosceptic, Europhile and centre.[51] His conclusion was that Hague got into a winning position because he was not disliked by either Euro group and could command general support from the centre. When Duncan Smith defeated Kenneth Clarke for the leadership in 2001 – the first time the membership had voted – his victory could only be accounted for by members' relative positions on Europe.[52] Instead of a nationally popular former Cabinet minister they chose a totally inexperienced rebel.[53] But then, the ground of his rebellion had been Europe. Only with the defeat of the European constitution in the referendums in France and Holland in 2005 and the lack of any serious consideration of Britain's joining the European Common Currency did the issue subside. After the 2005 election, Euroscepticism consolidated itself within the Conservative Party to the extent that the division can be said to belong to the past. There are Conservative Europhiles still but not enough to pose any challenge to prevailing wisdom.

The Shadow Cabinet that Cameron selected in 2006 contained 63 per cent who had been privately educated and about 60 per cent who were products of Oxbridge.[54] Of the twenty-four (including two peers) only two were not upper-middle class and only six represented constituencies in the North (as defined earlier) or the Midlands. None at all represented an urban constituency. Predominantly in their forties and fifties, they included three women, two Scots and one working-class male. Cameron's Shadow Cabinet, in short, represents a body of well-educated, middle-aged, chiefly male, well-to-do suburbanite southern English. To all intents and purposes this Shadow Cabinet resembles more a Macmillan team than a Thatcher or even a Heath team. In July 2007 Cameron reshuffled, bringing two women in via nominations to the House of Lords, Dame Pauline Neville-Jones and Sayeeda Warsi, with security and community cohesion responsibilities respectively. He also promoted three back-benchers from the 2005 intake.

Party members

We turn now to that body of citizens which, unpaid, works for the return of Conservative governments, and we have the advantage of Whiteley, Seyd and Richardson's study of party membership, *True Blues*, whose findings remain very relevant.[55] Before turning to this study, however, we shall consider a detailed study of the motivations and aspirations of the members of one local party. Philip Tether examined in detail the structure of the local party in the city of Kingston upon Hull.[56] He argued that local parties provide a framework for aspirations that are only tangentially connected to politics. Tether distinguished two levels of membership, the total and the visible. The first compromised all who pay a subscription; the second was restricted to activists and comprises, in the constituencies he looked at, between twenty and fifty members (though in more successful constituencies the figure would be substantially greater). He continued:

> The party is seen by much of this visible membership as a social organisation. It serves the function of a social club for a limited type of clientele – middle-aged to elderly, predominantly female but not exclusively so and completely middle-class in origin.

This visible membership sets the tone of the association. 'They tend to regard the party proprietorially since they are all long-established members. Membership of the group is by co-option through evolution.' The social goals that this group set are straightforward: the maintenance of an agreeable and congenial coterie of companions and the organising of social events. The status goals of the 'visibles' are provided by their office, a confirmation of local social prestige.

Tether emphasised that local associations differ one from another, but his cameo of the personalisation, what he calls 'privatisation', of constituency party politics was, he felt, applicable to all but the best organised and most active of constituencies. One final point: Tether highlighted the importance of married women in the local structure, but constituency parties being run – though seldom led – by women are becoming rarer as more married women return to full-time employment. The work of a number of local associations has clearly suffered as a consequence.

On now to the broader picture, and we can begin with an interesting reflection: nobody currently knows how many members the party has. Not only are commentators guessing (however intelligently) but so also is the party bureaucracy, and indeed so are the constituency associations themselves. Whiteley et al. discovered that the differences between claimed and actual membership could vary from an overestimation of 69 per cent to an underestimation of 194 per cent.[57] Perhaps the best recent indications of membership numbers are these: when Cameron won the 2005 leadership election, 253,689 voted, some 6,000 more than voted in the referendum the following year on the leader's *Built to Last* policy statement. A membership of about a quarter of a million, then, is the most reliable current estimate.

If there is some doubt as to the size of membership, there is much less doubt regarding socio-economic characteristics. The party in the 1990s, according to Whiteley et al., comprised men and women in almost equal number; only 16 per cent of members were under 45 whereas no fewer than 43 per cent were over 65. In terms of occupational background 23 per cent worked for a private company or firm but 32 per cent were employed in the public sector. No fewer than 91 per cent owned their own homes, although only 13 per cent enjoyed a household income of more than £40,000. Not only was and is the Conservative Party nationwide an overwhelmingly middle-class party but also only a minority of its members (29 per cent) were in full-time work, most having retired. The Church of England is traditionally seen as the Conservative Party at prayer: 70 per cent of party members in the 1990s were members of the Churches of England or Scotland compared to 7 per cent who were Roman Catholic and 7 per cent Non-conformist.

It will come as no surprise to discover that the political views of Conservatives are informed by the Tory press: only 8 per cent took a paper other than the *Daily Express*, *Mail*, *Telegraph* or *Times* – and these included readers of the previously loyal *Sun*. All in all then, the party membership has always represented a remarkably homogeneous group. But what motivates them to join and to become active?

Tether's cameo of local party membership emphasises the psychological motivation of key members, Whiteley et al. provide a broader picture of ideological motivation. They quote an arresting statistic for a party which prides itself on its 'statecraft': when asked if the party should stick to its principles even if it meant losing an election, 81 per cent replied in the affirmative. Members saw themselves as patriots, proud of Britain's achievements and institutions and approving of authority and discipline. Although in many senses progressive – 81 per cent felt that governments should spend more money to eliminate poverty, 80 per cent wanted more money spent on the NHS and 64 per cent wanted to give workers more say in the workplace – attitudes towards immigrants presented a different picture: 70 per cent thought a future Conservative government should encourage their repatriation. Although immigration and asylum have traditionally been important to Conservatives,[58] we can be certain that nowadays repatriation would no longer be so strongly supported. Nevertheless in both the 2001 and 2005 elections, when the leadership was keen to sustain its core support, immigration issues played a large part in the campaigns.[59] In a survey of members in 2004, strict limits on asylum seekers were preferred by 95 per cent of respondents.[60]

As to whether Margaret Thatcher's leadership transformed the ideological disposition of the rank-and-file members, the authors found some ambivalence. We have already seen the strong support for acting to abolish poverty and improving the NHS; 57 per cent also favoured protection against the effects of the free market. These findings suggest that Thatcher failed to convince her supporters that there were no such things as society and its concomitant, the mutuality of social obligations. It is true that 61 per cent believed that the welfare state undermined self-reliance and enterprise and 60 per cent wanted to reduce government spending generally, but it is hard to believe that these figures had been much inflated by the influence of Margaret Thatcher. The study of party members concludes that 'in many respects the grass-roots Conservative Party is rather anti-Thatcherite': 41 per cent of members described themselves as left-of-centre, and only 20 per cent as being on the right.[61] 'Many grass-roots Conservatives', the authors conclude, 'are…more progressive than conventional wisdom suggests'.[62]

Whiteley et al. also explore levels of activism within the membership and make some interesting discoveries: only a relatively small proportion (20 per cent) of members 'frequently' undertook even the minimum activity for the party – delivering election leaflets. Even fewer (15 per cent) frequently attended meetings. For the majority of members, then, membership seems to constitute some way of making a statement; after all, however inactive they generally are politically, 83 per cent described themselves as 'fairly or very strong' Conservatives, and 55 per cent claim to have been motivated to join the party to support Conservative principles (or oppose Labour ones). The authors conclude their study into activism by observing that the better-educated members with relatively high incomes are likely to be the most active, and their reasons are a mixture of the psychological, social and ideological.

Although Conservatism in Scotland and Wales is not significantly different in terms of psychological, social and ideological factors, it has special problems, more particularly in Scotland. Peter Lynch used the word 'disaster' to describe the consequences of Thatcherism for the party north of the border.[63] He makes an important point: for Conservatism to prosper in Scotland it will have to dilute its enthusiasm for the Union. Indeed, in 2006 several leading supporters forsook the party for the Nationalists because they could see no future for Conservatism in Scotland while the party was connected in the public mind with Englishness. The party in Scotland is flirting with the idea of fiscal autonomy. Perhaps Scottish

Conservatism needs to abandon the Union in order to thrive, unless (as does not currently seem likely) its fortunes can revive under Cameron's leadership.[64]

As for the great European divide, it is evident that the majority of party activists are opposed to further European integration, as the 80 per cent support for Hague's policy of opposition to European Monetary Union shows. In a survey of members taken in November 2004, 70 per cent agreed with the statement: *The Conservatives have to toughen their stance on Europe or risk losing members like me to UKIP.*[65] In a referendum to join the Single Currency no fewer than 87 per cent would vote against. In contrast to John Cleese's parrot, Euroscepticism is emphatically not dead, merely sleeping.

Conservative voters

The third and final category of Conservative that we need to consider is the voter. The traditional relationship between class and voting has been clear enough at least since 1945 with the middle and upper-middle classes tending to vote Conservative and the working class and the very poor tending to vote Labour. Further, support for the Conservatives has traditionally been strongest in the upper-middle class (about 75 per cent) and the further down the middle class the less substantial was Conservative support, though these voters were more important because there were many more of them, and many tended to be located in the more marginal constituencies.[66]

Even with this substantial middle-class vote, the Conservatives always needed the support of a sizeable number of working-class voters to secure election. That they managed this so frequently since universal male suffrage was granted has been described as 'one grand historical paradox'.[67] It might be heretical to ask, but why should it be considered paradoxical for working-class voters to support the Conservatives? The answer, as everybody knows, is because of the established relationship between class and voting. But that relationship cannot be proved to be strictly causal and anyway it is a long way from being exact. The generalisation 'class determines voting' (more correctly, 'class and voting are related') has never been much more than 70 per cent accurate, and no predictive theory that is wrong on about every third time can be considered definitive. Stuart Hall described Thatcherite Conservatism as authoritarian populism and it is on these terms that we might consider that to call the working-class Conservative vote a paradox makes little sense, indeed it may be considered somewhat patronising. Paradox or patronised, however, the working-class Conservative has always been of interest to the political sociologists who have sought to explain such 'deviant behaviour'. Three theories have been developed in this attempt, those of deference, embourgeoisement and generation cohort.

The theory of deference argues that a number of working-class voters see the Conservatives as the 'natural rulers of Britain – sensitive to her traditions and peculiarities and uniquely qualified to govern by birth, experience and outlook'.[68] Deference theory also speaks of a second category of working-class Conservatives who vote more instrumentally; they believe quite simply that the Conservatives' record shows them better able than their opponents to run the country. The first category of voters has been called 'deferential' and the second 'secular'; moreover, although the loyalty of the first category could be relied upon, the second had to be persuaded. According to McKenzie and Silver, writing in the late 1960s, the second category was younger, larger and growing.

The second theory, generated by the Conservative victories of the 1950s, held that as workers' disposable incomes rose, so they acquired more middle-class attitudes among which was support for the Conservatives. According to this, the theory of embourgeoisement, the better sections of the working class were simply becoming middle class, or bourgeois. This thesis – which was not without influence on the Labour leadership at the time, and indeed since – was generally held to have been invalidated by Labour's victories in the 1960s, though, not surprisingly, it resurfaced in the 1980s.[69] Yet even the elections of the 1950s, when analysed in detail, showed the theory to tell only part of the story, for working-class Conservative voters were by no means exclusively the better off.

The third traditional explanation of working-class Conservatism was that of the generation cohort. 'Given the extent to which party loyalties are transmitted in the childhood home,' said Butler and Stokes, 'time was needed for historic attachments to the "bourgeois parties" to weaken and for "secondary" processes to complete the realignment by class.'[70] This theory had an obvious potential for self-fulfilment or self-destruction, for it predicts that the working-class Conservative vote would decline with the passage of time. The elections of the 1960s and 1970s seem to corroborate the theory, but nobody seems to have explained its workings to Margaret Thatcher, for there were wholesale working-class defections to the Conservatives in 1979, 1983 and 1987. In 1992 John Major's electoral victory blew the theory out of the water.[71] The subsequent collapse of the Conservative vote, including working-class Conservative support, is better accounted for by other explanations.

Perhaps we should regard the working-class Conservative vote not as a paradox at all, but as at least in part a rational appraisal of self-interest (instrumental voting). The lives of a considerable number of people have been changed by totally different patterns of consumption, by social mobility, greater educational opportunities, and so on. This may have led not necessarily to a permanent switch of allegiance but at least to instrumental voting. When he led the Labour Party, Harold Wilson targeted these instrumental voters with considerable success by presenting his party and its policies as theirs, though Labour later lost their allegiance with the Winter of Discontent. However, research published in 1988 indicated that the working class as a whole was more disposed towards Conservative moral values (not related to welfare provision) than they were to Labour's, with working-class Conservatives more in favour of these values even than their middle-class counterparts.[72] In its election campaign of 1992 Labour moved perceptibly towards this agenda, especially on issues such as law and order. By 1997 New Labour had committed itself very largely to the values of what had become known as the 'aspiring' working class,[73] and this shift has been maintained in subsequent elections.

Instrumental voting is another dimension of the process which Crewe, Barrington and Alt referred to as partisan dealignment: that is, the steady erosion (but not demise) of the class–party correlation.[74] This is a general development, well documented by the authors, in which voters are seen to be less and less tied by traditional party loyalties. The Conservatives were the chief beneficiaries of this process in 1979 but in 1983 and 1987 had to share these non-aligned voters with the Alliance parties. Yet as 1997 demonstrated, these votes are not the Conservative Party's or indeed the Liberal Democrats' as of right; all parties must compete. Of course there have always been instrumental voters among the so-called floating voters; what is new is the growth of the dealigned instrumental vote. Partisan dealigment means, quite simply, that instrumental voters have grown in influence and numbers so as to be decisive in most modern general elections.

Moving finally from the general to the specific, let us examine the Conservative vote in more detail. Traditionally it comprised around 60 per cent of the managerial and professional group, that is, social classes A, B and C1; about 40 per cent of the skilled working class, social class C2, and between 30 and 35 per cent of the unskilled working class and the poor, that is social classes D and E. These social differences may also be expressed geographically. In 1979 the Conservatives won 146 of the 193 seats in the south of England while losing support in the north. In 1983 this apparent re-emergence of 'two nations' was reinforced; the Conservatives won no fewer than 183 of the 186 seats south of a line from the Wash to the Severn (excluding London) whereas there were swings to Labour in the northern cities. The net result of this trend was a voting pattern (when adjusted to a 50:50 ratio) of 61.4 per cent Conservative support and 38.6 per cent Labour support in 'the South' – what Butler and Kavanagh referred to as Tory Britain – and exactly the reverse of this in what they refer to as Labour Britain – what we have called the North, but with the addition of Inner London and the West Midlands.[75] This division, replicated almost exactly in 1987, was considered by some commentators to have become permanent. It should not be thought of as a new phenomenon, however; the Conservative Party has traditionally been the party of 'the South' since before the advent of universal male suffrage, with sometimes as many as 80 per cent of its MPs representing southern constituencies. But the extent of the polarisation in the 1980s was new in the democratic age.

In 1992 the pendulum began to swing back, and in 1997 it swung through the whole arc: Labour, massively victorious in its own territories, also managed to do well in the Tory South. In fact Labour won 85 seats to the Conservatives' 104 in 'the South', and in 'the North' Labour took 277 seats to the Conservatives' 23. The swing to Labour, though more or less uniform, was in fact proportionately strongest in parts of 'the South' (no doubt because it was building on a smaller base). In 1997 the two nations explanation of voting behaviour, which appeared to indicate that 'the South' would be permanently Conservative and the Conservatives in a permanent majority, was in need of considerable refinement to say the least.

We know that voters who supported the Conservatives in the election of 2005 were not sufficiently numerous to unseat Labour but what else do we know about them? We know that support among the party's natural supporters, the professional middle class, continued to decline. In 1992 they had a lead over Labour in this category of 32 per cent; it has declined consistently since and in 2005 stood at only 9 per cent. Although small gains were made among the C1s and C2s, these were largely confined to the South East. Support for the party among the young and the middle-aged, too, continued to trail Labour and though small gains were made among younger males, they were offset by further declines among females generally. Only among the over-65s did the Conservatives lead.[76] In 2005 the Conservative vote rose by 0.5 per cent overall, but this was due to advances made in the South East. In Yorkshire and the Northern Region the Conservative vote actually fell by twice as much. All in all, the Conservative share of the vote remained lower than at any time since between 1857 and its last electoral victory in 1992.[77] Voters were generally unenthusiastic for Labour but did not see the Conservative Party under Michael Howard as a viable alternative. This is the level of support that Cameron inherited in 2006.

To say that this need not be so is to state the obvious. As we have seen, not only have the Conservatives traditionally secured the majority of their votes from the working class but also from 1979 to 1992 they actually secured more than half of the working-class vote. Norton and Aughey felt sufficiently confident to conclude that Conservatism

> Can be seen as the articulation of the interests not only of those who benefit from the present institutional structure and who wish to preserve the privileges they derive from the status quo, but also those who prefer, despite not having these privileges, what is known and predictable in the present system, and who believe that this is how things should be.[78]

Disraeli is widely considered to have developed a kind of Conservatism with which working men could identify, Salisbury incorporated the interests of the new suburban middle class, Macmillan tempered his style of Conservatism to the aspirations of the affluent 1960s working-class consumer and Thatcherism was in part a response by the party to populist-authoritarian issues which concerned 'Essex man'. Commentators claimed that middle-class leaders such as Tebbit and Major destroyed the 'old boy' network in the party and were in the process 'insidiously destructive' of its values, thereby bringing the party closer to the people.[79] Perhaps the power of the 'old boys' was broken (more likely weakened) but it was not permanently replaced by the power of the 'new lads'. We should not forget that a very substantial number of Conservative voters of all classes – no fewer than 49 per cent in 1983 for example – were motivated primarily by fear of Labour; in that election only 40 per cent of those who voted for the party actually 'liked the Conservatives'.[80] As 1997 was to show, an electable Labour party could challenge for the newly dealigned instrumental vote with every prospect of success.

The defeat of 1997 was nothing less than spectacular for the Conservatives. Curtice and Stead saw it as an 'expression of a long-standing nationwide political disenchantment that almost undoubtedly set in the moment that the pound fell out of the European Exchange Rate Mechanism (ERM) in September 1992'.[81] This conclusion suggests an instrumentalist voting pattern – 'it's the economy, stupid' – but this seems too clever by half. Few ordinary voters could have been aware of what ejection from the ERM signified, and anyway the economy soon began to improve almost visibly. What ordinary voters, especially natural supporters of the party, would have been aware of was weak leadership, party divisions, and perhaps above all the seemingly endless stream of sleaze. So great was the disenchantment of Conservative voters and so profoundly changed was Labour, that for three successive elections a sufficient but declining number overcame their fear of Labour and gave that party an historic three-term tenure of 10 Downing Street.

Conclusions

The Conservative Party seems still to be in the throes of fundamental change. We have seen that the changes that commentators wrote and argued about in the parliamentary party especially from the 1970s paled into insignificance when compared to the changes to the party after the leadership of Margaret Thatcher. In rejecting the notions of consensus, intra-party coalition and compromise, Thatcher changed the historic role of a non-ideological party that believed in Pearce's 'chug-chug' government. She exchanged that role for a dynamic, ideological Conservative Party that had a mission; exchanged it for Thatcherism – and with Thatcher. What the party failed to realise was that the latter was more important than the former and when it sought, under Major's leadership, to secure the benefits of Thatcherism without Thatcher, it actually finished with the worst not the best of both worlds. Bereft of its great warrior leader, shorn of its traditional self-belief, the party foundered. The leadership became fatally split; the parliamentary party lost its cohesion, the party organisation lost its sense of direction, the historic relationship with capital became much weaker, party members deserted in droves and Conservative voters jumped ship by the hundreds of thousands.

Max Hastings, then editor of the *Evening Standard* and a Conservative supporter, said in a radio interview that his party did not deserve to win the election of 1997; had the government been an old dog, he added, it would have been put down long since out of kindness. A BBC correspondent reported that Tories stayed at home because they could not bring themselves to vote for a party so 'discredited and so tainted'.[82] Faced with an opponent that had striven so hard and to such good effect to make itself electable, the Conservatives simply collapsed. It was fashionable to compare the Conservatives' 1997 position to that of Labour in 1983. This was underestimating the size of the problem. In 1979 the Conservatives moved to the right, offering Labour the option of occupying the centre, which Michael Foot declined. But in 1997 Blair occupied the centre and so for the Conservatives it became necessary to stabilise their core support on the right before any attempt to retake the centre could be contemplated. This William Hague sought to do. The 2001 election was fought on a right-wing agenda. Conservative fortunes reached their nadir under the hapless leadership of Iain Duncan Smith. If by 1997 the Labour Party had shown an enviable capacity to transform itself into a 'catch-all party' then the Conservatives appeared, under Duncan Smith, to have managed the unenviable transformation into a 'catch-nothing' party. Michael Howard took the party into the 2005 election on a right-wing agenda. If he managed nothing else he stopped the haemorrhaging of support to the Liberal Democrats and to the UK Independence Party (UKIP),[83] but when, on his departure, activists were asked who his replacement should be, William Hague was the favourite with only 9 per cent support, but still nearly twice the support for David Davis, the second favourite.[84] David Cameron did not even feature in the list. It would be fair to conclude that the party had no idea where it was going or whom it wanted at the helm.

We have already noted Cameron's vigorous attempt to focus his party on moving back to the centre ground. He has the charismatic appeal that his three predecessors so clearly lacked and he is not constrained by ideology (to put it another way, his opponents say his party has no policy at all). He gained and held a lead over Labour in opinion polls for several months and this makes the party potentially more appealing to its natural allies in the business world. He is poised now to mount a serious challenge to Labour's new leader Gordon Brown.

7 Labour politicians, activists and supporters

In the first edition of this book, Chapter 7 had a question as its title, a question that, with later editions, became increasingly less appropriate: 'Who are the socialists?' Nowadays such a question might prompt a similar response to the famous rhetorical Scots question: 'Wha's like us?' The customary response is: 'Damn few and they're a' deid!' Socialism, once claimed as the dominant ideology of half of the world, now seems to be dead, and in Britain the few socialists who remain in local and national politics are without influence. So instead we shall be more prosaic and simply examine the social and ideological background of Labour politicians, activists and supporters.

The parliamentary party: background

The Labour Party was established expressly to represent organised labour directly in parliament, and so it will be no surprise to discover that in its early years (between 1906 and 1918) no fewer than 89 per cent of Labour MPs came from the working class; indeed even after the party assumed government for the first time, the proportion was 71 per cent.[1]

The backbenches: social background

The great majority of Labour MPs were workers representing working-class constituencies. But politics is a middle-class profession and it was always going to prove difficult for Labour to retain such strong links with the class it claimed to represent as the first cohort of MPs began to lose numerical preponderance, especially with the great wave of new MPs who entered the House after Labour's triumph in 1945. Who does the party represent these days?

Perhaps the first distinctive feature that would strike a student of parties when looking at the Parliamentary Labour Party (PLP) would be its age profile: it has tended to be an older party than its rivals. In a typical parliament the PLP would comprise more than 20 per cent over 60 and more than 50 per cent over 50. Although the landslide victory of 1966 brought an increase in younger MPs, the safer seats were still held by older members and because a safe seat was often the reward for lengthy service to the movement, a poor electoral performance overall would tend to leave these older, usually working-class trade unionists in a dominant position. But 1997 changed all that. The average age of the new cohort was 44 compared to the incumbents' average of 53, and this new cohort comprised the largest intake by far of new MPs since 1945. With Labour's continued electoral success, however, the PLP is once again the 'oldest' of the main parties, with an average age, after the 2005 election, of 52.[2]

In terms of educational background, around three-quarters of Labour MPs in the inter-war period had been to school only for the minimum period prescribed by the state; in the next thirty (post-war) years less than one-third of Labour MPs were in this category.[3] Elementary school children were being replaced by the grammar school/university products, who formed what Mellors described as a meritocracy. In part this process was the result of a conscious effort by the leadership to improve the 'quality' of Labour MPs. As one Fabian put it: 'With all the education there is about these days Labour must show that its candidates are as well qualified as the Tories'.[4] Even the incumbents in the safer Labour seats those older union-sponsored gradualists were being replaced by younger better educated members. Following the introduction of comprehensive schools in the 1960s, the definition of minimal formal education lost the sharp meaning it had in the days of elementary schools. Even before the 1970s, however, no fewer than 19 per cent of Labour MPs had been educated in public school.

Moving on now to the 2000s we can see that the unmistakable embourgeoisement of the party continued. While the percentage of public school MPs remained fairly constant, the percentage of university-educated MPs has risen to 64 per cent, with 16 per cent from Oxbridge. Moreover, although the percentage of university-educated Conservative MPs has hardly changed since 1945 that for the PLP has doubled.[5]

Consistent with the changing educational background of Labour MPs has been the changing occupational background. The expansion of graduates has been matched by the expansion of professionals. By the mid-1970s more than half of Labour MPs were professionals whereas the proportion of manual workers in the PLP had been more than halved. Mellors characterised this process as the 'displacement of workers by teachers'.[6] Studies of graduate employment have indicated that it was predominantly the graduate children of manual workers who moved into teaching,[7] and thus the increase in Labour's professionals is another manifestation of the march of the meritocrats. Teachers and lecturers have more than doubled their representation among Labour MPs since the war. Kavanagh noted that this trend reflected similar changes in society as a whole and was therefore unlikely to be reversed.[8] Indeed in the current PLP, professionals comprise 40 per cent, with university and college teachers forming the largest single category.[9]

Another important feature of the make-up of the PLP after the 1970s was the number of trade union officials. They formed a relatively elderly group, ballast as it were, who did not often go on to achieve office. Originally union sponsorship was a reward for active participation in the affairs of that union but increasingly unions began to actively compete for promising candidates to sponsor. Though not the force they once were trade union officials, together with other 'political organisers' provide 17 per cent of the current PLP.[10]

Since the war the PLP could be said to comprise three principal occupational groups: professionals, political organisers and manual workers. What we have been talking about is the transformation during the 1970s and 1980s of what used to be a working-class party into something quite different. By 1997 49 per cent of the PLP were professionals, an astonishing 26.8 per cent 'political organisers' and only 8.9 per cent manual workers; indeed the new intake contained as many millionaires as it did manual workers.[11] This New Labour government was less representative of organised labour than the Liberal Party of Campbell Bannerman and Asquith that Labour had striven to replace. However, possibly because of contraction, this transformation has not developed. The current PLP contains more manual workers than business people, though there are still four college or university teachers for every miner.[12] The backbencher Sîon Simon has argued that these changes, representative as Kavanagh said, of social change generally, do not represent the break with tradition that they appear to. Speaking as a member of this cohort of new professionals, he argues: 'We were not privileged or posh. We were rooted in the party and the unions. Any sense that we were less so than any previous generation is simply wrong'.[13]

In 1983 thirteen Conservative and ten Labour women sat in the House; in 1997 there were still thirteen Conservatives (not the same ones) but a hundred and one Labour women. Were they in any sense different in terms of social background from their male counterparts? In educational terms they were hardly distinguishable, but they were somewhat younger. They were even less working class: a slightly higher proportion had been professionals, teachers and political organisers, but a lower proportion had been in business. Fewer women had had experience in local government, although they nevertheless formed a majority. In short they were very much like their male colleagues, just a little more in the New Labour mould. Nicknamed 'Blair's Babes' by the media it would be impossible to make a judgement as to whether they have, as women, made an impact on the way the House of Commons goes about its business, though the greater sociability of working hours might be ascribed to women's influence. Although there are currently fewer women MPs in the PLP (ninety-eight) they form a higher proportion (28 per cent). As we shall see, they have achieved significant roles in the party hierarchy.

The backbenches: ideological background

What kinds of changes in ideology have been associated with the social transformation we have outlined?[14] We should begin with the caveat that influxes into the parliamentary party in the years between 1950 and 1997 were not very great. Even the landslide victory of 1966 brought only sixty-seven new MPs. In 1974 and again in 1979 the party acquired only thirty-nine new recruits and in the calamitous election of 1983 a mere nine. The influx of over seventy new members in 1987 might have had an ideological impact, though with the party remaining in opposition it was less noticeable.

In terms of ideology MPs from the older-established professions have been traditionally associated with liberal attitudes towards, for example, humanitarian issues and overseas development, and by their nature these professions made it possible to combine careers, perhaps giving a broader perspective to the PLPs' political attitudes. The 'new' professionals of the 1960s and 1970s tended to become full-time politicians and 'much more strongly associated with the wider issues and principles of "socialism"' than the traditional professionals or the group which they were displacing, the manual workers.[15] Traditionally manual workers proved 'strong on the bread and butter issues and more moderate on ideological positions'.[16] According to Mellors, the changing structure of the PLP would be certain to have a major effect upon the party's ideological stance.

Fundamentalist opposition to the parliamentary leadership is as old as the party itself. James Maxton and the 'Red Clydesiders' could bring debates to a halt in the 1920s with a boisterous rendition of singing *The Red Flag*. Much later Tony Benn set out how he saw his parliamentary task:

> I see our job…as being to use the statute book to redress the balance in a way that allows the bubbling up of socialism from beneath to take place. I see a Labour House of Commons as…a liberator unlocking the cells in which people live. If you do that, you find you have actually created socialism.[17]

The parliamentary leadership never saw its prime task as to encourage the bubbling up of fundamentalism. Indeed Kinnock believed that his job was to bring the so-called soft left round to support him precisely to contain this radicalism. But to attempt anything like Benn's programme, the party first had to achieve power and the biggest obstacle to that, Kinnock believed, was Benn himself. In replacing nationalisation by social ownership as the party's goal (without even referring to Clause Four) Kinnock posted notice of what had been a considerable success for the social democrats in isolating the fundamentalists. Among the new intake in 1987, however, were the former leader of the Greater London Council, Ken Livingstone – 'the Borgia of the hard left'[18] – and a number of others who found Kinnock's leadership too right wing. The Target Labour Government group declared: 'We are not interested in reforming the prevailing institutions…through which the ruling class keep us "in our place". We are about dismantling them and replacing them with our own machinery of class rule.'[19] All the same, Kinnock, buoyed by his creditable election campaign, did manage to marginalise the unconvertible in a way that might have proved impossible had Labour actually won in 1987.[20] Not that Kinnock's leadership of Her Majesty's Loyal Opposition was unproblematic; in 1988 he failed to prevent forty-four Labour MPs from defying the party line on the Prevention of Terrorism Bill and lost two members of his Shadow Cabinet.

Kinnock and his allies made a concerted attempt to move the party towards the perceived interests of those whose votes it had lost. At the party conference in 1987 support was given for a wide-ranging policy review, which resulted in the publication of *Aims and Values: Statement of Democratic Socialism*. This shift to the centre-right prompted the fundamentalists Tony Benn and Eric Heffer to contest the leadership and deputy leadership against the social democratic ticket of Kinnock and Hattersley. The fundamentalists were decisively beaten.

Electoral defeat in 1992 strengthened the leadership's hand still further against the fundamentalists and the PLP was swept along, like much of the rest of the movement, by the subsequent Blairite 'project' of modernisation. Nevertheless as Cowley and Norton showed, between 1992 and 1997 Blair's parliamentary party was by no means submissive; thirty-eight MPs dissented from the party line on more than twenty occasions. Cowley and Norton foresaw a Blair government being encumbered by its fundamentalists. They did not envisage a New Labour majority of 179.[21]

Neither did these authors envisage that Labour's new recruitment process would produce a predominantly social democratic cohort including no fewer than a hundred and one women. Attitude surveys of the 1997 cohort undertaken by Norris indicated:

> A clear and unambiguous shift away from traditional socialist values....The principle of state ownership of public services was endorsed by...70 per cent in 1992 but by...48 per cent in 1997...moreover the proportion of Labour members who believed that it was the government's responsibility to provide jobs fell from two-thirds to one half...the last five years have seen a significant shift towards abandoning Keynesianism and embracing the market economy.[22]

Norris concluded that Blair's project was not foisted upon a reluctant party but seemed 'to reflect the attitude and values of most backbench Labour MPs'. And women generally were among New Labour's firmest supporters.[23] Fundamentalist MP Brian Sedgemore (who later joined the Liberal Democrats) compared the new intake of women to the Stepford Wives with 'chips inserted in their brains to keep them on message'.[24]

Some fundamentalists slipped through the tight selection procedures but hardly enough to worry the leadership.[25] Nevertheless over eighty MPs signed an early-day motion opposing the government's cuts in benefits to single parents (though only nine were women) and forty-seven went on to vote against the government, with fourteen others abstaining.[26] Further rebellions followed, but Cabinet with its massive majority was hardly shaking at the knees. Over the next ten years it put on the statute book, sometimes only by virtue of Conservative support, a raft of policies that transformed the provision and performance of public services in a manner that Labour backbenchers of previous decades would have considered inconceivable. And yet New Labour loyalists consider themselves to be part of Labour's tradition. 'The New Labour project', wrote Sîon Simon, 'was never an aberration, bolted on to an ageing workerist party by middle class opportunists. It grew in a straight line, right through the core of Labour's tradition'.[27] He describes the New Labour project as 'updating' the party's policies, rhetoric and analysis. 'The truth is once you compromise your core values you cease to exist'. Simon argues that New Labour, rather than being 'some kind of middle-class, Islington chatterati conspiracy', represented rather

> a move away from exactly those kind of left-liberal, 1970s...assumptions to a politics that was recognisably derived from the kind of working-class

communities from which Labour was supposed to draw its core support, but with whom it had lost touch.[28]

Simon confronts Benn's criticism of New Labourites as representing not ideological signposts for the voters but weathervanes, moving this way and that with every wind. He is partly right, Simon accepts. Benn and his supporters *are* signposts of a kind: they are wooden and have been pointing in the wrong direction for a long time.[29]

Party leadership

Moving up the PLP hierarchy to the Cabinet, we encounter a problem: the numbers are necessarily small until recently because there have been few Labour Cabinets. It would not be helpful simply to substitute Shadow Cabinets because traditionally these have been elected by the parliamentary party and not chosen by the leader and, to that extent, represent a rather different phenomenon. For obvious reasons there are no developments between 1979 and 1997 to analyse. Nevertheless, earlier trends were clear enough. The student of parties will immediately observe that, in Kavanagh's words, 'the higher one ascends the political hierarchy, the more socially and educationally exclusive it becomes'.[30] With three exceptions, every British Prime Minister since the Second World War was Oxford educated.[31] All the same, Labour Cabinets traditionally comprised nearly 50 per cent of ministers with elementary education; more than half of Labour ministers had not been to university though just over 25 per cent had been to public school. Moreover, 55 per cent were from working-class families. Many of Labour's 'great names' of the past came from this background, including its first Prime Minister, Ramsay MacDonald, and leading members of Attlee's 1945 administration such as Ernest Bevin and Aneurin Bevan. It was during Wilson's period as leader that the trend of the replacement of workers by meritocrats gathered momentum. When Wilson left office in 1970 only three Cabinet ministers came from the working class. It is true that Callaghan's ministry contained four but none was senior. Burch and Moran agreed that there had been a 'changing balance in favour of those who have practised a middle-class profession, at the expense of those who were, at some stage of their adult life, manual workers'.[32] Party leader Neil Kinnock came from a working-class background, though he was never a manual worker.

Burch and Moran pointed out that the influence of aristocratic and upper-middle-class families has also been in decline; since 1970 Labour Cabinets have contained not a single Harrovian or Etonian, not a single aristocrat. If we follow Kavanagh, though, and consider patrician rather than aristocratic influence, a different picture emerges. Now we find continuities: patricians include Attlee himself, Dalton, Cripps and Gaitskell in the 1940s and 1950s, and Crossman, Crosland, Gordon-Walker, Jay and Benn in the 1960s and 1970s, Jenkins, Owen, Foot and Williams later. It is hard to refute the argument that these patricians were disproportionately influential in the development of the party.

Our attention is drawn by Burch and Moran to what they take to be 'the most striking long-term alteration at the top of the Labour Party': the substantial number of those meritocratic Cabinet ministers who were actually born into the working class but who rose, through education, into the middle class and the new professions. These meritocrats are the beneficiaries of the improved state education system – the scholarship generation – and include many senior figures, such as Wilson, Kinnock, Hattersley, Shore, Healey and Castle. It was they who ran the Labour Party for a quarter of a century before Blair. These leaders might be thought to bring the best of both worlds: to put it crudely, humane working-class hearts and educated middle-class heads. This was not a line of reasoning shared by the fundamentalist Dennis Skinner, who wrote scathingly of the 'smooth-tongued, generally tall, dark, handsome men…[who] weave a series of ten-minute speeches out of a concoction of the 1926 strike; the beauty of pigeon and whippet racing'.[33] This phenomenon, the ex-working-class meritocrat, is 'of the people' only by self-ascription; certainly he or she is seldom considered as such by the people themselves

Tony Blair's Cabinet did not have the ideological divisions that bedevilled its Labour and Conservative predecessors, yet it was torn by personal rivalries that proved almost equally damaging. The rivalry is said to date from the succession to the leadership after the death of John Smith when Peter Mandelson, unknown to Brown, kick-started Blair's campaign during an agreed moratorium.[34] In December 1998 it was disclosed that Mandelson had accepted a loan of £300,000 from fellow Cabinet minister Geoffrey Robinson, whose business activities were about to become the subject of an inquiry by Mandelson's own department. It was generally believed that a Brown aide was involved in this disclosure, though he denied it. In any event it caused Mandelson to resign – a blow not simply to Mandelson's career but also to the Prime Minister, who relied greatly upon his advice. Blair sought to contain these rivalries by instituting the role of Cabinet 'enforcer' at the head of the revamped Cabinet Office with the formal responsibility to 'cajole departments, co-ordinate policy and initiate cross-departmental action'.[35] The Prime Minister's press secretary Alastair Campbell also acted as a less official enforcer, enquiring of two Cabinet ministers why they had given interviews to *Woman's Hour* and *The World at One* without clearing them with his office. How remarkable that an 'unelected hireling, a mere press officer [can] write to a Cabinet Minister with such peremptoriness'.[36] Coincidentally both ministers were later sacked from the Cabinet. No previous Labour Cabinet was dragooned in this way.

In Blair's final Cabinet, personal divisions flourished but ideological divisions were far less obvious. This Cabinet was naturally substantially older than the PLP, with only six members in their thirties or forties. Although women comprised 28 per cent of the PLP, they comprised 36 per cent of Cabinet, including Baroness Amos, the only member of Cabinet of non-Caucasian ethnic origin. Also 36 per cent of Cabinet was educated at Oxbridge, compared to 16 per cent of the PLP. The greatest disparity in Blair's Cabinet, however, was that 68 per cent of its members in the House of Commons represented 'Northern' constituencies (though not necessarily from the North themselves), an area which includes only about one-third of the British population, but is Labour's historic heartland.[37] Two members of Blair's Cabinet had been workers, both representing Kingston upon Hull, and there was a handful of members from working-class backgrounds. In its proportion of women and in its geographical skew, this was an unusually representative Cabinet (of the party) but its seniority and educational elitism were neither representative nor unusual.

Party activists

In one of the few detailed studies of Labour constituency parties in the 1960s, Janosik investigated the background of local activism and his analysis explained the genesis of the problems which came to beset many constituencies in the following two decades.[38] In contrast to the Conservatives, there was no preponderance of business people and professionals in constituency party work but there was instead a powerful trade union presence, which had no equivalent in the Conservative Party. In educational terms, though, the general pattern was not so dissimilar: the more important the position, the more likely it was to be held by somebody with post-secondary education. In some Labour constituency parties, there was a substantial component of manual labourers with a basic state education. Janosik found it helpful to distinguish between 'strong' and 'marginal' constituencies. The typically 'strong' party in the 1960s tended to be led by older men, many of whom were workers with little formal education.

Although the importance of the role of the trade unions in the constituency parties was widely acknowledged, especially in a typical strong seat, one aspect of trade union dominance seems to have escaped critical attention. The unions have traditionally put up much of the money locally and this has meant that in many strong seats the constituency party, unlike its competitors, did not need to engage in fund-raising activities. Fund-raising tends to bring people together, producing camaraderie and, equally important, an informal network of communications. This kind of continuous, non-ideological (hence less divisive) communal activity, with specified and attainable goals, was one of the reasons why Janosik's strong parties did not compare in membership or enthusiasm with many of his marginals; perhaps this was why they proved easy pickings for the determined groups of younger, well-educated fundamentalist activists.

Like Martin Harrison earlier,[39] Janosik discovered that, on the whole, activists were by no means as extreme as was generally depicted. When asked to assess the party's policies, more than half of Janosik's local activists in both strong and marginal constituencies were generally supportive of the leadership, with around 40 per cent of both in favour of discreetly moving 'slightly to the left'. As we might expect 11 per cent in the marginals favoured a move 'sharply left' as compared with only 2 per cent in the strong constituencies. Those who favoured moves sharply to the left thought, as fundamentalists have always thought, that this would prove both electorally advantageous and bring greater unity to the party.

Janosik emphasised the imprint of the socio-economic character of the constituency on the values of local parties, a point that emerges even more forcefully from Turner's later study of three London constituencies.[40] Strong Labour seats are almost invariably in stable working-class communities and activists tend to remain associated with the party over a long period of time. 'As veterans in a party that is never threatened by the opposition, they develop routinised ways of dealing with problems…[and] the party's goals remain unchanged',[41] leading to a preference for strong 'bread and butter' policies. Marginal constituencies, on the other hand, usually had to contend with a higher rate of mobility and a more rapid turnover of personnel, and hence a continuous influx of 'new ideas'. These constituency parties were prone to 'intellectual jousting' and 'the likelihood that ideological splits will be interwoven with personal rivalries'.[42] It is ironic that one of the constituencies that Turner studied was the 'safe' seat of Bermondsey where 'the crisis threats of an opposition were but memories'. Five years later Bermondsey fell to the Liberals at a by-election, having earlier fallen prey to a take-over from a determined minority of able, better-educated young activists, whose political vocabulary and imagery were more global and more ideological than those of the old guard. In Bermondsey, the old guard hit back and the consequent split allowed the Liberals to win the seat.

What was true of Bermondsey was true of a considerable number of seats in London, Liverpool, Manchester, Sheffield, Glasgow and other large cities. The elderly well-entrenched establishment did little to encourage new members to participate in the constituency's affairs and so, when the fundamentalists and, more dangerously, Militant tendency demanded entry, the old guard could muster little support to keep them out. Many marginal constituencies, by contrast, made a virtue of necessity and possessed organisational structures that were far more open and more receptive to new activists and new ideas. They too were influenced by the move towards greater militancy but were not such easy prey for take-overs. The consequences of these differences became apparent in the kinds of candidates adopted by the Labour Party for general elections during that decade when the party generally was moving to the left.[43] The fundamentalists won strong representation in many of the safer seats, but in the marginals it was soft-left or social democrat candidates who tended to be selected. Collectively these fundamentalist constituency activists and their parliamentary representatives had a more profound impact upon the party than did their predecessors, especially in securing the constitutional changes which, so they believed, democratised the party (and which the social democrats systematically began to reverse after 1987).

The growth of fundamentalist influence took place at a time when, as Paul Whiteley showed, Labour Party membership was falling substantially.[44] Whiteley argued that the failure of the Labour governments of the 1960s to solve the various 'bread and butter' problems that affected many traditional supporters had a disproportionate effect upon working-class activists. Equally important, said Whiteley, the working-class activists began to find themselves at odds with a party that was becoming increasingly middle class and ideological. Whiteley concluded that these small groups of articulate middle-class activists might 'paradoxically' drive out older working-class activists.[45] Why Whiteley should consider this to be a paradox is a mystery.

It was not until the late 1970s that the general shift towards the left changed the way the party did its business. For the constituencies, mandatory reselection of MPs was the most important. In January 1981 the Campaign for Labour Party Democracy produced a booklet entitled *How to Select and Reselect your MP*, with an analysis of how every Labour MP had voted so that activists could make a judgement on the extent of their MP's socialist commitment. Only eight MPs were deselected in this first round (for the 1983 general election), though a number of those who joined the SDP 'jumped before they were pushed'. Criddle describes the deselection of the eight as a 'take-over' by groups of left-wing ideologists caricatured as 'the polyocracy'.[46] One deselected MP in East London was specific, blaming his defeat on 'the bed-sit Trotskyists from the North East London Polytechnic'.[47] Denis Healey found the replacement of MPs by 'professional ideologues' distasteful but others saw the new fundamentalists as 'sources of resistance and radicalism' that would become an important force in British politics.

Of the various groups of ideologists who helped to 'fundamentalise' the Labour Party in those years, driving out working-class activists as they did so, none received more attention than the Militant tendency. The Militant tendency was a nationally organised far-left organisation with a ruling central committee (many of whom were members of the Labour Party) plus, so it was estimated, about 200 full-time workers – approximately the same number as the Labour Party[48] – and a regional and district structure. One of its principal objectives was to infiltrate the Labour Party and the trade union movement and move them towards a fundamentalist agenda. It enjoyed a considerable measure of success, particularly in Liverpool. The Labour Party was sufficiently concerned to establish three major inquiries into the activities of Militant and finally to take action to expel Militant supporters from the party. The principal charges against them were that they were in breach of the constitution in belonging to a party-within-a-party and that they acted in a grossly undemocratic manner, for example 'swamping' of delegate meetings with unelected members, selective notification of meetings, false accounting of membership and, most serious of all, intimidation of ordinary members.

Militant and other hard-left activists were able to devote themselves full time to politics because many were employed by neighbouring councils.[49] Most famous of these was the Militant deputy leader of the Liverpool council, Derek Hatton, who was employed by the neighbouring Knowsley council. The report of the third inquiry, the Widdicombe report, uncovered 'a web of patronage' in which up to 200 councillors in London, nearly all Labour, were provided with jobs in neighbouring authorities, which enabled them to be full-time politicians at ratepayers' expense. In Glasgow almost one-quarter of the council was employed by the Strathclyde region.[50] The fundamentalists, especially Militant, were well entrenched.

The steps taken after 1987 halted the flow of Militant influence and the reassertion of control by the leadership through the NEC began to have an increasing affect. What is not so often acknowledged in Labour circles, publicly at least, are the defeats inflicted on fundamentalist activism by the Thatcher government. It was Thatcher's resolve (and their own strategic incompetence) that led to the defeat of the miners in 1985 and the subsequent loss of influence and prestige of Arthur Scargill, a champion of fundamentalism. It was the Thatcherite press which exposed the (sometimes fictitious) extravagances of 'loony left' local authorities and the Thatcher government that confronted them through rate-capping. What Kinnock and his advisers, and later Smith and then Blair, sought to do subsequently was to limit the influence of 'unrepresentative' fundamentalist activists by both strengthening the party bureaucracy and, as we have seen, moving from delegate democracy to representative democracy, thereby giving the greater say to ordinary members at the expense of activists. It remains open to question whether Kinnock could have saved the Labour Party without the assistance of Thatcher.

How different are the rank-and-file of the 'saved' party nowadays? The most detailed study of Labour Party members in more recent times was undertaken by Seyd and Whiteley in the 1990s.[51] Their findings reinforce everything that we have observed regarding the previous decades: the changing character of local parties, especially in the inner cities. Labour Party members at this time were disproportionately male (61 per cent), disproportionately middle-aged (average age 48) and middle class (only 26 per cent were classified as working-class). Although over half (58 per cent) had only the minimum state education, 29 per cent held a degree. Seyd and Whiteley found a 'very sharp divide' between these two groups.[52] Almost two-thirds of Labour members held a public sector job in local government, the local health authority or college, or a public corporation. Manual workers comprised only a quarter of members. On the other hand, 70 per cent of this patently middle-class group considered themselves to be working class. Seyd and Whiteley concluded: 'The "new model" Labour Party of the 1990s may perhaps be in danger of becoming too responsive to the demands of the affluent radical rather than the poor proletarian',[53] and thus further excluding working-class membership. In all respects, at any rate, party members were substantially more middle class than Labour voters.

Given their self-ascribed class status, it is not surprising that 66 per cent of activists thought that the central issue in British politics was the struggle between capital and labour. Indeed they exhibited a strong commitment to what the authors describe as four socialist touchstones: they believed in public ownership (71 per cent wanted further nationalisation), were strong defenders of the legitimacy of trade unions, were sceptical about the benefits of defence expenditure (66 per cent were unilateralists) and, almost unanimously, they believed in high public expenditure even at the cost of higher taxation. Yet the local parties were atrophying at an even faster rate than the working-class communities they claimed to represent. The downgrading of local government and the changes in the party structure were leaving the local party 'increasingly "de-energised", an organisation in which members are increasingly passive rather than active, disengaged rather than engaged'.[54]

Kinnock's plans to increase rank-and-file membership as a balance to 'unrepresentative' activists failed but Blair's did not. Despite the dispiriting picture that Seyd and Whiteley painted, by the time of the 1997 election, the Labour membership attracted more new members than the entire membership of the Liberal Democrats, from whom it regained a number of former SDP members, including several ex-Labour-ex-SDP MPs. The average age of new members was 39. Over 62 per cent of new members were under 45 and just under half were women. The largest single age category were those under 27 – a group that Seyd and Whiteley had felt obliged to write off – and thus members of Young Labour. The bulk of these, according to Mandelson and Liddle, were 'university-educated and professionally employed, as much in the private as in the public sector'.[55] (A survey of new members showed that 47 per cent described themselves as professional, 25 per cent as retired, 9 per cent as students, 9 per cent as unemployed and – significantly – only 10 per cent as manual workers.) No doubt the party took comfort from the fact that 60 per cent of new members came from the Midlands and South of England.

A significant factor in the growth of membership was certainly the change in the method of applying. Previously to become a member one made written application. The application was then scrutinised by the branch before being formally endorsed by the management committee. Normally one would have to be a member of a trade union. 'The system', say Mandelson and Liddle, 'seemed designed to keep people out rather than recruit them'.[56] In 1995 a new national membership scheme allowed people to join directly, for example by simply answering a newspaper advert. Prescott promoted a 'recruit a friend' campaign, which was responsible for 28 per cent of new recruits. Less successful was individual recruitment from the affiliated trade unions.

Writing in 1996, Mandelson and Liddle referred specifically to changes in the way that New Labour perceives local government. With more local councillors than ever, they say, the days of 'loony left' councils are over:

> In London (for example in Lambeth), and in Liverpool, Manchester and Sheffield and many other cities where problems previously existed, there has been a sea change in attitude among Labour councillors. Where once they were out of touch…they are now pragmatic and innovative…involving the local communities…advocating close partnership with the private sector, and prepared to take tough decisions.[57]

Was this picture of 'pragmatism and innovation' typical of the traditional Labour heartland of the West of Scotland, South Wales or the West Riding of Yorkshire? In these and other parts of the United Kingdom, Labour operated almost as a one-party state and charges of corruption and nepotism were just as rife when Mandelson and Liddle were writing as at any time. These heartlands had not been all but destroyed in the 'bad days' of the early 1980s,[58] but the whiff of corruption often associated with 'one-party' government prevailed too often. In 1997 the NEC suspended the entire Doncaster district party for corruption and abuses of privilege.[59] During 1998 the Labour Party conducted inquiries into 'irregularities' in Glasgow, Paisley, South Tyneside, Doncaster, Birmingham, Coventry and Hackney.[60] In Hull the police investigated the expenses of one Labour councillor who, in his year as Lord Mayor, enjoyed a civic hospitality bill of £342,000 – double the previous mayor's bill.[61] All the same the white knights of New Labour, with their reforming zeal, were not universally welcomed in these heartlands. In Blair's own Sedgefield constituency, three elderly Labour councillors were dese-lected as part of the modernising project. One, a 72-year-old with twenty years' experience, was replaced by a young female transsexual.[62] In the last few years Labour has lost control of such bastions as Sheffield and Hull, and following the switch to proportional voting in local elections, its Scottish local government base has been decimated.

The New Labour assault on decadent and unrepresentative constituency and ward parties that so enthused Mandelson and Liddle was based upon increasing the membership and empowering it via one member one vote. But as the Blair premiership continued, so the initial expansion of the party began to falter and go into reverse. During his third term this reverse became dangerous. In December 2006 membership stood at 198,026, fewer than half the 1997 number and indeed the lowest it has been at any time since Ramsay MacDonald's defection in 1931.[63] One backbench critic pointed out that if the decline continued at the same pace, the party would have no members at all by 2013.[64] John Harris, writing in the *Guardian*, suggested that Labour was losing not simply members but devoted activists. He interviewed activists in the Manchester area in an attempt to under-stand their disillusion. He found strong anecdotal evidence of constituency branches unable to hold quorate meetings, of by-elections being fought with paid help. He quoted an MP who described a visit to the London constituency of a senior Labour minister, where he found 'there was literally nothing there. No canvassing, no leafleting. In effect, there was no Labour Party'.[65] In Stockport, Harris met a woman who had left the party and who claimed: 'There's nowhere for me to go. And that's one of the reasons I feel angry with Blair. He's hijacked our party. He's stolen it and made it into something different'. The Blairite newcomers, she felt, did not share the principles of the older members. In Wilmslow he met the daughter-in-law of the late Sidney Silverman, a Labour backbencher long remembered for his private member's bill to abolish capital punishment, who had also resigned.[66] 'You think about the people who came here before you and how they would regard you…but for us it's like a religion'. Her husband, too, had resigned, telling the party: 'You've obviously got bigger and better sources of cash, so I'll take mine back'.[67] In a Manchester constituency, on the other hand, Harris found activists who were highly supportive of Blair. He had 'absolutely smashed' the 'liberal intellectualism' of the 1980s, they believed, and replaced it with a pragmatic, problem-solving activism that had achieved much. Another study in Birmingham spoke of the bad days of Militant and the constituency infighting that occurred among the teachers, lecturers, accountants and managers. The rout of Militant led to a thriving local party but by 2005 the three wards of the local constituency had to meet as one, and were lucky to attract twenty people. Activists believed that their party had been taken over by 'an ideologically driven group with its own agenda' comprising policies with which they fundamentally disagreed, such as the introduction of private capital into the provision of health and education, aggressive law and order policies and, of course, the war in Iraq.[68] In short Kinnock was perceived by some to have removed one elitist minority and Blair was perceived by others to have replaced it with another.

These are snapshots of individual wards and constituencies but in 2006 Channel Four commissioned a YouGov survey of Labour supporters whose findings lent weight to Harris's and Coulson's studies.[69] Surveyors found an ageing membership, 46 per cent of whom had been active for more than ten years; 32 per cent described themselves as 'fairly left wing' and 42 per cent as 'slightly left of centre' compared to 12 per cent who described themselves as centre and 4 per cent as 'slightly right of centre'. Activists were asked to respond to a series of questions about motivation for joining the party: 58 per cent joined to meet people who shared their 'ideals and hopes' and 49 per cent joined because, they said, 'I am a socialist and I wanted to join a party that would put my aspirations into practice'. Although 15 per cent were attracted by the repeal of Clause Four, mostly newer members, even this group was substantially more attracted by socialism. Nevertheless the allure of socialism was far more important to activists with more than ten years' standing. Whereas 38 per cent of members over 60 had once been members of the Communist Party, 38 per cent of those under 40 had been members of the Green Party. All in all support for the government was strong in terms of its running a sound economy (78 per cent) and helping poorer families, through the minimum wage and tax credits (77 per cent). Only one policy attracted the opprobrium of more than half of members: the invasion of Iraq (52 per cent), although only 25 per cent had seriously considered resigning as a consequence. Too much privatisation of service provision was opposed by 46 per cent. Finally 71 per cent of members wanted Blair to resign before the 2007 party conference, and this reinforced Harris's and Coulson's findings. Even in a Blairite constituency one councillor commented: 'Round here, we would have a list of doors we would knock on as soon as Brown became leader'. It is too early to say whether Brown's accession to the leadership will prove an effective catalyst for regeneration but the early signs have been mixed.

We have concentrated on just the highlights of the substantial YouGov survey. If it shows a party in the country that is a long way from suicidal, we should remember two things: first, these are the members who have not left. Second, although only the Iraq invasion was opposed by a majority, most of the government's more important policy initiatives were opposed by between one-quarter and one-third of all members. And we should certainly remember that, even among his supporters, Blair had outstayed his welcome long before he finally left office.

Labour voters

Karl Marx was absolutely convinced of the eventual political triumph of the working class, given universal suffrage, and he was equally convinced that the triumph of the working class would be synonymous with the triumph of socialism. Other commentators expressed a similar view more prosaically, pointing out that

Labour had only to mobilise its natural class support to win every general election. It seldom managed to do so, and anyway it has been clear for some time that this is no longer true. The history of the Labour Party, over more than a hundred years, shows that the preponderance of support for the party, organised labour, was not strictly socialist: Hardie's description of their ideology was 'labourism'. However, until the Labour governments of the 1960s a clear identity of interest existed between socialism, labourism and the interests of the working class in general. Each camp, for example, would have supported policies designed to promote greater equality of all varieties. This was because a substantial section of the population, substantial enough to vote in Labour governments, considered itself underprivileged in most respects. But to the extent that the Labour government of 1945 actually succeeded in creating greater equality, it diminished its bedrock of natural, instrumental support (i.e. those who saw it as being in their interests to vote Labour). The interests of the recently elevated – the upwardly mobile elements of the working class (loosely referred to as Essex Man) – no longer necessarily coincided with those who remained underprivileged. Essex Man now had something to lose and his vote could not be taken for granted by a party seeking to create even more equality. The interests of a generally better-paid, fed and housed workforce are not necessarily the same as those of unemployed people. A Labour government committed to egalitarian policies would not nowadays always be representing the interests of the majority of workers.

The success of Thatcherite Conservatism in representing populist-authoritarian values was a major factor loosening Labour's hold on the working-class vote. Labour's policies on these issues were not shaped by the perceived interests of the working class but by humanitarian considerations or simply by socialist ideology. All mainstream parties will feel some moral obligation to pursue policies that they consider to be morally right, even if the electoral consequences are likely to be damaging in the short term. But if they are wise they will ensure that the damage is limited by a comprehensive explanation of what they are doing and why; if they are wise they will listen to what those whom they claim to represent have to say; if they are wise they will also pursue policies favourable to their supporters. A party which purports to speak for the mass of ordinary people must, when it is departing from their perceived interests, take care fully to explain why it is doing so.

The Labour Party, in the 1970s and 1980s, moved increasingly away from its traditional voter without taking any of these precautions. In his report to the annual conference in 1982, for example, general secretary Jim Mortimer said:

> It is not the party's policy, but public opinion, which needs to be changed. No socialist worthy of the traditions of the Labour movement should refuse, on occasions, to go against a strong current of public opinion if…he believes that such a course is necessary for the purpose of social progress.[70]

The election manifesto of 1983 which Mortimer helped to prepare produced what Butler and Kavanagh referred to as a 'spectacular retreat' from Labour among working-class voters: only 38 per cent of manual workers and 39 per cent of trade unionists voted Labour, while 32 per cent of trade unionists voted Conservative. Moreover, as Kellner demonstrated, many who did vote Labour did so in spite of, not because of party policy.[71]

Failure to persuade the majority of the working class to support it was highly damaging to Labour but to return to a point made earlier, the working class – 47 per cent of the electorate when Wilson won the 1964 election – had shrunk to 34 per cent by the time Kinnock became leader in 1983, whereas the middle class had grown from 36 per cent to 51 per cent in the same period.[72] Commentators calculated that by the election of 1987, Labour's 'natural' constituency comprised no more than 37 per cent of the electorate and was still shrinking.[73] Kinnock and his advisers, especially Mandelson and Philip Gould, realised that recapturing the majority working-class vote would never again be enough to secure electoral victory. Britain's social structure had evolved, in Skidelsky's phrase, 'from a pyramid to a light bulb' with 'an increasingly large majority...[regarding] themselves as part of the middling curve'.[74] Defeat in 1987 only seemed to prove the point. When he became leader Kinnock signalled his intentions to broaden Labour's appeal to voters by 'gaining votes from the home owners as well as the homeless, the stable family as well as the single parents, the confidently employed as well as the unemployed, the majority as well as the minorities'.[75]

Despite what was widely acknowledged to have been a very effective campaign, the party was defeated in 1992, although Labour gained what Butler and Kavanagh called 'a modest reversal of the long-term [regional and social] pattern that dates back to 1959'.[76] In 1997 Blair built spectacularly on this 'modest reversal', making gains among classes A and B (up 9 per cent), and massive gains among the crucial C1 and C2 classes (up 15 and 19 per cent respectively). The party also gained among homeowners (up 11 per cent), actually overtaking the Conservatives (41 to 35 per cent) for the first time ever. Moreover Labour also overtook the Conservatives in terms of support among women. The party made significant gains in all age groups save those over 65. That these changes reflected a great disillusionment with the Conservatives rather than a newfound admiration for Labour must be acknowledged.[77] Butler and Kavanagh point out that Labour's share of the vote (43.2 per cent in 1997) was lower than that secured by Harold Wilson after thirteen years of Conservative rule in 1964 (43.4 per cent) – yet Wilson's majority was 4 and not 179. But what 1997 showed very clearly was that Labour *could* win seats across the whole social and regional spectrum, that voters *did not fear* a Labour victory, and in that sense if no other, this election marked a watershed. Gaitskell, Crosland, Kinnock and Smith could consider themselves vindicated: voters were willing to support a broadly reformist programme run by a party which had shed its fundamentalist image. In terms of those who voted for it, this was indeed a New Labour Party.

Labour's electoral success was maintained in 2001 and 2005, though the extent of the victory diminished: in 2001 Labour won 40.7 per cent of the vote, securing an overall majority of 165; in 2005 the Labour vote fell to 35.2 per cent and its overall majority to 66, indicating that Labour's ability to hold on to significant numbers of its new social constituency remained uncertain. Nevertheless, unlike Harold Wilson, it was not at all fanciful for Blair to claim that Labour had become the new natural party of government.[78] One worrying feature however was the low turnout: only 59.4 per cent voted in 2001, the lowest since universal adult suffrage, and only 61.2 per cent in 2005. The fall in turnout had affected Labour disproportionately, especially after the Iraq war.[79] Disillusion grew regarding the justification for war and the conduct of the occupation, but more generally with the party's perceived propensity for 'spin', associated with which were a growing reputation for control freakery and for dealing in 'lies, damned lies and statistics'. Labour sought to address this disconnection with the electorate (especially its core supporters) through the Big Conversation in 2003, when organisers tried to promote a dialogue between supporters and ministers. It was not a success, perhaps because the government continued to undertake a legislative programme key elements of which were antithetical to members' values.

Given the comparative weakness of local organisations, the party campaign in 2005 relied substantially on professionals working from the centre and resources were directed mostly on key marginal constituencies.[80] This did little to halt the kind of structural decline described earlier. There is little about the 2001 and 2005 general elections to suggest that Labour under Blair has lost its capacity to win votes among the middle- and upper-middle-class constituency cryptically referred to as Middle England, but it lost 4 million votes in 2005. Though Iraq may not have been a very salient issue for most voters, one in four who voted Liberal Democrat admitted that they would have voted Labour 'but did not do so because of Iraq'.[81] It was the unlanced boil of Iraq that weakened Labour in the Scottish and Welsh elections of 2007 and again the harm was greatest among Labour's traditional voters.

Conclusions

Accounts of the death of the Labour Party, common enough between 1959 and 1992, proved to be much exaggerated. The party is in power having won three consecutive elections. This chapter has presented a picture of an evolving party, a party that came into existence to redress the balance of parliamentary representation in the interests of organised labour. In so far as it won the votes of ordinary working people, the infant Labour Party destroyed much of the base of support for the old Liberal Party. However, since its halcyon days of 1945–50 the Labour Party has slowly become less of a people's party in terms of those who represent it, those who are active on its behalf and those who support it in the polling stations. The drift towards a middle-class, public-sector-dominated party with a more fundamentalist socialist ideology gathered pace during the 1970s and early 1980s, but it found little support in the polls and indeed suffered a series of defections from social democrats who left to found their own party. From the low point of 1983 when Labour received a smaller percentage of the vote that at any time since 1918, modernisers brought the party back towards the centre and, as we have seen, consciously aimed at making itself more acceptable to all voters. In making the party less of a class-based party Labour came more and more to resemble the Liberal Party it had been created to replace. Blair's New Labour Party in parliament appears to be a party of the centre or even centre-right but the party activists retain more of Labour's traditions. Blair's attempts to build up a mass membership party, initially very successful, have foundered and been put into reverse: the party, say left-wing critics, has been 'hollowed out'. It is not clear how Gordon Brown will attempt to rebuild the party but if he is to avert defeat in the next election, he must certainly do so. But if Brown's government simply takes on the mantle of Blair then traditional Labour supporters, to some of whom modernisers are little better than traitors, will exact revenge. Fukuyama notwith-standing, social democrats should not be over-confident that they have reached the end of the historical confrontation with the fundamentalists, and the policies of the Labour government must in future be more careful to appear to reflect that historical accommodation between social democracy and fundamentalism that has defined Labour traditions. Brown will need to construct a Fourth Way.

8 Liberal Democrats – always the bridesmaid?

If we wish to understand the genesis and *raison d'être* of the Liberal Democrats, we had better begin where all good stories start, at the beginning. The difficulty in this case is that there is no obvious beginning. Was it the establishment of the Liberal Democrat party in 1989? Was it the founding of the Liberal–SDP Alliance in 1981? Was it the Orpington by-election of 1962 when the Liberals showed that the post-war two-party system might not, after all, represent the telos of British party politics? Or was it instead the founding of the Liberal Party a hundred years earlier? We can discern an unbroken if sometimes tenuous thread connecting the Whigs of Charles James Fox, Grey and Russell, to the Liberals under Gladstone and Lloyd George, to the recharged Liberals of the 1960s under Jo Grimond, to the Alliance party of the 1980s, to the Liberal Democrats of today, so it seems most appropriate to start with the Liberals in the nineteenth century.

The Liberal Party

The Liberals were one of the two great parties of state until 1918.[1] Their unantici-pated demise was largely the consequence of a Labour Party better geared to serve the interests of the industrial working class and this process has been famously recorded.[2] Its apparent suddenness, however, was the direct consequence of personal rivalry between Asquith and Lloyd George. The former was party leader and Prime Minister at the outbreak of war in 1914 but the Conservatives would participate in a wartime coalition only under the leadership of Lloyd George. When the latter sought to continue as leader of a peacetime coalition in 1918, he refused to endorse the 'Squiffites', Asquith's supporters who were consequently forced into opposition.[3] Lloyd George in effect broke the Liberal Party. 'Dazzled by his own light,' as Simon Jenkins poignantly put it, 'he could not see the darkness until it overwhelmed him'.[4] In the face of this irreparable split, the party ceded its position as the main progressive force to Labour in the inter-war years, and Labour's dominance was endorsed by the totemic victory of 1945 when the Liberals returned only twelve MPs on 1.9 per cent of the national vote.[5]

Worse was to follow in 1950: only nine Liberals were elected and no fewer than 319 deposits were lost. In 1951 and again in 1955, six Liberals sat in the House of Commons, representing only 1 per cent of voters. The 'strange death of Liberal

England' seemed almost complete. But only almost. As the Conservative governments of Eden and later Macmillan became unpopular, so the Liberals showed small signs of recovery. Derided as a Celtic fringe party, they broke out of their familiar territory with a spectacular by-election victory over the Conservatives in the safe London suburban seat of Orpington. The Conservative vote fell by 18 per cent and the Liberal vote increased by an unprecedented 31 per cent. It was the most stunning of all such victories. For the next thirty-five years the Liberals and their successors would garner protest votes with assiduity and increasing tactical nous, usually from unpopular Conservative governments. They were often dismissed by their opponents as ideological scavengers – feeding off the votes of the disgruntled, rather than representing something that might be called a Liberal tradition – but they could not be ignored.

Liberal ideology

Liberalism has a long and on the whole honourable history in British parliamentary politics. Drawing from the philosophical traditions that originally gave them political shape, the Whigs and later the Liberals were concerned with the nature and practices of the constitution. Although in many other respects Liberalism can be seen to have changed over the years, with Manchester Liberalism and Lloyd Georgian Liberalism exhibiting almost polar-opposite economic policies for example, a concern with the protection and enhancement of civil liberties through the constitution has been constant.[6] And this tradition has marked modern Liberalism and Liberal Democracy just as clearly as it marked the Liberal Party of Jo Grimond, setting it apart from the Conservatives for whom constitutional issues were taken as more or less settled, and the Labour Party, which traditionally sought a strong central state capable of creating and managing socialism.

Constitutional reform is not the only debt that Liberal Democrats owe to their tradition. They have also been shaped by the forces that emerged in the 1890s. The political currents of the late Victorian period included three distinct but generic traditions on the centre left: the radical liberal, the social democratic and the fundamentalist socialist; distinct but not separate because of overlapping support. There was a fluidity regarding political allegiances at the time with new groups forming and reforming almost continuously.[7] There were, for example, the 'new Liberals', who claimed to speak in the interests of the industrial working class. They argued strongly that the state ought to be prepared to intervene in the economy in the interests of the individual liberties of all citizens. About the same time as the new Liberals were changing the contours of liberalism, socialism was beginning to establish itself. There was much in common between the movements, not least the friendship between the leading members. Collaborative groups of intellectuals were established, such as the Rainbow Circle.[8] The liberal magazine *The Nation*, declaring that left-wing liberalism merged imperceptibly into socialism, believed that the progressive agenda would be set by adherents to a broad left-of-centre platform that it called social democracy.[9]

Within a comparatively short time however, the Liberal Party ceased to be a major force and social democrats, and indeed many former Liberals, were to join the ranks of the Labour Party. But the Liberal tradition lived on, if at times precariously, and it continued to develop ideologically. The Liberals believed in a society in which the individual was able to participate in the decisions that shaped his or her own life.[10] It represented one of the basic tenets of traditional liberal faith: in human rationality. Grimond argued that people are bound by a common rationality; for him it took the form almost of natural law.[11] 'Certainly it is impossible to make men self-directing responsible citizens,' says another Liberal writer. 'They must do this for themselves. But society can create opportunities for them to become so, and encourage them to take them.'[12]

Post-1955 Liberals were never happy with the label of 'centrists' or 'middle-of-the-roaders'. 'By any strict language Liberals are the true Left, the real progressives,' said Elliot Dodds.[13] Donald Wade rejected the whole idea of a left–right spectrum based on attitudes to public ownership; for Liberals it was more important to measure from libertarian values to authoritarian ones and in terms of this classification the extremes of left and right (in standard terminology) fused into each other around the authoritarian pole. There were only two senses in which the Liberal Party was unequivocally centrist: first, its attitude to the 'public versus private ownership' debate was largely pragmatic, and second, it enjoyed substantial support from the middle classes. Liberals supported the nationalisation of coal and opposed that of steel, they supported the sale of council houses in some areas and opposed it in others. As for middle-class support, it was after all chiefly this sector which sought to become 'self-directing, responsible citizens': that is, to participate.

Participation became the keyword of modern Liberal policies and it stood in contradistinction to the bureaucratic elitism of fundamentalist socialism and the social elitism of conservatism. At the popular level participation was a feature of the life of a real community, defined as a group of individuals with something in common: nationality, neighbourhood, religion, work, workplace or victimisation.[14] Community politics for the Liberals was both a means and an end. It was a *means* of creating a less unequal society superior to the fundamentalist socialist's schemes of public ownership and it was an *end* in so far as giving as many citizens as possible a say in the decisions affecting their lives was a goal of traditional liberalism. Liberals rejected the notion of class politics, claiming that Labour discouraged the political participation or ordinary people and that the trade union movement stood in the way of industrial participation.

At the representative level, participation was a basic ingredient of the policy of decentralising government, of giving more not fewer powers to democratically elected local authorities, of inserting a regional tier into the British system of government which would require devolving executive powers to assemblies in Scotland and Wales and returning them to Northern Ireland. The Liberals (and Liberal Democrats) were the only party traditionally to advocate devolution as a positive good in its own right. Above all, Liberals sought to encourage participation at all levels through a fairer electoral system. In short Liberal ideology represents both change and continuity.

Liberals, social democrats and fundamentalists: back to the melting pot

Given the collapse of the Liberal Party after the First World War there were good reasons for social democrats to remain within Labour and to continue the struggle with the fundamentalists for control of party policy-making, especially since they usually won. Writing before the end of the 1974–79 Labour government, Peter Jenkins argued that these social democrats wished to transform their party into a northern European-style social democratic party.[15] He assumed that the struggle between social democrats and fundamentalists would take place, as it always had, *within* the Labour Party. It did not. Jenkins suggested that the social democrats' success would depend upon Denis Healey becoming party leader after Callaghan. He did not.

Michael Foot won the leadership election for the fundamentalists and the party subsequently lurched to the left. In January 1981, three leading social democrats, Shirley Williams, David Owen and William Rodgers, together with Roy Jenkins, a former Cabinet minister,[16] left the party and promulgated their Limehouse Declaration, establishing the Council for Social Democracy and promising to set up a new party before Easter.

What did these social democrats stand for? Roy Jenkins had already set out his own manifesto in the 1979 Dimbleby Lecture. He took as his starting-point the ossification of the British party system and the deleterious effects, especially on the economy, of adversarial politics. He argued that the two great parties were coalitions but that no real community of interests existed within them any longer. He argued for the building up, through a proportional electoral system, of 'living' coalitions, dismissing arguments that such coalitions could not provide effective government.[17] Jenkins argued that Britain suffered from an inability to adapt consistently, together with too great a capacity to change inconsistently. 'The paradox is that we need more change accompanied by more stability of direction.'[18]

It was important to devolve decision-making, giving parents a voice in the school system, patients a voice in the health system, residents a voice in neighbourhood councils, and so on. Above all Jenkins believed it to be necessary to involve in politics the considerable number of people who felt alienated from the business of government; only their engagement offered a guarantee against extremism of right or left. The three former Labour ministers, Owen,[19] Rodgers,[20] and Williams,[21] wrote at length along similar lines to Jenkins. Their principal concern, too, was to re-establish a sense of community involvement in politics. This, then, was the ideology of what became the Social Democratic Party (SDP).

The irresistible rise of the Alliance

It soon became apparent that the social democrats, or Social Democrats as they officially became, had much in common with Liberals, including firm commitment to electoral reform. For the Liberals the rationale for an alliance with the SDP was clear. Since their first major post-war by-electoral triumph at Torrington in 1958, the Liberals secured an average of 23 per cent in by-elections during Conservative governments, yet they managed only 15 per cent under Labour governments.[22] The Liberals simply could not win enough working-class votes to make a sustained challenge to the major parties. An alliance with the SDP, who were, after all, brought up in the party of Hardie and McDonald, might enable the Liberal leader David Steel to fulfil the vision he had inherited from his mentor, the former leader Jo Grimond: a non-socialist realignment of the centre-left. A formal alliance came about later in 1981 and with immediate success. For more than six months in 1981–82, popular support for the Alliance registered over 40 per cent and the next election in 1983 could not come soon enough.

But Alliance leaders reckoned without the Falklands War of 1982 and the great boost it gave to the Thatcher government. The Alliance campaign of 1983 lacked punch and Roy Jenkins was replaced as SDP leader by the younger David Owen, immediately creating a personal rivalry with David Steel, the Liberal leader. The expected additional working-class support did not materialise: the 23 former Labour MPs who had joined the SDP were, with few exceptions, defeated in the election. Nevertheless history was nearly made in 1983. Ineptly led, divided and generally unpopular, Labour held on to its status as the main opposition party – just. The Alliance (at 25.4 per cent of the popular vote) came agonisingly close to overtaking Labour (27.0 per cent) but it returned only 23 MPs in comparison to Labour's 209.[23] There could hardly have been a more stunning indictment of the electoral system. David Steel's lengthy sabbatical from political life immediately after that election told its own story.

The decline and fall of the Alliance

By 1987 two developments were beginning to shape the Alliance. At ground level most Liberal and SDP local groups were cooperating fully and acting more or less as a united party. At the leadership level precisely the opposite was happening. Owen firmly opposed local cooperation as 'merger by the back door' and, from start to finish, he opposed merger. Meanwhile under Kinnock, Labour had won back most of its defecting voters; in contrast the SDP had become a predominantly middle-class Home Counties party, with more members in the borough of Camden than in all of Yorkshire. The Alliance election campaign of 1987 was a comparative failure. In securing 23 per cent of votes cast and returning 22 MPs, the Alliance did less well than in 1983. Support for the Alliance had slumped in working-class seats and so the original rationale for two parties working in tandem had collapsed. Henceforth they would be competing for the same middle-class votes. Unless, of course, they combined.[24]

The emergence of the Liberal Democrats

Steel called for merger discussions immediately after the election. When negotiations began, however, they proved to be such a charade of ineptitude that Steel, their godfather, felt obliged to resign. Fresh negotiators were assembled and a new proposal was put to both parties for endorsement. At a special meeting held in

Blackpool in 1988 the Liberal Party voted for merger by a huge majority (2,099 to 285). At Sheffield a week later the SDP council also voted massively in favour (273 to 28, with 49 abstentions). The merger proposals were finally put to the membership of both parties and were duly endorsed by both.[25] Finally in March 1988 the Liberal and Social Democratic parties merged to form the Social and Liberal Democrats (SLD).

The Owenite SDP lived on, causing considerable confusion in the public mind and splitting the diminishing third-party vote. At Richmond in Yorkshire for example, the Conservatives won a by-election in 1988 though the combined votes of the former Alliance partners was hugely greater than the Conservative vote. A young William Hague was the beneficiary of their failure to combine.[26] Support for the SDP began to decline thereafter and when, in 1990, the party was overtaken in a by-election by the Official Monster Raving Loony party, Owen wound up the SDP.[27]

In the meantime the SLD had become engaged in a leadership contest. By the closing date only two candidates, the Liberal MP for Yeovil, Paddy Ashdown, and the Liberal deputy leader, Alan Beith, had declared themselves. No former SDP candidate stood. The election campaign was a relatively quiet affair that Ashdown won decisively.

The Ashdown years

Ashdown's first major test as leader was the European elections of 1989, when the SLD received only 6 per cent of the vote to the Greens' 15 per cent, putting its status as third party in jeopardy. The party was demoralised and nearly bankrupt. Ashdown set about turning round the fortunes of his seriously ailing party before the next election and the first crucial step was to rename the party the Liberal Democrats (polls having revealed that some three-quarters of the population got the party's former name wrong).[28] Shortly after the Liberal Democrats took Eastbourne from the Tories at a by-election, overturning a majority of 17,000, and soon after captured Ribble Valley, the thirteenth safest Tory seat. By the time of the 1992 general election the party was in good fettle. The result (twenty seats won), hardly a triumph but certainly no failure, was followed by four stunning by-election victories and the defection of a leading Conservative MP, Emma Nicholson.

Ashdown built on this foundation. The Liberal Democrats enjoyed unparalleled success in the years of Tory decline. Across the United Kingdom the Liberal Democrats became the second party of local government after Labour. In the European elections of 1994, too, the party had enjoyed its first successes, winning two seats and coming close in five others. Parliamentary by-elections in winnable seats boosted morale and the additional four seats, together with two Tory defections, gave the parliamentary party twenty-six members, more than at any time since the heady days of the Alliance in the early 1980s. Party membership had passed the symbolically important 100,000 and finances were on a relatively sound footing. Party strategists identified winnable seats at the next election and resources were ruthlessly directed towards them.[29] The party approached the 1997 election in good heart.[30]

The end of 'equidistance'

In 1995 Ashdown had heralded the demise of equidistance, the principle according to which the Liberal Democrats would consider working with whichever party secured most seats after an inconclusive election.[31] Ashdown now declared:

> People must know that if they kick the Tories out through the front door, we will not allow them to sneak in through the back door{...}every vote for the Liberal Democrats is a vote to remove this Conservative government and the policies they stand for.[32]

In reality equidistance had seldom been more than symbolic.[33] It is true that in the 1950s agreements had been reached through which Liberals and Conservatives allowed each other a free run against Labour opponents in Huddersfield and Bolton, true also that in the 1987 election David Owen had refused to rule out the possibility of a post-electoral arrangement with Margaret Thatcher's Conservatives. Nevertheless the historic function of the Liberal Party in the twentieth century had been to provide a non-socialist radical alternative to Conservatism, not hold some mythical balance.[34] When in the late 1950s Jo Grimond was helping to re-establish the Liberals as a major national party he, too, called for a realignment of the left, adding significantly that he 'didn't give a tinker's cuss' what a realigned party should be called.[35] In 1974 the Liberals refused to make a post-electoral arrangement with Heath's Conservatives despite their having received most votes at the previous election, although in 1978 they were willing to keep a minority Labour government in office. Later still, after the 1992 election, David Marquand (then a Liberal Democrat) argued that the party should have 'come clean' to the voters: it was a left-of-centre party and should not have masqueraded as an equidistant, centre party. (He later rejoined Labour, a party that had become pleased to be considered a centre party.)

The problem for the Liberal Democrats in 1992 was exactly what it had been since 1950: it professed a preponderance of left-of-centre policies but in the main was supported by disgruntled centre and right-of-centre voters. The Liberals and the Liberal Democrats may well have needed a Labour victory to have any hope of sharing power, but they continued to rely principally on defecting Conservative support for the electoral successes which would allow them to bargain with Labour about power. The irony during the years of the Blair government, and especially since the Iraq invasion, was that though for the first time the Liberal Democrats showed that they could take numbers of disaffected Labour votes, their success makes the notion of power sharing more problematical: they would be just as likely to hand victory to the Conservatives.

Liberal Democrats and New Labour

Why did Ashdown in 1995 signal the end of a policy that he knew had never really existed? To abandon the myth of equidistance was to signal a change in the ideology not of his own party but *of the other parties*.[36] He was right to signal the changing positions of the major parties: in the Littleborough and Saddleworth by-election later that year Labour spokesmen denounced the Liberal Democrats as a high-spending, high-taxation party and claimed the Liberal tradition of Keynes and Beveridge for their own party.[37] When the pro-Labour *New Statesman* advised Labour supporters to vote tactically and support the Liberal Democrats, it drew an extraordinary storm of invective on its head from the Labour leadership. (However, in the by-election the Liberal Democrats stuck to their guns: taxation was the price of a civilised society, they claimed. And they won.)

By attempting to 'fix' his own party's policy stance, however,[38] Ashdown was actually hoping to make possible some post-election arrangement with Labour without alienating those who were hostile to Labour within his party, by showing that Labour had moved towards the Liberal Democrats and not vice versa.[39] He felt confident enough to pursue an active policy of engagement with Labour before the 1997 election. One of the fruits of this was the Cook-Maclennan Report on Constitutional Reform that set out the programme which, to some extent, the Labour government subsequently followed. Both parties were committed to this wide legislative programme, but it reflected policies that the Liberal Democrat (and Liberal) Party had advocated for many years.[40]

Although Labour came into office on such a massive majority in 1997, Blair was prepared to discuss the possibility of two Cabinet positions for the Liberal Democrats,[41] acknowledging both the electoral cooperation between the parties,[42] and also what the parties had in common in respect of constitutional reform. The offer was somewhat reluctantly declined, but this period nevertheless marked the highpoint of Liberal Democrat influence. Blair told Ashdown that he was 'absolutely determined' to mend the schism in progressive politics that had lasted a century.[43] In 1998 Blair established a commission on electoral reform chaired by Roy Jenkins, though he did nothing to implement its pro-reform recommendations. Nevertheless these early years of Blair's governance saw the enactment of the Cook-Maclennan programme in large part. Although history may have overlooked the fact, Ashdown's strategy turned out to be very successful vis-à-vis the enactment of party policy, though not vis-à-vis party fortunes.[44] Labour's early legislative programme represented something of a retrospective victory for Grimond, Steel and their colleagues.

If Liberal Democrats were as far away from the handles of power in Westminster, the same was not true either for the Edinburgh or the Cardiff administrations. First in Edinburgh then in Cardiff, the party entered a coalition with Labour to form the administration; in Wales the coalition did not survive the 2003 elections, but in Scotland it lasted for eight years until May 2007, when Labour lost its status as Scotland's major party to the Scottish Nationalists. In that period Liberal Democrats managed to persuade Holyrood to legislate on their policies in respect of student fees and care for elderly people, and on changing the electoral system in local government to Single Transferable Vote.[45]

When in 1999 Ashdown resigned as leader, Charles Kennedy proved much less inclined to offer Labour the support that his predecessor had proffered,[46] especially as government responded to the so-called war on terror with policies that threatened individual liberties.[47] Unlike the Conservative Party, the Liberals opposed the Iraq war from the outset and Kennedy's more critical stance towards the Labour government was continued by his successor Sir Menzies Campbell.[48] From the Liberal Democrat perspective it was not merely Labour's Iraq policy that drove the parties apart, but Labour's health and education reforms. Once again, it was not so much the Liberal Democrats whose policy stance shifted but Labour's, so that although equidistance was not formally reinstated it had become the reality, at least at Westminster. In Edinburgh, nevertheless, the party was in a coalition with a Labour administration whose policies were similar though not the same.

Party organisation

The history of Liberal Democrat organisation is necessarily short and recent. Its most noteworthy features are the distinctive federal structure, unlike that of other major parties, and the absolute commitment to participative politics.[49]

The party leader

Leaders of major parties can deflect the task of representing the party to other influential and preferably photogenic leaders: thus even as forceful and dynamic a leader as Thatcher could confidently defer to other leading figures such as Tebbit or Parkinson. Liberal Democrat leaders have rarely had that advantage. The leader of the Liberal Democrats is elected by all members of the party, and once elected is in the job till death, incapacity, resignation, loss of support, or loss of his/her seat forces him or her out. A party leader enjoying a favourable public image has considerably greater influence in the affairs of his/her party than even the leaders of the major parties. It is an interesting paradox that in a party dedicated to maximising participation, leaders from Grimond onwards have had a reputation for dominating their parliamentary colleagues and party. 'Ashdown very much controlled the party', one activist rather despairingly remarked, 'and very often dragged the party where it didn't necessarily want to go'.[50]

On the other hand the party hierarchy can be ruthless too, as the 'resignation' of Charles Kennedy as leader in 2006 demonstrates. Kennedy's leadership style was far less affirmative than any of his predecessors since Clement Davies;[51] he was more of a 'chairman'. Many of his senior colleagues believed that a drink problem was hindering his performance as leader. In January 2006 a letter from twenty-five MPs stated that the signatories would not serve on a frontbench under Kennedy. A survey for BBC's *Newsnight* discovered that only seventeen of sixty-two MPs wanted him to stay on. After a visit from the 'men in grey sandals', Kennedy reluctantly resigned on 7 January, triggering a postal ballot of all members. Of the candidates to replace him, Sir Menzies Campbell was the most experienced (and at 64 the oldest) and represented the traditional mainstream of Liberal Democracy; party president Simon Hughes represented the left of the party, Mark Oaten, who was associated with the *Orange Book* group,[52] the right. Chris Huhne, an environmentalist and an MP only since 2005 but an MEP for six years previously, was a late entry. Disaster overtook Oaten when a newspaper report of a liaison with a male prostitute caused him to resign. Later Hughes, too, was obliged to admit previously denied homosexual relationships.[53] Although he remained in the race, support for Hughes ebbed away. Victory in this rather tawdry competition went comfortably to Campbell, but few in the party greeted his triumph with enthusiasm.[54] The anxieties that many felt concerning his ability to galvanise the party or win over the electorate were not relieved by the party's poor performance in the 2007 local government elections, which saw the loss of 246 seats in England and setbacks in Scotland and Wales. As Michael White pointed out, the prospect of the party going into an election in 2010 with a leader by then approaching 70 became, in 2007, a distinctly unappealing idea.[55] It says much about the role of the Liberal Democrat leader that competence is not enough: the party has been treading water since the departure of Ashdown. Campbell chose to resign in October 2007 and though deputy leader Vince Cable was no doubt justified in claiming that Campbell was not actually 'pushed', little enthusiasm for his leadership was evident at any level. Cable's brief spell as acting Leader gave a glimpse of what the party had missed under Campbell, artfully 'muscling his way into the headlines'.[56]

The parliamentary party

David McKie argued that the modern parliamentary party compares unfavourably with more colourful predecessors, when the Commons was graced with Liberals of genuine public stature such as Jo Grimond, Jeremy Thorpe, David Steel, Clement Freud and Cyril Smith, not to mention David Owen, Roy Jenkins, William Rodgers and Shirley Williams in the days of the Alliance.[57] McKie feels that this is almost certainly the consequence of a style of regionalised candidate selection, which tends to reward local service and hence to produce, in McKie's words, a 'sound but pedestrian parliamentary party'. It is more likely to have to do with the fact that more Liberal Democrats get elected nowadays. Before the Alliance, only very fortunate or larger-than-life candidates tended to secure election. Earlier Liberal leaders would have been delighted to lead a sound but pedestrian party.

Before 1997 there were too few MPs to make worthwhile generalisations, but we *can* comment on the post-2005 election parliamentary party of sixty-two. Currently the parliamentary party comprises 40 per cent with a professional background, of whom the largest single group comprises school teachers. A further 29 per cent have a business background. The party has one former manual worker. Some 39 per cent of the parliamentary party were educated privately (almost exactly 'equidistant' between the two main parties) and 79 per cent went to university (31 per cent to Oxbridge). Some 40 per cent of MPs went to state comprehensive schools.[58] In terms of age 31 per cent of the parliamentary party are under 40, and overall the party is significantly younger than its major competitors. There are ten women among Liberal Democrat MPs, again making it almost equidistant between Labour (at 32 per cent) and the Conservatives (at 9 per cent).[59]

Parliamentary strategy

Under both Conservative and Labour governments, the party in the House of Commons sought to establish itself as an independent party of opposition, opposing the government on issues of principle but not 'for the sake of opposition'. This position was frequently derided by both the major parties when in government and opposition. In European matters, for example, both parties attacked the Liberal Democrats for inconsistency.

The Liberal Democrats earned the Conservative government's displeasure when supporting a successful Labour amendment to provide that the United Kingdom's representatives on the new EU consultative committee of the regions should be elected by local authorities and not nominated by government. Here the Liberal Democrat stance was clearly taken on principle. The party then earned Labour's displeasure when, with Liberal Democrat support, the government won a paving motion to proceed with its Maastricht Treaty legislation. Defeat for the government, said Labour, would have led to its fall, something to be aimed at by any Opposition. But the Liberal Democrats favoured the Treaty. Further Labour opprobrium followed when the Liberal Democrats supported the government on the European Communities Finance Bill. Labour had proposed an amendment not to sanction any increase in the United Kingdom's contribution to the EU budget 'without action by the government to curb fraud and waste in Europe'. The Liberal Democrats supported the government, accusing Labour of opportunism, and the government secured a comfortable majority.[60] In truth the party was not inconsistent: it had voted from principle.

'Principled opposition' to the Conservative government grew into 'constructive opposition' to the incoming Labour government. Ashdown and four of his senior colleagues sat on a Cabinet committee concerned with constitutional reform and at the end of 1998, formal cooperation between the two parties was extended to European defence and foreign policy issues. This kind of limited opposition fitted the party's traditional rejection of adversarialism but it earned the opprobrium of the Conservative opposition, and indeed of some Liberal Democrat backbenchers, who felt inhibited in their role as critics. When the debate on a Conservative motion of censure on the government's policy of cutting single parents' allowances began in December 1997, there were only three Liberal Democrats in the chamber and when the vote was finally taken, the party half-heartedly supported Labour.[61] If this was not a sacrifice of party principles for expediency, it certainly looked like it. However, with the resignation in 1999 of the chief architect of 'constructive opposition', Ashdown, following the demise in late 1998 of one of its most influential Labour supporters, Mandelson, the whole project of centre-left realignment fell and with it support for constructive opposition under Kennedy and Campbell. The 'war on terror' transformed domestic politics as it did foreign affairs, but most Liberal Democrats would have found great difficulty in supporting the policies of successive Home Secretaries.

The Shadow Cabinet

Ashdown's Shadow Cabinet comprised only a dozen MPs, each monitoring several departments. Campbell's Shadow Cabinet comprised twenty-three, and two members of the House of Lords. In terms of age, four were in their twenties or thirties, nine in their forties and ten in their fifties and sixties. Nine represented 'northern' constituencies (in our terminology), nine southern constituencies and six western, a category devised especially for the Liberal Democrats, whose traditional heartland is in the Celtic south-west. All had been to university, with twelve having been to an Oxbridge college. Eleven had local government experience. All had a professional background, some lawyers but more in some form of managerial or consultancy work. Eight had been in politics all or nearly all of their professional life, as researchers, advisers or administrators. The Shadow Cabinet included five women. In the 1950s the Liberals used to be derided as the party of the (loosely defined) Celtic fringe. No less than 50 per cent of the leadership of today's modern national party comprises representatives of that same Celtic fringe.[62]

In the current House of Lords there are seventy-seven peers, led by Lord McNally, who take the Liberal whip. They meet every Thursday with either the leader or deputy leader in the Lords taking the chair. These meetings are often addressed by the relevant Commons spokesperson. The party in the Lords, additionally, has its own committees, but the entire party in the Lords is supported by only three paid officials, and so Liberal Democrat peers feel there is a limit to what they can accomplish. Short of assistance, cramped for space, they nevertheless concentrate resources on producing their own amendments to legislation rather than simply responding to Labour's amendments.

There are twelve Liberal Democrats in the European Parliament, led by Andrew Duff, with at least one from every English region and one from Scotland. They sit in the Alliance of Liberals and Democrats for Europe group, of which Graham Watson is the leader. In 2006–07 Diana Wallis, MEP for Yorkshire, was appointed Vice-President of the European Parliament.

The party's federal structure

Before the merger of the two parties, the Liberals had already moved towards a federal structure but time did not allow the many problems that emerged to be satisfactorily addressed. The Scottish Liberal Party operated in many respects as an autonomous unit but the federal executive of the national party, with prime responsibility for policy and indeed for strategy, was often perceived by the Scots to render federalism more a myth than a reality. The original move for federalism had arisen chiefly in Scotland, though Welsh Liberals were generally supportive. The position of England had always posed a major problem by virtue of its disproportionate size and wealth and in order to 'square' England, the new federal structure that emerged from the merger negotiations incorporated eleven English regional organisations.[63] The merger negotiations establishing the English regions (potentially one of the more contentious issues) proved successful. There has been no renegotiation of regional boundaries, despite the relocation of some local parties into other regions. English regional parties can, if they choose, seek the status, like Scotland and Wales, of state parties. None so far has done so.

In order to belong to the Liberal Democrats it is necessary to belong to a local party or a specified associated organisation (SAO), such as the Association of Liberal Democrat Councillors, the Youth and Students Association, or the Parliamentary Candidates' Association. These associations are themselves semi-autonomous. Liberal Democrats Youth and Students, for example, is organised federally, like the party itself, meets in conference twice a year and runs specific national campaigns, especially on issues relating to higher and further education but also on issues such as development aid, homophobia and so on. Formed in 1993 with the amalgamation of separate groups for youth and students, the group caters for Liberal Democrats under 26. Any thirty SAO members may form a local party, based upon at least one parliamentary constituency. Local parties are directly represented at the twice-yearly federal conference, proportionately to membership. Standing Orders provide for consultative sessions at the September conference in which any member may speak, so in theory it is possible for ordinary members to participate in policy-making.

One of the pivotal groups in the party structure is the federal policy committee (FPC). Its principal tasks are to approve party publications and to make interim policy decisions on topical issues. FPC, with twenty-five elected members who are broadly representative of the party, has the additional function of making detailed policy of the kind needed to implement the broad policy outlines adopted by conference. The FPC chair is elected by the parliamentary party. FPC prepares election manifestos for general and European elections in consultation with the parliamentary and European parliamentary parties. It has the power to set up policy working groups that have a remit to consult as widely as possible. Most important of the party committees is the Federal Executive (FE), which comprises some thirty-five members and is representative of the party in the country and the administrative structure. It serves as the hub of a system of subordinate committees and subcommittees. It establishes, among others, subcommittees for publicity and broadcasting, campaigning and elections and international relations. The FE also has the power to conduct consultative ballots of all party members but its own views are taken as representative by the leadership. For example it was from the FE that Ashdown sought endorsement for extending cooperation with Labour in late 1998.

The constitution of the English party recognises the existence of regional party structures. These parties have the power to make policy on matters that relate exclusively to their region and they can draw up a regional manifesto for use in general elections provided that this manifesto is consistent with federal policy. The structure of the two state parties in Scotland and Wales is broadly similar, though in practice the electoral decline of the Welsh party allows much less scope for autonomy. The Scottish party has its own constitution, its own leader and officers and its own policy-making structure. Moreover the Scottish party holds two conferences a year, making it difficult for many members to find the time to play much of a part in federal conferences. The Scottish party jealously guards its autonomy and clearly finds it difficult on occasions to subordinate itself to federal (especially as it is often seen as 'English') policy objectives.

The status of the Scottish Liberal Democrats has been greatly enhanced since devolution. They spent the first eight years of devolved politics in government at

Holyrood and their refusal to enter a coalition with the SNP after the 2007 Scottish election was decisive in shaping the minority governing system that has presided over Scotland since.[64] Liberal Democrats might say that their regional structure allows for the accommodation of national divergences but in truth nobody knew whether the structure would work in practice. We know now that despite tensions, it has more or less worked.[65] It was always considered that subnational (state) parties would be constrained in their policy preferences by the demands of the national electoral priorities but that national policy-makers would, in their turn, be influenced by subnational (state) imperatives.[66] It was further assumed that where the competencies of national and subnational (state) parties overlapped functionally, the pressure towards convergence would be the greater.[67] One factor that most theories do not deal with is the operating of different electoral systems at national and subnational levels, systems that tend to produce different outcomes requiring different strategies. Coalition government was always going to be likely in Scotland and unlikely in the United Kingdom. What the Scottish Liberal Democrat (SLD) leader Jim Wallace struggled – successfully – to establish was that negotiations on forming a Scottish coalition would not be run 'by remote control from London'.[68] Wallace became Scotland's Deputy First Minister and his party took two of eleven Cabinet portfolios. After the 2003 elections, Wallace was able to claim a third Cabinet seat. In Wales the Liberal Democrat leader Mike German was able, with greater difficulty, to come to a similar arrangement with Labour, but after 2003 Labour was able to govern alone and chose to do so. Following the elections of 2007 the leader of the Scottish Liberal Democrats, Nicol Stephen, and the Welsh leader Mike German, are in opposition.

The Liberal Democrats, like the Conservatives, have a presence in Northern Ireland, but do not contest elections there. Instead they support the Alliance party; indeed the Alliance leader David Ford is also a member of the Liberal Democrats.

Federal structures can be problematical. At the 1994 national conference a major contribution to the uncertainties of the debate on decriminalising cannabis stemmed from the fact that the conference of the SLD had already declared itself to be in favour. What sense would voters have made of Liberal Democrats in Scotland favouring decriminalisation but English and Welsh Liberals Democrats opposing it? Realists at party headquarters continue to believe that the structure of power within the federal party has more to do with financial resources than constitutional theories. In addition to the 20 per cent of their subscriptions which headquarters returns to the regions and the states, the parties, SLD included, need headquarters' funding to survive, and in effect that means funding from the English party. The SLD has its own bureaucracy in Edinburgh, the Welsh party and a number of the English regions have offices but none could be run effectively without federal funds. This, together with its strong national profile based in large part on ideological preferences, holds the party together.

Policy-making

Policy-making in the Liberal Democrats represents a rough balance of power between the leadership, the parliamentary party, FPC and the federal conference. FPC exerts the greatest influence since it decides the membership of the working groups, which draft policy proposals, and which papers shall be discussed at conference, plus the content of the election manifesto. The parliamentary party is well represented on FPC, although its influence has been described as largely negative, delaying the development of policies it deems to be potentially electorally damaging.[69] The role in policy formulation of the leader has been enormous, not the least because he chairs FPC. As Duncan Brack explained in respect of Ashdown, he was 'able to stamp his ideas so firmly on the party's policy programme because of the respect and admiration he has enjoyed among party members'.[70] It is no secret, however, that tensions started to grow between the leader and FPC and more so between the leader and conference (the 1994 debate on decriminalisation of cannabis is still the best example). Leaders become impatient with the processes of policy formulation from time to time and the membership becomes wary of the leader's long-term strategy. Ashdown's forging a closer relationship with Labour was closely monitored; Campbell's ditching in 2006 of the party's commitment to a 50 per cent tax band for incomes of over £100,000 caused initial concern. The process of policy-making, however, is inclusive. The policy review embarked on in 1998, for example, established eight representative commissions, with outside experts, to shape a mid-term manifesto that was taken to conference for endorsement. As we have seen, Liberal policy in Scotland and Wales is substantially in the hands of those national parties.

Candidate selection

In Scotland and Wales candidates' committees, which draw up a list of approved candidates for parliamentary and European elections, coordinate procedures for selection and adoption, publish criteria for the assessment of candidates, train them and make rules governing the selection and adoption of candidates. In England it is the regions that operate candidates' committees and provide candidate lists for parliamentary and European elections. A federal joint candidates' committee, chaired by the chief whip and with state representatives, meets at least once a year to oversee the operations at state level. Shortlists must include at least one member of either sex and 'due regard' is required for ethnic representation. Hustings are arranged and every member receives a copy of the shortlist and, if requested, a ballot paper.

Selection procedures designed to secure fairer gender representation, have been reasonably successful: 30 per cent of all Liberal Democrat councillors are women.[71] Although there are no women-only parliamentary shortlists, the party traditionally fielded more women than either of its rivals.[72] In 2005 there were 145 women candidates (23 per cent) of whom 10 were elected. The party has been less successful in terms of ethnicity; although it fielded 42 ethnic minority candidates, none was elected.[73] In 1992 the party candidate in Bethnal Green (London) had been obliged to resign just before the election, because of a 'a high level of racism in the party'.[74] Although untypical this incident represented a potential tension in the nature of community politics. Communities under pressure might well respond in ways that, to outsiders, seem illiberal.

Party finances

Although the financing of political parties has been a perennial issue in Britain,[75] the Liberals and Liberal Democrats have seldom been subjected to much criticism. They have traditionally been more open about donations, perhaps making a virtue out of necessity since they have never received many. They were not much supported by large business interests, wealthy individuals or trade unions. As one *Economist* article contended, 'Liberal Democrats don't really seem to get any donations at all, but many of them [*sic*] come from Liberal clubs all over the country'.[76] A perusal of donations after the election year 1997 showed a number of donations from the Joseph Rowntree Reform Trust and a range of smaller donations totalling some £400,000. Although election expenses for the party do not compare with those of the major parties, in 2005 the party received a donation from the Scottish businessman Michael Brown who, at the time of his donation, was living in Marbella. The donation came from a company that, it later transpired, was not trading at the time in the United Kingdom (indeed it was not trading anywhere; it was fraudulent) so any donation was illegal. The Haydon Phillips inquiry acknowledged that the party accepted the donation in good faith at the time, though the donor was later sentenced to two years in prison. At £2.4 million this donation was ten times bigger than any donation the party had ever received before. It is not surprising that in his evidence to the Haydon Phillips inquiry, Campbell argued for a limited extension of state funding and lower national limits on election expenses.

Party activists

Liberal Democrat activists have traditionally inhabited a paradoxical world in which the party they worked for was unlikely to achieve power nationally and yet offered reasonable prospects locally for power, or power sharing; in fact a number of the present party membership are or have been local councillors.[77] Nevertheless, the theory of instrumental participation (serving one's self-interest or the interest of one's social group or class through political involvement) was hardly appropriate for Liberal activists. Nowadays, however, the party has a higher national profile having shared power through devolution, gained representation in the European Parliament and built a solid local government base. Crucially it might find itself in a pivotal position in Westminster at the next election.

Whiteley, Seyd and Billinghurst have produced a study of Liberal Democrats 'at the grass roots';[78] the authors assure us that although the party represents a merger between two separate parties there are, by now, few observable differences between the two.[79] They are, as a party, almost as old as the Conservatives, with 35 per cent over the age of 65.[80] Women form 47 per cent of party membership. Liberal Democrats are the most highly educated activists among the main parties: 42 per cent are graduates compared to 30 per cent (Labour) and 19 per cent (Conservative). A considerable majority (65 per cent) thinks of themselves as religious, and although they have a distinctive moral attitude that, not surprisingly, could best be summed up as liberal, 73 per cent were in favour of stiffer sentences for lawbreakers and 84 per cent thought a life sentence should mean exactly that. (These were among the strongest opinions expressed.)[81] Party members overwhelmingly thought of the party as being united and as occupying the centre (58 per cent) or left of centre (36 per cent).[82] What distinguishes Liberal Democrats ideologically is a concern with institutional reform and civil liberties and support for Europe.[83] Whiteley et al. concur with the Bennie et al. study of ten years earlier that the Liberal Democrats are very much the party of 'the public sector middle class'. The old Liberal Party was perceived as a party of bearded men and beaded women wearing sandals. The SDP, on the other hand, was characterised as the 'nice people's party' comprising owners of Volvo estate cars who drove sedately. Liberal Democrats today do not correspond remotely to either stereotype. The party exhibits a high level of activism, similar to that of Labour, and fund-raising is an activity which involves and connects party members both with each other and with the party as an institution.

In most respects Liberal Democrats are closer to Labour activists than Conservative ones in terms, for example, of their attitudes towards redistribution of wealth, though they show greater support for the free market. Liberal Democrats are prepared to pay more taxes both to safeguard the environment and to eliminate poverty.[84]

Liberal Democrat voters

The traditional Liberal vote, speaking generally, suffered from a number of disadvantages: it was socially spread, lacking a distinct social base; it was geographically spread, and it was highly volatile, capturing or failing to capture the protest vote – the votes of those disenchanted with the larger parties. The impact of the alliance with the SDP modified this picture only marginally. The Liberal Democrat vote nowadays, however, is not so fragile. As John Curtice tells us it is distinctly higher among the salariat and the better educated.[85] It also has a stronger regional base, having established itself firmly through much of the south-west of England and to a lesser extent in rural Scotland. Moreover its strength has grown at the expense of Labour as well as the Conservatives. Curtice predicted in 1995, on the basis of its regional strength, that the party could lose votes nationally in the 1997 election but still win at least thirty-eight parliamentary seats. He was right.

Curtice found that Liberal Democrat voters were making 'inroads into Labour's traditional ideological territory', identifying with traditional Labour preferences, such as increased public spending. Liberal Democrat voters' attitudes, too, were better measured along a liberal–authoritarian axis rather than the traditional left–right axis: they saw themselves as liberal, not centrist.

However, the party still lacks what Curtice calls social reinforcement. Only 33 per cent (compared with 45 per cent for Labour and 58 per cent for the Conservatives) reported that the person to whom they spoke most often about important matters was a fellow Liberal Democrat. They were not part of a social-political culture. On the other hand Kavanagh and Butler found in 2005 the entire electorate 'more fractured that at any time since...the years immediately following the First World War',[86] so perhaps this traditional disadvantage is becoming less relevant. Nevertheless the party has come to dominate the non-Conservative vote in certain parts of the country, and with its substantial strength in local government its vote is more stable than it used to be. One of the more interesting trends of the 2005 election was the fact that the Liberal Democrats replaced the Conservatives as Labour's main opponent in a number of urban areas. Many of the party's gains came in urban areas previously held by Labour, for example Manchester Withington, Cardiff Central and Birmingham Yardley. The party had already controlled local councils in Liverpool, Sheffield, Newcastle and Stockport. In 2007 it took Hull. In 2005 the party won second place in more than 100 Labour-held seats, making it almost impossible for the Conservatives to win a working majority at a general election. The Liberal Democrats not only were strong in northern cities, but also formed the largest anti-Labour group in Bournemouth, Bristol, Cardiff, Leicester, Norwich, Portsmouth and Southampton.[87] In short we can say that today's Liberal Democrat voters, while socially little changed from Curtice's 'better educated salariat', are ideologically more diverse. The party is able to take votes from Labour as well as from the Conservatives. Support for the party is not classless, Curtice concluded: it is distinctly stronger among the educated middle class.[88] The government's decisions on Iraq and university tuition fees had been powerful recruiters for the Liberal Democrats. Indeed a Sky News poll found that no fewer than one Liberal Democrat voter in four would have voted Labour but for Iraq.[89] Despite stronger foundations the Liberal Democrats can never forget that, as ever, the protest vote is the flakiest vote. They remain, in Polly Toynbee's words 'profoundly conflicted by electoral necessity'.[90]

Conclusions

We have examined the continuities and discontinuities, showing the thread that bound together the ideologies of 'new' Liberalism and social democracy, both at the end of the nineteenth century and towards the end of the twentieth. We considered the formation of the Alliance in some detail; it represented the most important development in British party history since 1931. But we concentrated on the Liberal Democrats and considered their development and the role that they have sought to play in modern British politics. The ten years that coincided with Ashdown's leadership were extraordinarily successful. 'More than any other Liberal leader in living memory,' said *The Times*, 'Mr. Ashdown shaped the party of his time'.[91] When he resigned the party had over 5,400 local councillors, 100,000 members, forty-six MPs and two MEPs. In 2007 it had only 1,973 councillors and something over 70,000 members. On the other hand it had sixty-three MPs and twelve MEPs. Moreover the party has witnessed the securing of some of its most cherished policies: devolution for Scotland and Wales; the prospect (not as distant as it might appear) of regional government for England (indeed a reality as far as London is concerned); proportional representation (for London, European and Scottish and Welsh elections); the incorporation of the European Convention of Human Rights into British law, and freedom of information legislation. 'Labour measures but Liberal Democrat victories', as *The Times* called them.[92] When he resigned as leader Ashdown predicted that the Liberal Democrats would be in national government within ten years.[93] The next general election could make this hope a reality but since 2006 the party has been confronted in the south and especially the south-west of England with a reinvigorated Conservative Party. It could well face a Labour opponent in the north reinvigorated by the leadership of Gordon Brown. In these circumstances the Liberal Democrats would surely advance no further; indeed they would have to fight tooth and nail to hold on to what they have. John Maynard Keynes noted that the Liberals really comprised two 'parties', the Whigs (perfectly sensible Conservatives) and the Radicals (perfectly sensible Labourites). As such the party is susceptible to pressure from the major parties when both claim the 'sensible' centre ground. As Rachel Sylvester has argued, this is precisely the situation in which today's Liberal Democrats find themselves. They must take great care that they 'do not end up looking like the eccentric political fringe'.[94]

The party needs a charismatic, energetic leader; it needs an Ashdown (affectionately known as Action Man). It also needs astute elder statesmen but not, surely, as leader. In a study published in 2003 David Walker suggested that circumstances were more propitious for the Liberal Democrats than ever before.[95] This proposition is dubious today. Nevertheless in the first seven years of the new millennium, the Liberal Democrat Party has looked a more permanent feature of the political landscape than at any time in the previous eighty years. Yet these are increasingly volatile times and permanence is as permanence does. The choice of leader, and the ability of that leader to construct a political strategy that the party will find acceptable, are crucial considerations. Campbell's age was not so much the issue – though he himself sometimes makes it an issue[96] – but his caution was.

When it became clear, in October 2007, that Brown had decided not to hold a general election in the short term, Campbell's position became less tenable, especially following the publication of an ICM poll showing that support for the party had fallen to 14 per cent. In the face of considerable media speculation Campbell decided to resign, precipitating a leadership contest between the party's environment spokesman Chris Huhne and the home affairs spokesman Nick Clegg. With either likely to lead the party for a decade, the stakes were high and under media scrutiny the two-month campaign always had the potential to become abrasive; in fact at one stage it became rancourous with Huhne's team producing a dossier of alleged policy 'flip-flops' entitled 'Calamity Clegg'. [97] The campaign veered from the personally abusive to the downright soporific. As a democratic process it left a great deal to be desired, as a party cohesion building device it was counter productive. In the end Clegg won with the narrowest of margins. He has much to do to mend fences and to sustain the party at its current strength. To make the party a truly key player in the British political system will be a Herculean task.

9   Britain's other parties

In the course of this study we have been concerned with Britain's three major parties, largely because it is principally they who constitute the British party system, but mention has been made here and there of smaller or minority parties. The phrase 'minority party' is in general use, and is convenient as a kind of shorthand term, but we shall not be using it here systematically because it suggests a single category of party about which useful generalisations might be made. In Britain however this would be misleading.

On 16 May 2007 Alex Salmond, leader of the Scottish National Party, a minority party in British terms, became Scotland's First Minister, heading a minority government; indeed the SNP held only 36 per cent of seats. Very few minority parties actually form governments, we might think. But we would be wrong. At Westminster Labour's first government in 1924 was a minority government – it was not even the largest party – and so was its 1929 government. In February 1974 Harold Wilson came to office with a minority. Elsewhere, as Kaare Strom has shown, no fewer than 35 per cent of all governments in fifteen parliamentary democracies since the Second World War were formed by minorities.[1] Indeed the Swedish Social Democrats governed for almost half a century, often as a minority. Strom's influential book on the subject, *Minority Governments and Majority Rule*,[2] captures the essence of his (to British minds) counterintuitive argument about minority parties: with allies, they can justly claim to represent the majority of voters.

In Wales, too, following the One Wales agreement in July 2007, the Welsh National Party also entered government. It formed a coalition with Labour under which its leader Ieuan Wyn Jones became deputy to Labour's Rhodri Morgan as First Minister. This imaginative move means that Wales is managed by a government representing a substantial majority of voters.

By contrast, we know that in United Kingdom elections, no 'majoritarian' government in the past hundred years could actually claim to have represented a majority of voters. On the other hand it would come as something of a surprise if Britain's Official Monster Raving Loony party, for example, were to help form a government (though judging by the number of abstentions in general elections these days, some voters seem to think that they already have!). Some minority parties are more important than others. In short to call a party a minority party is really to say very little about that party and its relationship to power.

There are currently (late 2007) over four hundred political parties registered with the Electoral Commission to fight elections in the United Kingdom, including fifty-eight in Northern Ireland. Apart from the three that have been the focus of our study so far, a further eight parties are represented in the House of Commons, the largest of which is Northern Ireland's Democratic Unionist Party (DUP) with nine MPs; the Scottish National Party and Plaid Cymru (the Party of Wales) work as a single group and between them they also have nine MPs; Sinn Féin has five MPs, though they do not take their seats; the Northern Irish Social Democratic and Labour Party has three, and the Ulster Unionists, the Respect Coalition and the Independent Kidderminster Hospital and Health Concern Party each has one. There are an additional seven parties that are represented either in the devolved institutions or in the European Parliament. The overwhelming majority of parties are represented either only at a local level or not at all. Some are predominantly local or regional. Mebyon Kernow (the Sons of Cornwall), for example, has twenty-three local councillors in Cornwall and contested four parliamentary seats in the 2005 election. The Community Action Party, unknown outside the county of Cheshire, is the second largest party in Wigan. Even the Official Monster Raving Loony party, with its 198 members, furnished Ashburton town council in Devon with its mayor for a time. In May 1990 the party overtook David Owen's Social Democratic Party at the Bootle byelection, a result that caused the SDP to disband. In the following year it won a seat on the East Devon district council. Its minor successes have been no guarantee against schism. Environmentalists broke away to form the Racing Loony Green Giant Party and libertarians later formed the Rock 'n' Roll Loony Party. There are exclusively Scottish, Northern Irish and Welsh parties, such as the East Kilbride Alliance, the Socialist Environmental Alliance and Cymru Rydd; there are far-left parties, including five separate Communist parties, and far-right parties, including the British National Socialist Movement; there are religious parties such as the Christian People's Alliance and the Islamic Party of Britain, and there are 'joke' parties such as the Fancy Dress Party. Many combine categories, like the Liverpool Protestant Party. Some parties are very dependent upon the personality of a charismatic leader and if that leader loses public support, the party might disintegrate. In 2007 the Scottish Socialists lost all their four Holyrood seats due to the recriminations following party leader Tommy Sheridan's court case – which he won.[3] They ceased to be a significant player in Scottish parliamentary politics overnight. The great majority of these parties have one thing in common: they attempt to influence the decisions that affect those they represent. But not all small parties fall into this category. Some parties that contested elections before the law on names was amended, such as the Literal Democrat Party or the Conversative Party, had, we might guess, somewhat more mischievous goals.

What factors do we need to know about 'minority' parties in order to understand how they operate? Whenever Winnie the Pooh's friend Piglet was informed about the arrival of some new animal in the Hundred Acre Wood, he would always ask apprehensively if it were 'one of the larger animals'. He was right to ask. The larger the newcomer, the greater the likely impact upon Piglet's activities. So too with parties. Large parties generally command many more sanctions than smaller ones, though we need to add a rider to this. In the 1970s the SNP's influence was greatly enhanced by the successful extraction of North Sea oil, which the nationalists claimed to be Scottish oil. It goes without saying that North Sea oil was a resource of great economic importance and those who had a plausible, though not uncontested, claim to own it were not to be ignored. Although it was a small party, it was influential enough to cause the Labour government to devote a great deal of legislative time to devolution, and indeed to seeking to create, unsuccessfully in the event, legislative bodies in Scotland and Wales. Devolution, seen as a policy to head off growing support for the SNP's policy of independence, had the support of the strategically placed Liberal Party, but it was the potential threat posed by nationalism to Labour's hegemony in Scotland and Wales, with the ultimate possibility of Scottish independence and control of oil revenues that sensitised Callaghan's government to the importance of the issue of devolution. At its strongest, in 1974, the SNP returned only 11 MPs to Westminster compared to the Labour government's 319 seats. Even relatively small animals can bite.

Moreover, although in the context of the House of Commons the nationalist parties are relatively small, within their own devolved political systems they are not minority parties nowadays but major players. So, too, populist parties like the right-wing British National Party (BNP) might gain considerable influence in certain parts of Britain or certain sections of the electorate as a consequence of large-scale immigration locally. Governments' attention will become focused upon these issues as a consequence. When assessing the influence of 'minority parties', we need to know what potential sanctions they might bring to bear directly upon social cohesion and indirectly upon the electoral prospects of the larger parties.

What follows is an account not of British minority parties as a category, then, but an analysis of the structure, support, ideology and electoral strategies of the more prominent of Britain's 'other' parties. We shall begin with the most prominent, the nationalists.

The nationalist parties

In Britain there are four main nationalist parties in the three Celtic countries. There is no English equivalent, though the British National Party has more support in England than elsewhere. The largest of the nationalist parties is to be found in Scotland.

The Scottish National Party

The SNP, led by Alex Salmond, who currently sits in both the House of Commons and the Holyrood parliament, was founded in 1934, when the former Party of Scotland and Scottish Party merged. Its first parliamentary seat was gained in a by-election in 1945. The seat was lost in the subsequent general election and thereafter the party lost its way. Weakly organised and poorly financed, the party was unable to take advantage of the generally favourable mood towards some form of home rule manifested in the Scottish Convention and the seizing of

Scotland's ancient Stone of Destiny from Westminster Abbey in 1950.[4] In fact there was no other victory until 1967, when the safe Labour seat of Hamilton was taken in another by-election. The aftershock of this astonishing victory was a contributing factor leading to the establishment of the Kilbrandon Commission, which considered the governance of the whole United Kingdom and opened the possibility of constitutional change. SNP electoral gains in 1974 were achieved with the support of something like one-third of the Scottish electorate and, as we have seen, the Labour government was moved to seek reform. However, with the defeat of Labour's attempts at modest measures of devolution for Scotland and Wales in 1979 and the advent of a Thatcher government opposed to constitutional change,[5] SNP fortunes declined. Although the party was able to argue that the radical policies of the Thatcher government had not been mandated by Scottish voters, the party lost support. When in the general election of 1993 Alex Salmond claimed independence as his goal – 'free in '93' – the party performed badly, returning only three MPs; it was taunted by its Labour opponents – not free in '93 but three in '93. But that taunt was a sigh of relief, for under Salmond's leadership the party had achieved the status of posing a genuine threat to Labour. In his history of the party, Peter Lynch refers to this period as 'the search for credibility'.[6] It was successful and was followed by a process of structural and ideological modernisation under Salmond. To general surprise, however, Salmond resigned as party leader in 2000;[7] his replacement, the 36-year-old John Swinney, was unable to prevent the party continuing to haemorrhage support. Nevertheless the party had consistently polled well in Scottish regional and local elections, for example winning 181 seats in the local elections of 1995 on 26 per cent of the vote, so that when the first election for the new Scottish parliament was held in 1999, it was no surprise that the SNP became the official opposition to the Labour–Liberal Democrat coalition: it won 29 per cent of the vote and thirty-five seats. Its position deteriorated in 2003 – only twenty-seven seats – but it was still the official party of opposition and, significantly, the main beneficiary of any disillusion with the governing coalition. And disillusion with the governing coalition there was, though not as great as the disenchantment with Blair's Labour government in Westminster. So in 2007 the SNP won 33 per cent of the votes and forty-seven seats, becoming the largest party. With the support of the two Green MSPs, Alex Salmond became First Minister and leader of a minority government. Labour's hegemonic control of Scottish politics, a *sine qua non* before 2007, had been broken.

The SNP's most distinctive policy has always been independence. But how to implement such a policy? With a Scottish parliament sitting at Holyrood, the answer is to hold a referendum in Scotland empowering the Scottish Executive (renamed by First Minister Salmand as the Scottish government) to enter into negotiations with the government at Westminster to repeal the Act of Union of 1707, thereby making Scotland an independent state once again. Most surveys of Scottish opinion on the matter show a majority against independence, however, and all of Scotland's other major parties are opposed to the idea of a referendum. Perhaps the SNP Executive will concentrate on other policies, hoping to establish the party as a competent party of government and thereby strengthen support for independence indirectly. Writing in 2002, Lynch referred to 'independence by stealth' and envisaged the enlargement of Holyrood's current power to vary taxes by 3 per cent into full-blown fiscal autonomy.[8] Indeed there is wide support among the other parties for such a development, and not merely among the other parties: the Scottish business community too is showing greater interest in such a possibility. The problem here, as Lynch points out, is that such policies, if they led finally to independence, might take ten years or more to unfold. There are those within the SNP who would not be prepared to wait so long and would strongly urge the party leadership to be more precipitate.[9] Gradualism and fundamentalism have always vied for dominance in SNP thinking and hitherto Salmond's great skill has been in managing both factions. But Salmond is not going to lead the party forever. In the meantime the party is in office, though perhaps not unambiguously in power. This experiment with minority government constitutes a genuine innovation in modes of governance in Britain as a whole and should be watched with the greatest of interest.

The SNP claims to be a European social democratic party, to the left of centre. It is committed to nuclear disarmament, redistribution of wealth through progressive taxation, free university education and membership of the European Monetary Union. However, the SNP has stated its opposition to NATO though it would continue its membership of the Commonwealth and, despite a republican element, has no plan to abolish the monarchy. If at the heart of SNP thinking lies a belief in the value of 'Scottishness', it is not entirely clear what is being valued. There are those who see Scottishness embodied in the Gaelic traditions of the Highlands and Islands and those who think the opposite: that the Gaelic tradition is essentially Irish and foreign, bound up with Roman Catholicism. There are those within and outwith the SNP who see Scottishness as an ethnic characteristic that *ipso facto* excludes the English, who should be persuaded to go back to England. The SNP leadership has sought to remain aloof from these struggles to define identity, to distance itself from those few who have sought to persuade incomers to leave through violence, and to champion instead an inclusive civic Scottishness that seeks above all that those who live in Scotland should govern themselves. Whether such comparative generosity could be sustained should an independent Scotland find itself at odds with its vastly larger neighbour is impossible to calculate.

Like most British parties, the SNP is built upon branch organisations and since the party was actually built up from the grass roots, they tend to guard their branch autonomy jealously. As the party grew so these branches formed constituency associations; these in turn form regional associations of which there are now eight. The party has an active youth and student movement and a trade union group. At the centre the party is controlled by the National Executive Committee (NEC), which represents conference, parliamentarians and local councillors, the trade unions and youth and student movements. It meets monthly, though it has various subcommittees that may meet more regularly. The structure is overseen by a representative body known as the National Council, larger than the NEC (with some 300 members), which meets four times a year. Policy is the formal responsibility of the National Assembly, which runs a series of ongoing policy committees. The party meets in conference once a year. In the 1990s the party established a Shadow Cabinet responsible in the first instance to the leader, thereby giving a much firmer sense of direction to policy development.[10] Around this time the financial stability of the party was assured by a series of very successful fund-raising activities. In 1994 Salmond felt able to suggest the appointment of a chief executive whose task was to oversee electoral strategy and to act as a media and communications expert – a 'spin doctor'. This appointment strengthened Salmond's position as leader since the appointee was an ally. All in all, the strength of the party organisation has always been a factor of its electoral fortunes.[11] It is fitting to conclude that in 2007 the party had over 12,000 members and was financially stable, and was thus in a good position to optimise its own popularity and the Labour Party's discomfiture. Following the election of that year, in addition to its forty-seven MSPs (Members of the Scottish Parliament), the party had six MPs (who cooperate at Westminster with Plaid Cymru) and two MEPs (who, again along with Plaid Cymru) belong to the European Free Alliance.

Plaid Cymru

The Party of Wales has much in common with the nationalists north of the English border. Founded in 1925, Plaid Cymru has chartered a similarly stormy passage. It too was formed from the amalgamation of two older groups, the Welsh Home Rule Army and the Welsh Movement. There are, however, significant differences between the two parties and the core of the difference is located in the status of the Welsh language. The primacy of Welsh, with the aim of making it Wales' only official language, took precedence historically;[12] this was in part because Home Rule for Wales had been espoused earlier by both the Labour and Liberal parties. By the 1930s the aims of self-government and independent representation at the League of Nations had become party objectives. It is nevertheless true to say that Plaid's support was largely confined to the Welsh-speaking middle classes of North Wales. In 1936 two Plaid members set fire to a new Royal Air Force base in Gwynedd. Their subsequent rough treatment in the courts gave the party a significant boost, however, though at the time of the Second World War membership was less than 2,000. Butt Phillip has pointed out that in these early days, Plaid was largely conservative in personnel and politics and the suspicion that some of its leaders were favourably disposed to the right-wing regimes of Europe was given some credence by Plaid's wartime pacifism and proclaimed neutrality.

Plaid contested seven seats in the 1945 election, including some in English-speaking South Wales. The party had no success. By 1959 Plaid was able to contest most Welsh seats, however, and the decision taken at Westminster in 1957 to flood a Welsh valley to provide extra water for Liverpool, a decision which no Welsh MP supported, strengthened its hand. Remarkably in 1966 Plaid won a stunning by-election victory from Labour and nearly followed it up with two others, on massive anti-Labour swings. In the 1970 general election the party contested every Welsh seat, and in the October election in 1974 three Plaid Cymru MPs were elected. However, with the defeat in Westminster of the devolution bills, Plaid, like the SNP, went into decline, and – again, like the SNP – it repositioned itself ideologically at this time, to become left of centre. In 1984 a signal victory was gained when S4C, a Welsh language television channel, was established. By now Plaid had shown itself able to win seats not only from Labour but also from the Conservatives and Liberal Democrats, so that in 1999, following the establishment of the Welsh Assembly, Plaid Cymru became the official party of opposition, winning seventeen seats to Labour's twenty-nine, including some in Labour's South Wales heartland.

If Plaid appeared to have found its place in the sun in 1999, the 2003 election result was decidedly chillier, for though it retained its position as the largest party of opposition, the party lost five seats, among which were the previous gains from Labour. Worse followed in the local elections a year later and the general election of 2005, when the party was reduced to three seats. In the Assembly elections of 2007 Plaid managed to win back three seats. As the largest opposition party, it made strenuous if finally unsuccessful attempts to form a three-party governing coalition involving the Liberal Democrats and Conservatives. With the Labour majority unable to govern alone, the possibility of a coalition between the two former enemies, One Wales, was forged. Like the SNP, Plaid is currently about to enter government for the first time. In short, Plaid's history since devolution has followed a similar trajectory to that of the SNP.

Plaid's organisational structure emphasises the popular participation that characterised the social movements from which the party emerged: like the SNP it was a 'bottom-up' party.[13] At the base is the branch and above the branch the constituency; these in turn send representatives to the National Council and have a major part to play in candidate selection. The annual conference is formally responsible for policy but the National Council is in reality the prime policy-maker. Party strategy is the responsibility of the National Executive Committee. Although the party president, until recently, was neither an MP nor a Member of the Assembly (AM), the party leader in the Assembly was designated as overall leader in 2006 and the incumbent president, a folk singer, became head of the party's voluntary wing. Plaid is not as financially stable as the SNP, its income being sourced largely from the membership and from public funding (known as Short money) but because its structure is based on grass-roots activism, it just about manages to live within budget. It has a national office in Cardiff and eight regional offices.

What distinguishes Plaid from the SNP is its firm cultural base. Although now a bilingual party, the defence of Welsh heritage and culture and especially language has shaped its ideology.[14] But the party knows that it has to flourish as a truly national party and not just a cultural pressure group if it hopes to win power in Cardiff: it must succeed in English-speaking, industrial South Wales. There are patriotic Welsh people who fear the Plaid's emphasis on ethnicity and who see Labour as the true vehicle for their Welshness.[15] Significantly Plaid is committed to the success of the Welsh Assembly and as Van Morgan has shown, this stance has ramifications, urging the party towards 'a greater willingness to engage in cross-party collaborative ventures, and has deflected attention from fundamental debates over Wales' place in the UK constitution'.[16] We easily recognise the difficulty of winning over traditional Labour supporters to some form of independence, but this is only half of the problem: less than one-third of Plaid's own members have traditionally supported independence.[17] No wonder Plaid's principal aim of 'full national status within the EU' remains a puzzle. In coalition Plaid will urge its larger partner to press for wider powers for the Welsh Assembly and no doubt either that they will be pushing at an open door.

Sinn Féin

The name Sinn Féin is said to originate from a local newspaper from County Meath and translates as 'We Ourselves'. The party was established in 1905 (though like many 'facts' about the party there is some dispute about this date) and although in the early years it was not revolutionary or even republican, it became both following the Easter Rising in 1916 and Britain's later attempt to impose conscription upon Ireland. The party became indissolubly associated with the movement for Irish independence. At the general election of 1918 Sinn Féin won seventy-three of Ireland's hundred and six seats, though not always democratically. In January 1919 some thirty of these MPs met in Dublin's Mansion House and proclaimed themselves to be the government of Ireland. Sinn Féin split over the Anglo-Irish Treaty of 1921 which ended the War of Independence and fought on both sides in the ensuing Civil War. There were at least three later splits leaving Sinn Féin marginalised in Ireland. What brought it back to prominence was the outbreak of the Troubles in Northern Ireland in the late 1960s and the formation of the Provisional Irish Republican Army (PIRA).[18] Under the leadership of Gerry Adams in the North, Sinn Féin's influence has been the consequence of its perceived status as the political wing of the PIRA. However, even after its legalisation by the British government, Sinn Féin never attracted the majority of Catholic voters, who did not support its campaign of violence. The newly proclaimed strategy of 'ballot paper in one hand and Armalite in the other' proved unconvincing to the majority of Catholics and anathema to loyalists.[19] However, when the party committed itself to constitutional politics and began slowly to disarm, so support grew; in 2001 Sinn Féin became the largest nationalist party in the North. The following year it took five seats in the Dáil Éireann. Following the 2003 Assembly elections Sinn Féin entered a power-sharing executive with the Ulster Unionists, then the largest loyalist party, and although this arrangement broke down amid ferocious recriminations, in 2007 a new power-sharing executive came into being, with Ian Paisley, the leader of the Democratic Unionist Party, as First Minister and Martin McGuiness of Sinn Féin as his deputy. Such an arrangement would have been unthinkable only a few years earlier.[20]

Sinn Féin's organisational structure encompasses the whole of the island of Ireland and its basis is the branch. Branches are organised into district and regional bodies. An eight-person standing committee nominated by the national executive is responsible for the day-to-day running of the party. The larger national executive is representative of the party structure (and must include at least 30 per cent women) and meets monthly. Policy is formally the responsibility of the annual national conference.

Sinn Féin's most distinctive policy is a united Ireland and nearly all of its policies have this all-Ireland context, so for example they campaign for free breast screening for women over 40 in both the Republic and the North. They campaign for all Northern Ireland's eighteen MPs to be allowed to sit in the Dáil Éireann as full members. As we have seen, the party contests elections in the Republic, though in 2007 its expectations to increase its numbers substantially (from five to twelve) so as to make it a possible contender for coalition were thwarted: Sinn Féin gained only one additional seat and so has five out of a hundred and sixty-six. Nevertheless the party also holds twenty-eight seats in the Northern Irish Assembly and shares power with the majority Democratic Unionist Party and has five Westminster seats. Unlike the other nationalist parties, Sinn Féin has no desire to contribute to the politics of the United Kingdom, but remains very influential in one part of the UK.

Democratic Unionist Party

There would be many members of the DUP who would disclaim the title of nationalist party because, like mainstream British parties, they are not motivated to change the constitution: quite the reverse in fact. Nevertheless their unionism is as much the core of their ideology as nationalism is to Sinn Féin. Formed by Ian Paisley in 1971, the DUP is now the largest of the unionist parties. It has the well-earned reputation of being the strongest opponent of concessions to Sinn Féin and in fact the party never endorsed the so-called Good Friday Accord of 1998, being against the early release of terrorist prisoners and the holding of office by Sinn Féin members while the IRA had not decommissioned its arms. Indeed it had earlier been opposed to the establishment of a power-sharing executive following the Sunningdale Agreement in 1974. More recently, in 2006, the party had published a four-page letter in the *Belfast Telegraph* setting out its views on power sharing and seeking consultation with the membership and the general public. As a consequence Paisley made it clear that his party would be prepared to consider sharing power with Sinn Féin if the latter endorsed the newly re-established police force and in May 2007 the party agreed finally to power sharing. The Northern Irish Assembly at Belfast was duly reconstituted and devolved government began again.

The DUP is predominantly a right-wing populist party and the party structure follows the pattern we have observed with other parties. It is managed by a central executive committee, with constituency representation, and the executive elects party officers. The 2,912 party members do not meet in conference every year. It is a feature of successful smaller parties that the leader's role is disproportionately important, but Paisley's is particularly iconic. It was Paisley's conversion to power sharing that brought the party into the executive, against the original opposition of a number of leading members, including some MPs. However, an overwhelming majority of the party executive eventually voted in support of restoring devolution, though the party's sole MEP resigned, as did seven local councillors. In short Paisley was able to take his party where probably nobody else could have taken them. Structural and even ideological considerations become secondary in the face of such a charismatic leader. Nevertheless the ideology of sustaining Northern Ireland's position in the United Kingdom covers a gamut of intensity, and issues arising from this ideology are likely to exacerbate fissiparous tendencies within the party. After all, the nationalists' goal of Irish unification is likely to drive their policies in government, and such a goal will remain anathema to many DUP members and supporters. To pursue such a policy through the ballot rather than the Armalite is hugely preferable, but it will not be lost on the DUP that those with whom it shares power wish to demolish the political system that they are currently helping to manage.

Following the 2005 general election the DUP has nine MPs; three former members sit as peers, though not under their old party label. It currently has 36 Assembly members (of 108); its sole MEP defected without resigning in 2004 and now sits as an independent, and the DUP is the largest party of local government in Northern Ireland with 182 councillors.

Others

Before leaving the nationalist parties, reference must be made to the Social Democratic and Labour Party (SDLP) and the Alliance Party, both Northern Irish parties. The SDLP, founded in 1970 under the influential John Hume, was for a number of years the main constitutional expression of nationalism. But as its name implies, it was never solely a nationalist party but also a democratic socialist party with ties to the British Labour Party. As nationalist voters grew more confident of Sinn Féin's democratic credentials so the SDLP influence declined. Nevertheless under Mark Durkan the party has three MPs and sixteen Members of the Legislative Assembly (MLAs) in Stormont: it is not a party to be ignored. The Alliance Party, also founded in 1970, is Northern Ireland's only non-sectarian party. It has strong ties with the British Liberal Democrats and has a similar ideological disposition. It is a pro-union party so long as that is the majority view. Although it has never won a Westminster seat, it currently has six MLAs and some forty councillors. Although the SDLP is in part a nationalist party, the Alliance is certainly not, but they are discussed here simply because of the context in which they operate.

Minority parties

We now turn to those other parties that might less ambiguously be referred to as minor parties, though we shall bear in mind our original caveat and not expect them all to be exactly the same kind of animal.

The Green Party

An article in *The Ecologist* magazine entitled 'Blueprint for survival' prompted a group in Coventry to form a movement called People in 1973. They were apprehensive about calling themselves a political party, however, and put their efforts into engaging with other environmental movements. Nevertheless when the February election came in 1974 they laid their misgivings to one side and fielded seven candidates, taking almost 5,000 votes. Despite attracting more members following the election, the October election of 1974 saw votes lost and members resigning. However, from the teething problems a new party, the Ecology Party, emerged in 1975; two years later Jonathon Porritt came onto the national executive and managed to give the party greater national visibility. In 1979 the party fielded fifty-three candidates in the general election, thereby entitling it to radio and television broadcasts. The party gained 40,000 votes but more importantly its membership increased tenfold to 5,000. With this increase came serious divisions between the traditionalists and those who advocated forms of non-violent direct action. The latter made their presence felt in a decentralist campaign that saw the executive stripped of some of its powers and a decision taken not to appoint a leader.

In 1985 the Ecology Party became the Green Party, but the tensions remained and attempts by the traditionalists to streamline party organisation were vetoed by the fundamentalists. Nevertheless the prominence of environmental issues, especially following the Chernobyl nuclear disaster in 1986, gave the party an opportunity to project itself, which it took eagerly. In the European elections of 1989 the Green Party received 15 per cent of the national vote and overtook the Liberal Democrats as the third party. As before, however, the party did not handle its growth well, and the schism between the traditionalists and the direct action groups remained acute. Moreover one of its spokesmen, a well-known BBC sports reporter named David Icke, brought disrepute on the party by proclaiming himself the son of God and predicting Armageddon. If this was largely an embarrassing distraction from the real issues, the schism seemed to ruin any effort to strengthen party organisation, causing leading members including Porritt to leave the party.

Although the party was originally founded to promote a keener appreciation of environmental issues, these are seen in a broad perspective. The party supports organic farming and opposes all forms of intensive farming and genetically modified foods. It opposes live exports, genetic manipulation and blood sports. Less well known perhaps is its opposition to circuses and zoos. The party is in favour of renewable energy resources and against nuclear energy: it has a target of reducing carbon emissions by 50 per cent before 2050. The party has what it thinks of as a progressive attitude to drugs, calling for the legalisation of all recreational drugs. Its crusade for sustainable economic development constitutes a rejection of the modern mass consumption lifestyle and a championing of small-scale, local economic units, such as community banks. The Greens are in favour of replacing the benefits system with a 'citizen's income' payable to all and funded by an increase in the higher rates of income tax. They seek to encourage small businesses through a progressive system of corporation tax and strongly support a 'polluter pays' eco-tax. The party also supports the renationalisation of basic service industries. All in all the party seeks to build a fair, prosperous society based on a zero-growth economy.

The Green Party is concerned, too, with issues of governance, seeking to reform the House of Lords, abolish the prerogative powers of the monarch, reform the electoral system and create regional and stronger local government. Its general outlook on issues of security is libertarian – for example it is opposed to identity cards. In foreign policy matters the party's position appears to be pacifist, or certainly non-interventionist.

As we have seen organisational issues have littered the history of the party. It has no leader believing that leadership is of its nature hierarchical and disempowers ordinary members; policy is made at a biannual conference. However, the party has an executive, elected by the membership. The executive sets up committees and draws up a panel of people who speak on behalf of the party for each policy area. In addition the executive contains a male and female principal speaker. The party consists of regional parties (one of which is the Welsh region, which has a 'leader', though the party is adamant that this leader has no 'powers of leadership') that, in turn, elect a representative regional council (with male and female co-chairs) that oversees the organisational structure and organises the conferences, where policy is made. The party has a youth movement, which is active in universities and colleges. It also has a lesbian, gay, bisexual and transgender group, a trade union group and a new anti-capitalist and eco-socialist group known as Green Left. A group known as Green 2000, which aimed to put the party into power by the millennium, was disbanded and so far no Green 3000 group has replaced it.

With the advent of devolution, especially coupled with electoral reform (for the new institutions and for Europe), greater opportunities presented themselves. In 1999 two Greens were elected to the European Parliament and they held on to their seats in 2004. Three Greens were elected to the new London Assembly, though one seat was subsequently lost. None was elected to the Welsh Assembly. The party has 111 councillors in England and Wales, with significant representation in several cities and indeed forms part of the governing coalition in three cities. Their candidate for Brighton Pavilion took 22 per cent of the vote in the 2005 general election. Overall the party fought 202 seats, securing an average of 3.4 per cent of the vote.[21] In addition the Green Party has one peer. The party has just over 7,000 members. In late 2007 the party returned to the issue of leadership and held a referendum in which fewer than half of members voted. Of these 73 per cent favoured the establishment of a leader and deputy leader.[22]

The Scottish Green Party separated from the mother party in 1990 and has since acted independently. In the 2003 Scottish elections it secured no fewer than seven MSPs but lost five of these in 2007. Nevertheless the party struck a working deal with the SNP (it has always favoured a referendum on independence) through which it will generally support the SNP and in turn will be given a committee chair in Holyrood and an early bill on 'climate change'. A study of Scottish Green membership, which these days stands at some 900, showed party members to be very largely middle class and well educated.[23] Not surprisingly therefore its current eight councillors represent the leafier parts of Edinburgh and Glasgow.

In Northern Ireland there is a small Green Party, which contested thirteen seats in the Assembly elections in 2007. Although none was successfully elected, one member managed to abseil down the Europa Hotel in Belfast.

The United Kingdom Independence Party

Commonly known as UKIP, the main *raison d'être* of the party is to restore self-government to the United Kingdom by seeking its withdrawal from the European Union. The party was founded in 1993 and immediately attracted interest from a number of Conservative Eurosceptics, for these were the days of John Major's attempt to ratify the Maastricht Treaty. Although the party mounted a challenge in the 1997 general election, its thunder was stolen by James Goldsmith's lavishly funded Referendum Party. However, Goldsmith died shortly afterwards and his party disintegrated. In the 1999 European elections UKIP won 7 per cent of the vote and three seats. But squabbles within the leadership prevented the party from attaining the higher profile its results might otherwise have generated. UKIP won no seats in the 2001 general election (securing an average 2.1 per cent of the vote) and none in the Scottish and Welsh elections in 2003. More leadership squabbles were to follow when the former television chat show host and then MEP Robert Kilroy-Silk made a bid for the leadership. Having been thwarted he resigned the UKIP whip at Brussels and then resigned from the party. As we shall see, he founded his own party, taking two UKIP London Assembly members with him. UKIP has since been dogged by financial problems and is currently facing a full financial review by the Electoral Commission. It is also considering changing its name to Independence.

In addition to its major policy of EU withdrawal, the party favours the abolition of the Scottish parliament and the Welsh and Northern Irish assemblies. It is opposed to identity cards and strongly in favour of nuclear energy and believes that the government should be investing into technologies that would replace fossil fuels. UKIP is also opposed to compulsory metrication. There can be no doubt, however, that withdrawal from the EU is the policy that attracts the party's supporters.

In the 2004 European elections UKIP took 16.8 per cent of the national vote (more than the Liberal Democrats), winning no fewer than 12 seats. In Brussels UKIP members sit in the Independence and Democracy group of 37, which is opposed to a European constitution and further measures of integration. It is ironic that UKIP's only significant successes have come in elections for an institution (the European parliament) that it wishes to leave. In the general election of 2005 the party fielded 495 candidates, an increase of 67 on 2001, and pushed its average share of the vote from 2.1 per cent to 2.8 per cent. Some have argued that UKIP is really a pressure group on the fringe of the Conservative Party whose real task is to persuade the Conservatives towards a policy of withdrawal from Europe and the party's electoral performance suggests that 'where UKIP does best, the Conservatives suffer the most'.[24] In early 2007 party leader Roger Farage wrote to every MP announcing that his party would not oppose any MP who signed up to the 'Better Off Out' Campaign, a clear gesture to sympathetic Tories.[25] Conservative leader David Cameron, himself a Eurosceptic, responded by describing UKIP members in a radio programme as 'fruitcakes, loonies and closet racists'. If it were to attract sufficient votes in British elections, it could conceivably pose a threat to the Conservative Party that might push the Conservatives into an even stronger

Euroscepticism. However, in the 2005 general election, it won only just over 2.4 per cent of the national vote and no seats, and posed no threat to anybody.

Like other parties, UKIP has a national executive that runs the party and organises annual conferences open to all members. The conference is nominally responsible for making policy, though the executive will develop such policies and has a series of committees to make this possible. The leader is chosen by a postal ballot of all members and has a Cabinet to offer advice. In 2006 the party had some 17,000 members. A major setback occurred in 2005, however, when their largest donor transferred his allegiance back to the Conservative Party.[26]

Currently UKIP has no representatives at Westminster, Holyrood or Cardiff. It has two peers and some thirty local councillors, but its two London Assembly members left the party. One of its twelve MEPs had the whip withdrawn in 2004, having been charged with fraud, and another was suspended in 2007 when he too came under investigation for fraud. A third, Kilroy Silk, resigned the whip.

Veritas

When in January 2005 Kilroy-Silk resigned from UKIP on his failure to mount a successful challenge for the leadership, he decided to form a different kind of political party, one that was 'honest, open and straight', one that would avoid 'lies and spin'. Hence the name Veritas, which as all potential voters would surely know, is the Latin for truth. Some 1,000 members joined the party, which quickly established a national executive with subcommittees and produced a constitution. The party's primary policy was opposition to immigration but Kilroy Silk was also in favour of a flat rate of taxation. Critics saw Veritas as little more than an embodiment of Kilroy-Silk's self-esteem and dubbed it Vanitas; its robustness was soon to be put to the test in the forthcoming general election. Sixty candidates were fielded and all but Kilroy-Silk lost their deposits. Fighting the Derbyshire constituency of Erewash, Kilroy-Silk won 5.8 per cent of the votes. Subsequently a Veritas Members Association was formed to challenge the leadership but the leader resigned;[27] a leadership election was fought in which only 22 per cent of the membership voted. Resignations came thick and fast and new parties were formed. In the local elections of 2006 the party put up four candidates, two each in Hull and Bolton: they averaged 98 votes each. Perhaps these events go to prove the old saw that the only place to find the truth is in wine.

British National Party

Founded in 1980 by a former chairman of the National Front (NF), the British National Party (BNP) announced itself with an inaugural march in London and in the next general election in 1983 it sponsored enough candidates to gain the right to a party political broadcast. Less overtly racist than the NF, the only obvious difference between the two, so the leader claimed, was that the BNP would bar homosexuals from office.[28] In the election the BNP candidates did less well than the NF had done in 1979 and financial difficulties thereafter restricted the party to putting up only two candidates. In 1993 however the party secured its first local electoral victory when, in a by-election, it took a ward in London's Tower Hamlets,[29] though it was lost at the subsequent election. In 1999 Nick Griffin became party leader and he strove to make the party's image less trenchant, in fact to adopt the kind of policies that had given right-wing nationalist parties in Europe significant electoral success; the party's fortunes began to improve. In local elections in 2002 for example, BNP gained three seats in Burnley. This comparative success brought closer scrutiny from the media. In 2004 a BBC documentary *The Secret Agent* showed footage of party meetings taken by an infiltrated filmmaker.[30] The footage contained examples of what appeared to be incitement to racial hatred, though in a subsequent court case Griffin and a co-defendant were cleared on all counts. In the meantime Barclays Bank had frozen the party's accounts. In the general election of 2005 the party fought 119 constituencies, 86 more than in 2001, and secured an average of 4.3 per cent, up from the previous 3.9 per cent. In 2006 a survey undertaken by the Rowntree Trust suggested that no fewer than one in four voters would consider voting BNP in those areas of high immigration where the party had concentrated its efforts. As a consequence of publicity arising from these findings, support for the BNP had risen to 7 per cent. In the ensuing local elections of 2006 the party won thirty-three seats, giving it a total of fifty-two councillors and was placed second in a further seventy, more than doubling its previous representation. Its greatest success was in Barking and Dagenham, where it won eleven of the thirteen seats it contested. Later in the year the *Guardian* published an exposé of BNP 'techniques of secrecy and deception' in order to conceal its real intentions.[31] More disturbing even was the disclosure that the membership had grown to include many professionals. For example one member was a prominent ballerina with the English National Ballet.

The substantial growth of immigration since the enlarging of the EU, fuelled by the terrorist threat posed principally by Islamist extremists, was winning increased support for the BNP from those who believed that the mainstream parties had failed to protect their interests.[32] However, the BNP is not a single-issue party: it would withdraw Britain from the EU; it supports capital punishment for paedophiles, terrorists and murderers whose guilt is beyond doubt; it would fund mothers to stay at home to bring up their children; it would establish a system of workers' cooperatives; it would reintroduce national military service and permit all those who had completed their service to take home their rifle, with ammunition; finally, and perhaps counterintuitively, it favours organic farming.[33] The party is currently under investigation over its funding techniques by the Electoral Commission.

Their comparative successes in local elections in England have not been matched either by comparable successes in Scotland and Wales (they have one councillor in Wales – a defecting independent – and none in Scotland, and no seats in Scottish parliamentary or Welsh Assembly elections) or in general elections. Although the party, and some of its critics, thought that a victory in the European elections was a possibility, it did not materialise.[34]

The BNP structure is based upon the twelve European electoral regions but opposition from anti-racist and anti-fascist groups makes it difficult to organise in the normal way. The party has struggled to organise annual conferences because of determined opposition from protestors, though two token conferences have taken place in Blackpool in recent years. It has proved difficult to get its material printed commercially and acquired its own press before the 2005 elections. A national advisory council is nominally responsible for overseeing the party's policy and administration, though the chairman has the last word in respect of policy. He works through an executive of fifteen.[35]

Respect – The Unity Coalition

Respect is inescapably associated in the public mind with the charismatic and enigmatic George Galloway, though he is not officially its leader,[36] nor its founder.[37] The party was formed in January 2004 in London and most commentators have seen the party as a one-issue party, opposition to the Iraq war, but in fact the party has a broadly based socialist agenda, and it includes among its supporters the film director Ken Loach and the playwright and Nobel laureate Harold Pinter. It has a current membership of nearly 6,000. The party claims the support of a number of left-wing groups, including two of Britain's Communist parties. Although it nominates a leader, the party is formally run by a national council, elected by conference. The party sought to challenge the Blair government in the London and European elections of 2004. In London the party did well in City and East London, where it polled over 13 per cent and gained third place. In the European elections it polled 1.7 per cent nationally, its best result being in London, where it polled 4.8 per cent. Like the BNP, Respect won its first council ward at a by-election in Tower Hamlets. In the 2005 general election Respect ran twenty-six candidates and secured its first parliamentary success when George Galloway won Bethnal Green and Bow. It came second in nearby East Ham and West Ham and also in Birmingham Sparkbrook. Overall its twenty-six candidates secured an average 6.8 per cent of the vote. In the local elections of 2006 Respect won twelve wards in Tower Hamlets, and three other wards. Although there can be little doubt that the party fared best in areas with a high Muslim population where animosity to the Iraq war would be strongest, this was by no means always the case. Nevertheless criticism has been made of Respect, in particular of Galloway himself, for pandering to Muslim prejudices.[38] In the 2007 local elections only three of forty-eight candidates were successful, though a number of others achieved second place. Respect did not contest the Scottish or Welsh elections, though Galloway has suggested that he might not defend his East London seat, and has also spoken of moving back to Scotland and contesting a Holyrood seat.[39]

Respect is too young and volatile a party to encourage optimism in its future. Its agenda brings many diverse interests into one camp and what holds them together at the moment is the larger than life personality of George Galloway. Indeed, towards the end of 2007 serious fissures appeared between the hard left and Galloway's supporters. A BBC report from November 17th 2007 told of one faction changing the locks of the party's East London headquarters to prevent their opponents entering. In that month the party's factions held not one conference but two competing conferences. In short Respect has become a fractious coalition with little sign of unity.

Conclusions

These, then, are some of the more significant of Britain's other parties. Although I said at the outset that they did not form a single category about which useful generalisations could be made, it seems clear that for many, though not the nationalist parties, it is the perceived failures of the major parties that allows them to pose as champions of a neglected community or interest. In Kavanagh and Butler's words, they 'represent distinctive strands of opinion that the traditional parties are unable adequately to represent'.[40] The strength and influence of these other parties will tend to ebb and flow according to the way the major parties respond. In a way the short-term success of a smaller party is likely to be signalled by its long-term failure, especially where the party is single-issue rather than broadly ideological. To take the example of environmental politics, if Green successes stimulate the major parties to give more attention to environmental policies, support for the Greens is likely to fall. If the government takes steps more actively to control immigration, and to make more affordable housing available, support for the BNP is likely to fall.[41] Put simply then, the success of smaller parties is likely to be measured by their demise. The prospect of any government bringing about the ultimate demise of the Official Monster Raving Loony party by enacting its major policy, to abolish Mondays, is probably less likely. And we have to remember Piglet's question with which we began this chapter. Are these animals large enough to give the major parties, or us the citizens, cause for concern? The overt populism and scarcely covert racialism of the BNP is generally perceived to be a threat to orthodox constitutional politics. The party's policies are extreme. For their part the nationalist parties have changed the political landscape of the Celtic nations of Britain, but the others (including BNP) collectively totalled 8.5 per cent of the votes cast in 2005. In Britain today by far the most common form of protest against the major parties is not to vote at all: non-voters constituted 30.8 per cent of the electorate in 2005,[42] and this in itself is surely a greater cause for concern.[43] We should bear in mind that all political parties contesting more than 50 seats at a general election have a right to present a party political broadcast on all terrestrial TV channels and the conditions under which they do so are governed by the Communications Act 2003. The four nations of the United Kingdom are treated separately except for general elections. They gain access to broadcasting if they contest more than one sixth of seats. There are, however, regulations regarding the content of such broadcasts in respect of 'taste and decency', litigious content. In the 1997 general election a BNP broadcast on Channel 4 was not transmitted because the party and the broadcaster were unable to reach agreement on content in time.

Among the many small parties that we have not had space to discuss, one at least merits a mention. In the electoral register for 2006 it recorded zero for its political activities for the previous year. Its total expenditure for the year had constituted the payment of £25 to the Electoral Commission for its registration fee. The party's income and assets were assessed at zero and it had a membership of two. Suitably enough that party was the End is Nigh Party.

10 The British party system – fit for purpose?

'Do you mean to say that the story has a moral?' said the Water Rat.

'Certainly,' said the Linnet.

'Well, really,' exclaimed the Water Rat in a very cross manner. 'I think you should have told me that before you began. If you had done I certainly should not have listened to you. In fact I should have said – "Pooh!"'

(Oscar Wilde, *The Devoted Friend*)

Let me come clean: it is time for the Water Rat to consider his position. This investigation into British parties and the system in which they operate has been motivated not only by a desire to extend our knowledge of the subject but also by the hope that this knowledge might stimulate an appreciation of the limitations of the system and the compelling case for change. This story has a moral.

If there is one characteristic of the Westminster model of government that sets it apart, it is disciplined adversarial parties: not even the superficially similar United States system is so dominated by party. Parties were not designed nor was their development planned; they seemed to grow as the sovereignty of parliament grew. The nascent party system of the eighteenth century allowed the monarch to continue to influence parliament but slowly it became clear that executive power, which parliament was supposed to inherit, was a target not so much for ambitious monarchs eager to claw back the losses of 1688, but for political parties who wanted executive power for themselves. True the process was a slow one, and there were periods in the nineteenth century when the House of Commons itself enjoyed considerable power; governments were defeated, legislation made, ministers bundled out of office. The House of Commons was responsible for its own timetable and, all in all, maintained a healthy control over the executive. But it was not to last.

As democracy grew and the franchise was extended, so parties began to organise in the manner that we saw in Chapter 1. The coincidental impact of the Irish Party's determination to disrupt the parliamentary timetable did much to strengthen party discipline indirectly so that by the end of the nineteenth century parties had become autonomous institutions within, or to be more accurate, outwith the constitution. As they came increasingly to dominate parliament, it became apparent that the historical attempt to wrest power from the hands of the monarch and invest it in the people through parliament had failed. Instead power had been usurped by party leaders. Moreover the party leader, as Prime Minister, had fewer limitations to his or her power than the traditional monarch. As Hayek pointed out, 'all those constraints upon the supreme power that had carefully been built up during the evolution of constitutional monarchy [had been] successfully dismantled as no longer necessary'.[1] Unlike the traditional monarch the modern Prime Minister can almost invariably count on party discipline to support his or her personalised power and to provide the engine to drive that personalised power in the form of policy. As Douglas Home wrote, 'a party can be elected on a minority vote, and in spite of that gain a parliamentary majority, and use it to force down the throats of the electorate policies which the majority do not approve'.[2] Let me be blunter than Home: modern parties are *always* elected by a minority and still they can do things the majority does not want.

The growth of party was accidental and we can be reasonably certain that the reformer of 1688 or 1832 would not wish to take any responsibility for the system that has developed but would argue, to borrow a phrase from T.S. Eliot: 'That is not what I meant, not what I meant at all.' On the other hand it would be absurd to argue that our current two-party system has had no merits, and it is useful to remind ourselves of these.

This fundamentally two-party system increasingly took the form and spirit of adversarialism as party discipline strengthened to the point of being decisive. We know that this was a series of responses to developments, but the form and spirit of adversarialism were not coincidental. After all the English Common Law system is adversarial and not inquisitorial like most European legal systems. Many leading politicians had a background in the law. Moreover the great universities championed adversarial debate. The Oxford Union debates, for example, were highlights of the academic calendar. Most leading politicians had been to the great universities. Crucially the British first-past-the-post electoral system encouraged adversarialism to flourish.

Adversarial or two-party politics has been uniquely successful, providing a visible check on abuses of government in a parliamentary system in which power is concentrated rather than constrained. By agreeing to stop fighting at dinner time whoever is winning, British parties have endorsed the legitimacy of the political system; they have diverted social and economic conflict into constitutional channels; they have selected priorities in the running of the state; they have constituted a framework of accountability; they have provided a non-violent outlet for people's natural propensity for taking sides and they have provided a crucial link between the many and the few. The British two-party system has been largely successful in overseeing the emergence of a reasonably stable, socially just and productive society. Over the decades it has allowed the integration of first the bourgeoisie and then the organised working class into the political system with little social disruption, an extraordinary achievement.

For more than a century the major parties represented the interests of the great social classes and articulated those interests in the form of competing ideologies, which spawned alternative policy programmes. The sanctioning, by means of a general electoral victory, of one or other ideology provided a mandate for the party concerned to legislate on the basis of its policies. This fundamentally adversarial competition began to provide a framework for policy within which the civil service and government agencies would operate. That framework represented the fruits of a complex interaction between party leaders, 'experts', activists and supporters, supposedly set within the context of the party's ideology. For the victorious party that framework enclosed a viable programme for government. The party defeated at the election had at its disposal a similar framework from within which it would criticise the government's policies, thus providing accountability and choice. In giving the world the concept of loyal opposition, in actually paying state funds to the Leader of Her Majesty's Loyal Opposition, the British adversarial system made an extraordinary contribution to the development of representative and responsible government. But that was yesterday.

Adversarialism and the party system

Jack Hayward questioned the relevance of the adversarial thesis. He suggested that Britain's economic policies, the most important area of policy, were determined by forces other than those commanded by parties in government. Leaving aside the cultural and international constraints over which governments have little direct influence, Hayward argued:[3]

> The major source of Britain's difficulties is to be located among the non-state actors and…the efficacy of a subsidiary state intervention cannot be great when industrial firms, banks, and trade unions – who are directly involved in economic activity and decide in a more direct sense than do British governments – are unable to invest, produce, and sell efficiently. Politicians in power prate and posture, taking the credit and the blame for the diverse fortunes that ensue from the interplay of international forces, without…usually being genuinely responsible for either the good or the bad results.

Hayward was not suggesting that adversarialism was rather a sham or sideshow, but that it was no longer the prime mover in economic policy or in any area of major policy. Changes in the complexion of government via adversarialism were simply not particularly relevant. A similar argument was expressed more pugnaciously many years before by Bernard Shaw in his play *Major Barbara*. The industrialist Andrew Undershaft explains what politics is *really* about to his politician son:[4]

> Do you suppose that you and half a dozen amateurs like you, sitting in a row in that foolish gabble shop, can govern Undershaft and Lazarus? No, my friend: you will do what pays us. You will make war when it suits us, and keep peace when it doesn't. …When I want to keep my dividends up, you will discover that my want is a national need. When other people want something to keep my dividends down, you will call out the police and military. And in return you shall have the support and applause of my newspapers, and the

delight of imagining that you are a great statesman. Government of your country! Be off with you, my boy, and play with your caucuses and leading articles and historic parties and great leaders and burning questions and the rest of your toys. I am going back to my counting house to pay the piper and call the tune.

Unlike Hayward, Shaw *did* consider that British adversarial democracy was a sham: parties played the tune called by major industrial and commercial interests.

Richard Rose, in an influential work,[5] examined the claim that 'adversarial' politics produces policy inconsistencies of such a magnitude (with party B coming to power and reversing the policies of party A) as to make medium and long-term planning impossible.[6] He attempted to show that, on the contrary, party politics do not seriously impact upon government policy because policies are shaped by a range of prior considerations; in short we do not need to worry about adversarial politics because they simply do not work. We are being fooled by appearances. 'What parties say', said Rose emphatically, 'is not what parties do.' The adversarial argument suggests that the consensus-based politics of the 1950s and 1960s gave way to the ideology-based politics of the 1970s: socialist planning versus market forces, public versus private ownership, high public spending versus low direct taxation and so on. Rose asserts that this division was largely rhetorical. Nothing is new, he tells us. 'Labour and Conservative governments have been complementary parts of a moving consensus; in office in the past, they have not acted upon mutually exclusive ideological principles.'[7] History suggests that in opposition, parties tend to move towards their ideological extreme but when in government they move towards the centre – so parties 'don't matter'. Even the supposedly ideological government of Thatcher was, according to Rose, predominantly consensual (that is, the House did not divide on principle on the majority of government bills).

Like Hayward, Rose found that major developments in the period he studied were not much influenced by changes of party in government: whether we examine economic inputs (matters within the government's own hands, such as the level of public sector borrowing and public expenditure) or economic outcomes that are only partially influenced by government (such as unemployment, public investment and economic growth), the conclusions would be much the same. The success of the British economy is influenced for the most part by long-term events that are independent of the ambitions of any government and not affected by changes of government. What is true for the economy is true for all areas of government activity. Rhetoric does not transform reality, or as Healey explained to the 1982 Labour party conference apropos economic policy, general elections do not change the laws of arithmetic. Other writers have attacked the adversarial thesis on different grounds, suggesting that such major policy changes as take place tend to occur not so much between governments as within them.[8]

Rose dug deeper, making a detailed analysis of the policies of successive governments. First he examined the party manifestos. For him a party manifesto is primarily 'an exercise in party management', its function being to build unity within the party.

It is particularly important for parties in opposition. Although both Conservative and Labour governments 'do the majority of things to which they pledge them-selves in their opposition manifesto',[9] which seems to contradict his substantive thesis, Rose argues that manifestos are, after all, predominantly non-adversarial and anyway form only a small part of a government's legislative programme.[10] On this analysis Rose contends that even the apparently partisan parliaments of the 1970s were characterised more by consensus than by adversarial politics. The sternest opponents of government policies, as Norton showed, came from within the party's own ranks.[11] Far from being an adversarial system, then, Britain's two-party system is predominantly consensual. Far from stopping fighting by dinner time, Tweedledum and Tweedledee, whose original *contretemps* inaugurated this study, don't ever get beyond bringing curses down on each other: they never *start* fighting.

British governments owe their position to popular election, and the British elec-torate tends towards agreement rather than disagreement on major issues. Once in office a party will not push its own ideology too far because of recognition that this will encourage its opponents to act similarly when they gain office. Prudent self-interest further limits adversarialist decisions. Finally, if these reasons were not sufficient to dispose parties towards consensual politics, the awesome respon-sibilities of running the state with the assistance of a permanent non-political civil service, together with the general constraints upon its freedom of manoeuvre iden-tified by Hayward, would certainly toll the knell for any government seeking to act in a consistently adversarial manner. New ministers will face old problems, and with the same advice as their unsuccessful predecessors. Rose, like Hayward, attaches great importance to the restraints that inhibit incoming governments, domestically what he calls 'long-term secular trends' and internationally the state of the world economy and the global political situation. All in all, if our critics are correct, there seem to be solid prima facie grounds for rejecting the adversarial thesis that party conflict matters,

Given these arguments it would seem only prudent to accept that there are indeed limitations to the adversarial thesis but to consider these limitations to be necessarily paralysing is to ignore those important occasions when nations have reversed 'long-term secular trends', with considerable repercussions for their economic and political world roles, where party ideology has made an obvious and immediate impact. In the early years of the twentieth century the radical Liberal Hobson wrote about the creation of a federal structure for the British Empire. There were huge difficulties involved in creating an imperial federation with common defence and trade policies but the economic advantages to British industry and capital were such that imperial federation would happen.[12] Writing from a different perspective, Lenin advanced a similar argument more forcefully; he too believed that British parties played the tunes called by their paymasters.[13] But no imperial federation was created and one of the major reasons for this was the replacement at a crucial time in 1906 of a Conservative government dominated by Joseph Chamberlain's protectionism (favourable to an enclosed trading system) with a Liberal administration dominated by free traders for whom such enclosure was anathema. Adversarial ideology made a major difference just around the time that Shaw's *Major Barbara* was first being produced.

There can surely be no doubt that Britain's economic and fiscal policies changed during Rose's and Hayward's time, with the advent of Thatcher's Conservative government in 1979 (even if it is also true that they did not change back when Labour returned to power). Government policies may be not as decisive as some politicians would have us believe but it is unrealistic to suggest that parties make no impact whatever. As for the neutralising power of the civil service, two factors need to be borne in mind. First is the ability of a party in government to generate a different perspective within the service by influencing key promotions, or by bringing leading figures into the service from outside, or by making use of expert advice from outside the service, all of which are commonly done. According to Peter Hennessy,[14] many permanent secretaries were selected personally by Margaret Thatcher. 'They have been promoted for qualities of style and commitment', said Hugo Young.[15] The second is that civil servants regard it as their duty not simply to advise, but also to advise from within the framework of known governmental dispositions. For example, civil service advice on taxation systems differed in the late 1960s and early 1970s to suit the attitudes of successive governments towards joining the EEC. The anti-EEC Labour government was advised by the civil service that Britain's taxation system of purchase tax and selective employment tax (SET) was superior to the EEC's value added tax (VAT), whereas the incoming pro-EEC Conservative government was told the opposite: in other words each was told what it wanted to hear. It is well known that departments of state prepare themselves for the implications of electoral victory for each of the major parties. Of course they will attempt to dissuade politicians from adopting policies they believe to be unworkable, but they will generally give loyal support to a minister's policies.[16] And to his or her successor's policies, however different.

Finally we come to Rose's most deep-rooted objection to the adversarial thesis: that it confuses rhetoric with reality, failing to distinguish between what parties say and what they do. This suggests that what people say is not part of reality, an argument that makes sense only if it is always and everywhere true that people do not mean what they say. If a man says to me, 'One day I shall kill you', then my reality would certainly be transformed even if he did not actually do so, or even if he never really intended to do so. Only if I can be certain either that he did not mean it or that he was incapable of carrying out his threat would my reality be unaffected. Rhetoric is very much part of reality. In S.H. Beer's words, 'party stances establish the framework of public thinking about policy'.[17]

Rose's and Hayward's work leads us to appreciate the limitations within which parties have to operate and to recognise the common ground between them, but we must conclude that parties do make a difference and that if we take any note of the influence of what Rose dismisses as rhetoric then they can make a substantial difference. To quote Beer again, 'parties themselves, backed by research staffs, equipped with nationwide organizations, and enjoying the continuous attention of the mass media, have themselves in great part framed and elicited the very demands to which they then respond'.[18]

A number of other studies have been concerned with the effect upon specific areas of policy of adversarialism and some reach conclusions very different from

Rose's. Andrew Gamble wrote: 'The surprising thing about adversary politics is not that it destroys continuity of policy in some areas, but that it protects a narrow and unreflecting consensus on some of the most important determinants shaping economic policy.'[19] Gamble is not the only writer to say so. Ashford argues that, 'superficial' adversarial politics notwithstanding, in times of stress an 'elite consensus' emerges which concentrates decision-making within Cabinet and the higher levels of the civil service, and this consensus acts independently of party ideology or indeed parliamentary influence.[20] Suddenly adversarial politics is exposed as some kind of conspiracy theory.

Gamble develops his own theory further. Political stability demands continuity of policy so the electorate 'can be offered an effective choice between teams of leaders but not between policies'; adversarial two-party party politics is like Bernard Shaw's theory of democracy: it is only 'a big balloon, filled with gas or hot air, and sent up so that you shall be kept looking up at the sky whilst other people are picking your pockets'.[21] Gamble concludes: 'If the two parties ever became genuine adversaries the system would cease to be workable.' It is true that real adversaries often beat each other over the head. It is also true that we defined the role of political parties in a constitutional democracy as being to contain conflict. But party systems differ and to call a system adversarial is a more sophisticated and comparative judgement than Gamble will allow. It is hard to imagine that many people working in the areas of health or education would dispute the claim that party policies differ and that the differences matter. It is hard to imagine that Scots and Welsh voters saw no differences between the major parties in 1997 when one promised devolution and one did not. Was this 'just' rhetoric? Was devolution only symbolic?

In short, adversarialism is real enough, or to be more precise, it has been at work over a long period of time. Now I wish to consider whether it works well.

Adversarialism in action

Adversarial politics operate not only at a general level but also in discrete areas of policy. In *Parliament and Health Policy* the authors consider in detail the influence of parliament in the creation and scrutiny of health policy in the period 1970–75.[22] Every major aspect of health policy in that period was considered and, although this had not been the purpose of the study, clear indications of the influence of adversarial politics emerged. The study began by analysing the kind of contributions which backbench MPs might make to policy formulation and scrutiny; this was done simply by asking a number of backbenchers what they considered to be their most important function. On the basis of their answers backbench functions were categorised as being fourfold. First there was a deputational function, in which the MP is deputed to protect and further the interests of constituents. Second was the custodial function, where the emphasis is on protecting customary procedures and the constitution. Third was the advocative function, in which the MP represents certain interests, for example tobacco manufacture. Fourth was the partisan-ideological (or adversarial) function, in which the MP offers support to the party leader. The purpose of these categories was not to label MPs but to attempt to categorise their contributions to debate on the floor of the House and in committee, so as to get the measure of the way parliament actually operates.

During the period under scrutiny one major piece of legislation passed through parliament, the reform of the administrative structure of the National Health Service (NHS), the first major overhaul in nearly thirty years. The need for structural reform was not at issue, no major reallocation of resources was involved, nor was any major ideological division apparent. Yet a tabulation of major contributions to the second reading debate on the Reorganisation Bill (measured in column inches of Hansard) shows that adversarial inputs comprised 36 per cent, by far the largest category. The authors conclude: 'For parliament to spend over a third of its time on partisan point-making, *with the full knowledge that it would have no effect on the shape of the policy before it*, is an over indulgence.'[23] What was true of the major debate on the floor of the House was true also of committee discussions. In fact the most successful influence upon the government – and it was successful only in detail – came from the House of Lords (where, incidentally, similar categorisation indicated that partisan-ideological inputs accounted for only 4 per cent of all contributions). None of the real issues of structure and accountability was discussed as both parties sought out adversarial advantage.

Within five years NHS reorganisation was back on the political agenda: the 1974 reforms were almost universally considered to have been failures. There is much more in the study to tell a similar story; indeed the House seemed able to perform effectively only in the area of detailed scrutiny and only then when, as with the creation of the NHS Commissioner (Ombudsman) and his committee, detailed and often technical discussion precluded adversarial inputs. The authors conclude their study by suggesting:

> If health is any guide, the nature of policy making is becoming increasingly technical and as a result less amenable to [adversarial] presentation. The British model of parliamentary government requires partisan policy inputs, requires that policies be presented as simple alternatives for public choice. Yet in an increasingly complex age, policies are far less amenable to presentation as simple partisan choices, and policy inputs come increasingly not from parties but from experts within the executive. The procedures for assessing these policies, however, continue to operate as if they *were* partisan-ideological and so remain basically adversarial.[24]

To conclude this discussion of the place of adversarialism in twentieth-century history, Rose argues that the consensus nature of British politics prevents power from being used in an adversarial way. Thatcher was elected in 1979 on a minority vote. Her governments transformed the structure of the British state, reducing the status of local authorities to little more than agencies of central government, creating new unelected public agencies, privatising major service industries and recasting the structure, functions and traditions of the civil service. Thatcher's ill-conceived attempt to reform the domestic rates, the poll tax, which she was able to promote, against the advice of nearly all her colleagues, through the instinctive if reluctant loyalty of her parliamentary party, managed to incite senior citizens onto the streets to demonstrate in towns like Cheltenham. Her policy of enforced council house sales transformed, for good and for ill, the housing market in Britain; the country has not yet come to terms with its ramifications. Is it remotely conceivable that a Labour government would have done any of this?

Adversarialism: beyond its shelf life?

Having established the case that parties *do* make a difference, that adversarialism *is* real, I propose to take the argument into a more normative dimension. What is more remarkable even than the transformation that Thatcher wrought in British society and politics is the fact that in none of the three elections that gave Thatcher her 'mandate' did she receive as much as one-third of the possible vote. Two-thirds of the electorate did not formally approve of what she proposed to do, or later of what she did. We are told that manifestos are not read by many voters and that of those who do read them, a good number disapprove of the policies of the party for which they then vote. If we assume that 10 per cent of the electorate read manifestos (though it is certainly fewer) then only 3 per cent of the adult population read the Conservative manifesto in 1979, and a good number of these would have disapproved of a lot of what they read, but voted Tory anyway. Thatcher's mandate, like that of most modern Prime Ministers, would have been endorsed by something less than 2 per cent of the electorate.

Nevertheless having attained power a Prime Minister will promote policies from the manifesto and, as time passes, other policies will be pursued. The opposition will seek to prevent the passage of legislation whenever it thinks it has a chance of doing so (not too frequently, as Rose shows). From time to time new leaders of the opposition will declare that they will operate a new kind of politics: they will not oppose just for the sake of opposition. As the Duke of Wellington is said to have replied to the man who asked if he were a Mr Smith: 'If you believe that, sir, you will believe anything'. Prime Minister's Questions, the high point of adversarial 'accountability', has become a comedy show, a very professional and amusing one, but nevertheless a show. Here is one example. When the Labour government was trying to prevent the candidacy of Ken Livingstone for London's mayor and to promote that of Minister of Health Frank Dobson, the leader of the opposition, William Hague, offered his sympathies to the Prime Minister and even suggested a possible solution: Blair should appoint two mayors, one for the daytime and one for night-time. Then Dobson could be the day-mayor and Livingstone the night-mayor (nightmare). The wit is not usually so benign, but if we were expecting genuine critical analysis of policy met by informative replies, we might as well forget it.

I have tried to show already how the nature of parliamentary debate in general is weighted heavily towards adversarial point scoring. Rose suggested that since much legislation was not opposed, this indicated consensus. This is simply not so; it indicates that opposition party managers have a good idea of how seldom they might be able to have any impact on government policy. Governments will make calculations before introducing legislation about how to minimise their vulnerability in the face of known oppositional views, but they will seldom if ever make major concessions. This in turn means that opposition is a very blunt instrument; its best hope is often not to persuade government to amend its proposal but to bring down the government. Iain Macleod told the story of his early days in the House of Commons in the late 1940s when he was a parliamentary private secretary to Sir Winston Churchill. There was to be a debate on infant mortality and Churchill had asked Macleod to prepare some statistics for him to use. In those days the information services available to MPs were basic and Macleod had been at considerable pains to prepare a series of relevant data, which he had duly presented to the great man. In the course of the debate Churchill made not a single statistical observation and Macleod had tackled him on this later only to be reprimanded: what Churchill had meant by statistics was irrefutable evidence that fewer children had died when he was Prime Minister than were dying under the Labour government.[25]

What made adversarial two-party politics viable in the past was the notion of an ideological confrontation based primarily on a class struggle. There were two basically different views on how the state should be organised. It is true, as Hayward and Rose tells us, that a number of extraneous factors always moderated that struggle. Gamble is also right to say that if it were taken seriously, adversarialism would make parliamentary politics impossible. Nevertheless British politics was driven primarily by a competition between champions of these views, who sought to balance the attainment of their ambitions with a general respect for the institutions of government (though for Labour that might not have stretched as far as the House of Lords or as far as 'loony left' local councils for the Conservatives). But now the two great parties have become ideological husks, 'hollowed out' as the critics have said, and the underpinning class antagonism has lost its vigour, so now we must question the appropriateness of our adversarial two-party system for managing modern Britain. Modern electoral politics have levered governments of both parties towards very similar approaches to domestic and foreign policy. Where does adversarialism fit in?

If ideological confrontation is beyond its shelf life, what drives modern parties? It is, above all, personality politics. And what drives personality politics are the media. Modern political leaders give far more attention to their relationship with the media than with the House of Commons or the party. The media, in turn, are driven by a ferocious competition for saleable copy and what sells newspapers are celebrity, gossip and scandal: the 'human angle'. The role of the media in an adversarial system is dangerously corrosive. Just before he left office Tony Blair make an attack on this corrosiveness, referring to the media as 'feral',[26] but rather than attack those agents of corrosion who might be considered savage, the tabloids, he mounted a bizarre assault on, of all papers, *The Independent*, blaming it for too little reporting and too much commentary.[27] This attack exposed the real problem: the Murdoch press was too important to his success to be challenged. In his autobiography John Major attributed his own downfall to the activities of the

Murdoch press.[28] To understand how truly corrosive the relationship is between the modern media and politicians, it is instructive to read the diaries of Piers Morgan, one-time editor of the *Mirror*.[29] Most commentators thought Blair's broadside against the media was singularly ironic,[30] since he had paid an unprecedented attention to media presentation, sustained by an unusually close relationship with his press secretary Alastair Campbell and an ever increasing number of special advisers, totalling more than sixty, and costing the taxpayer £1.5 million.[31] An adversarial party system is the perfect habitat for the 'feral' media and for scavenging political satirists. No wonder the latter are so prolific. If adversarialism as a means of constraining the executive is, by its very nature, increasingly inappropriate, it is surely also true that the kinds of problems faced by modern governments are not amenable even to functional adversarial management. What are these problems?

The political agenda today

Let us begin with a parochial concern. Had this book been entitled *The English Party System* it would have covered much of the same ground. Most textbooks on British politics imagine that the Celtic countries operate a form of party politics that is mildly and probably temporarily divergent from the English; and after all, the English do make up about 85 per cent of the population of the United Kingdom. British textbooks tend to focus on England. In their informative book on Liberal Democrat grass-roots organisation, for example, *Third Force Politics*, Whiteley, Seyd and Billinghurst make little reference to the party north of the border, nor do they attempt to show what effect power sharing has had upon the party.[32] Even in *The British General Election of 2005*, Kavanagh and Butler seem unaware that the Green Party in Scotland is quite separate from the English Green Party.[33] I have tried to explore the Celtic dimension wherever appropriate, but I want briefly to expand the discussion a little by looking at the politics of identity in Britain principally through the prism of Scottish politics.

The problem of British unity

The English have traditionally used the descriptions 'English' and 'British' more or less interchangeably. Unlike the other British teams, when the English soccer or rugby team takes the field the anthem which is played is not an English anthem, such as *Jerusalem*, but the British one, *God Save the Queen*. Until recently few would take the St George flag to sports fixtures – though they certainly do now – but the Union flag. The cross of St George was hardly ever seen flying from public buildings in England. Only in Northern Ireland would one see more Union flags than in England. In Wales it is the red dragon that flutters from most flagpoles and in Scotland the saltire is everywhere. What is Britishness and can one be both Scottish and British? Such questions are asked only when, as Mercer says, 'something assumed to be fixed, coherent and stable is displaced by the experience of doubt and uncertainty'.[34] It is a testament to the strength of Scottish and Welsh culture and sense of nationhood that even after three and five hundred years respectively of domination by a much larger partner, they have retained their sense of identity. It is paradoxical that when Anglo-centric, usually metropolitan, culture is at its most pervasive through television, Celtic cultures should be enjoying their most fertile period for decades. In fact it is not a paradox: the London-based media project their cultural values into the minds of all who watch and some of those who watch are stimulated to resist.

One aspect of national culture has attained an unprecedented visibility. After the 1992 general election, of which the Scottish National Party had such high hopes, deputy leader Jim Sillars despairingly dismissed his compatriots as 'ninety-minute nationalists'. They only cared for their country during a soccer or rugby game. It is true that for many men and a growing number of women, Wales or Scotland versus England assumes an importance quite beyond the scope of that particular sport. Thirty years ago one of Scotland's celebrated sports commentators said of an English defeat at the hands of the Scots in Glasgow: 'The poor English. They came expecting a game of football and what they got was a tribal war'. National pride has a visibility in international sport and as George Orwell pointed out some time ago, sport is not always a force for brotherhood and friendship. There is in truth much that the peoples of the United Kingdom have in common but they are not the same. This can be seen in art, in song, in architecture – and these days especially in sport.

Brown, McCrone and Paterson have asked why the sense of Britishness is weaker than it was.[35] The great achievements of the British, the creation of a vast empire (whether this was a moral achievement is often questioned; that it represented a political achievement cannot be), collective heroism and defiance during the time of the Fascist domination of Europe, the creation of a National Health Service, to name the more obvious, are in the past. The original political motivation of the Scots towards union, that lowland Protestant Scotland saw itself at risk from the Gaelic-speaking Catholics in the north and west, is no longer relevant. Protestantism, which brought most of the United Kingdom together, is not the socio-political force it once was and neither is Roman Catholicism so much of an enemy.[36] External pressures too have tended to impact upon the sense of 'Britishness'; fear or distrust of Europeans is not widespread.[37] The European Union, moreover, offers a viable safety net for those who might otherwise fear for Scotland 'going it alone'. In addition to the growth in influence of Europe is the pervasive influence of globalisation. Inward investment to the United Kingdom is generated by companies with headquarters in Tokyo, Beijing or Detroit. Holyrood cannot control them, but then neither can Westminster. It is in the face of these internal and external pressures that the desire has grown to control at least some aspects of national life, and these are often part of a Scottish, Welsh or Northern Irish agenda rather than a British one. This can be seen as part of a much broader development, the emergence of a post-industrial society, which rejects bigness wherever possible precisely because it connotes lack of identity.[38]

Scottish and Welsh politics have never been just like English politics. In the nineteenth century – after the Reform Act of 1832 anyway – Liberalism, with its emphasis on self-reliance and the improvement of popular education enjoyed hegemony in Scotland unparalleled in Britain as a whole.[39] The Conservative Party in nineteenth-century Scotland was unable to take the industrial working class with it in the way that Disraeli was able to do nationally. However Hutchison shows that when the Unionists switched their allegiance to the Conservative Party, the Protestants of the west of Scotland went with them.[40] Working-class Protestant voters gave the Conservatives considerable political strength. The rise of the Scottish National Party made serious inroads into Conservative support just as Protestantism was becoming less politically influential. As Fry says: 'Till 1974 they never got much less than 40% of the vote, and often rather more; afterwards they never got much more than 30%, and often rather less'.[41] But what really flattened the Conservative Party (which had now dropped the Unionist tag) was the advent of Thatcherism. For most Scots the Thatcherite project of self-reliance seemed a threat to their sense of community. But most damaging of all to Scottish Conservatism was the introduction – one year ahead of England – of Thatcher's dreaded 'poll tax'. Scotland perceived itself as a guinea pig. Although after her departure John Major revived the party's fortunes a little, the blow of 1997 could scarcely have been more crushing – only 12 per cent of the vote for the Conservatives north of the border and not a single seat won. So, too, in Wales – not a single seat. (But for contrast, not a single seat out of thirty-seven in the old 'People's Republic of Yorkshire' either.) The Conservatives in Scotland have not recovered, though in the Scottish parliament – which they had resisted – and through its proportional electoral system – which they had resisted – the party has regained visibility and retains some hope.

Just as the Liberals dominated Scotland in the nineteenth century, so Labour did the twentieth, its rise keeping in step with that of the party nationally; indeed the British Labour Party, as we have seen, was to a large extent fashioned by workers' representatives from Scotland and the North of England. But Labour's dominance of Scottish politics, which is echoed in Wales, is quite distinctive from that of England as a whole (though not from the North of England). Even in the disastrous election of 1983 the Labour Party in Scotland still won forty-one seats, just about twice as many as the Conservatives.

What is distinctive about Scottish and Welsh politics, however, is what we began with: the indestructible idea of separate identity, which manifests itself in, among other things, political nationalism. This distinctive identity has taken Scotland and Wales, via devolution to multi-party politics, coalition and minority governments. Devolution was supported in England by some political commentators, who hoped that it might produce some creative institutional approaches to problem solving. Well for some time it produced coalition government but in truth little else. Now Scotland has minority government and so the ruling party will have to persuade the parliament/assembly of the wisdom of each measure it wishes to pass. This is an experiment with wider possible implications and it establishes Holyrood as being significantly different from Westminster. In Wales too history has been made: a coalition between the old adversaries Labour and Plaid Cymru, with Plaid's leader Ieuan Wyn Jones as deputy first minister, may bring a much more inclusive, non-adversarial system of government to Wales.

There are those in Scotland and Wales who seek independence and those who seek broader powers for their devolved institutions but within a United Kingdom. If the future integrity of the United Kingdom is not a major issue then nothing is. How is the British adversarial system to deal with this problem? There is not one solution more consistent with Labour party ideology and another more consistent with Conservatism. The Labour government at Westminster has a selfish interest in 'playing the British card'. It sought to control the Executive (now government) in Scotland as far as possible and it used its cohort of Scottish MPs at Westminster to force through legislation on health and education that did not apply to their own constituents. Without those MPs the legislation would have been lost. In every sense of the word, this is acting irresponsibly. The Conservative Party too has a selfish interest in 'playing the English card'. It won a majority of votes in England in 2005; it knows that if Scotland were to cease to send MPs to Westminster, its hand in English politics would be far stronger. The Conservatives are currently seeking ways of limiting the influence of Scottish MPs in Westminster even if that would damage Scottish support for the Union. Before he succeeded Blair, questions were raised about the propriety of Brown, a Scot who represents a Scottish constituency (and whose constituents therefore look more to Holyrood than Westminster) becoming Prime Minister of the United Kingdom, because much of the legislation generated at Westminster no longer directly concerns Scotland. The question was asked primarily to gain adversarial advantage and to weaken Brown's position. When John Prescott sought to explore the possibility of a limited form of regional government in the North East of England, the tepid support his proposals received in a referendum were the occasion for opposition ridicule. Yet Mebyon Kernow seeks at least this status for Cornwall, and the early level of support for devolution in Wales was lower than that for the milk-and-water form of self-government offered to the North East of England. The Liberal Democrats and the Liberals before them have argued for a federal Britain, with a level of self-government for the English regions. Nevertheless for a quarter of a century there has not been, nor is there likely ever to be, a debate on the future of the United Kingdom that would not be distorted by adversarial considerations – unless it could be taken out of the political arena by, for example, the appointment of another Royal Commission.

Already Labour leaders in Scotland are seeking increased powers for Holyrood. Former First Minister McLeish declared that 'the UK is in danger from Westminster' unless the powers of the Scottish parliament are extended.[42] In November 2007, Labour, Liberal Democrat and Conservative MEPs agreed to establish a castitutional commission to advise how the Scottish parliament might achieve greater fiscal and economic powers. Interestingly David Cameron has signalled a willingness to consider a general review of spending arrangements, though Brown has made no equivalent response.[43]

When the Blair government established the new governmental institutions at Cardiff and Edinburgh, it expected administrations sympathetic to Labour in both and it expected to 'dish' the nationalists. The plans of mice and men! No consideration was given as to how to manage the system if and when conflicts emerge between the various governments – and they will: Alex Salmond will make sure of that. The British adversarial system has failed the nation in this issue as in so many others. It has shown no capacity for long-term planning. Its policy frame lasts from now until the next election, or even the next by-election.[44] Is there a distinctive Labour and Conservative ideological position on the future of Britain? If there were, would policy be improved over the long term by competition between them?

I have concentrated on the politics of British identity here, but there are numerous candidates for an analysis that shows the limitations of adversarialism. Energy policy, for example, requires long-term decisions of an essentially non-adversarial nature. These are difficult enough to handle in the present system, but impossible even to consider strategically until the future political structure of the United Kingdom is settled. Is there a distinctive Labour and Conservative ideological position on the future of energy supplies? If there were, would policy be improved over the long term by competition between them?

International problems

If there is cause for concern in respect of the inability of the adversarial system to come to grips with internal problems facing Britain, it pales into insignificance when compared to that in respect of the international problems that press on the country. Although the adversarial system was not responsible for the invasion of Iraq, it provided a framework within which a full debate on the causes of war was less likely. Subsequent debates on the causes of war and on the conduct of the occupation, however, have been and will continue to be shaped by considerations of adversarial advantage just as they are in the United States. We cannot say that a multi-party system would have prevented war or made the subsequent occupation less destructive, but we can say that adversarialism made these better outcomes less likely. Is there a distinctive Labour and Conservative ideological position on Iraq? If there were, would policy be improved over the long term by competition between them?

The so-called war against terrorism is likewise an issue of the greatest international importance but from the outset it has been marked by the two major parties seeking partisan advantage. The balance between protecting the citizens of the United Kingdom from terrorist attack and the maintenance of the very civil liberties that are under threat from terrorism is a fine one; adversarial parties, their eyes firmly on the next general election, are not the best institutions to achieve that balance. Is there a distinctive Labour and Conservative ideological position on terrorism? If there were, would policy be improved over the long term by competition between them?

Finally, let us consider the issues around climate change. These are highly complex, highly technical issues of the very gravest importance to all the people of the United Kingdom, as indeed to the rest of the planet. The world community is seeking to achieve a global response to the threat of global warming. The response in Britain is worth examining. Both major parties acknowledge the importance of cutting greenhouse gas emissions but neither has yet proposed a policy to cut the consumption of oil through, for example, restrictions on internal air flights, the insulation of all homes, the inducement through taxation of fuel economies and so on. A principal reason for the failure seriously to address these problems is the fact that if one party adopted any such measure the other would attack it, realistically expecting to obtain electoral advantage. This is precisely the logic of adversarial politics. Instead British politicians strike poses for the media. The Conservative leader David Cameron cycles to the House of Commons closely followed by his limousine carrying his papers. If we think Green, we are advised by his party that we should vote Blue: that is the way to tackle global warming. Is there a distinctive Labour and Conservative ideological position on global warming? If there were, would policy be improved over the long term by competition between them?

Parties and the future

Nearly everywhere in the West parties are less popular than hitherto, and new social movements more popular. Klingemann and Fuchs tell us that across Europe, 'there is a clear increase in non-institutionalised participation and a clear decline in attachment to political parties'.[45] These authors remain optimistic about the future for parties but they stress that a more politically aware electorate is turning increasingly to single-issue groups which bypass elections and parties and thereby tend to erode 'the legitimacy of the competitive party system'.[46] What also tends to erode the legitimacy of the party system is the fact alluded to earlier that policy decisions nowadays tend to be of a more technical and long-term nature and not so easily amenable to adversarial presentation.

Parties may indeed be necessary to parliamentary democracies but the merest glance at our European neighbours shows that not all party systems are the same and the British party system need not take the shape it does nor does it need to operate in the way it does. It is not within the scope of this study to consider in detail changes within parliamentary practice and procedure that might alleviate the excesses of adversarialism, though parliamentarians themselves have given much thought to this since the mid-1970s. Obvious possibilities might be to restrict the use of whipped votes to a certain number of key policies specified in advance so that most decisions in the House of Commons are taken on a real and not a fabricated majority; to anonymise voting in parliament so that the Whips could never be quite certain how their MPs had voted; to make the role of select committees *much* more central to the business of the House and to minimise party control over these committees. And above all a proportional system of elections could be introduced for Westminster.

There are arguments against electoral reform. Lord Hattersley noted that when Blair spoke of an end to the tribal politics of traditional Conservatism versus old Labourism he meant a divorce from 'the ideals which inspired the Labour party from Keir Hardie to John Smith'.[47] More generally Matthew Parris reminds us that those who

> cry 'beyond Party' from below, and leaders who cry 'beyond Party' from above, [forget] those who inhabit the gulf between them, the tens of thousands of men and women from door-knockers to councillors who owe their status and often their income to party.[48]

Klingemann and Fuchs assure us that a system's legitimacy rests on two factors: its performance and the extent to which it reflects the underlying values and norms of the people. Parties, they argue, are crucial to both. According to Schmitt and Holmberg, 'political conflicts are the raison d'être, the breath of life, for political parties. Without conflict parties languish...the ideological distinctiveness of parties is the single most powerful predictor of flourishing partisanship'.[49] Partisanship, they continue, contributes directly to the stability of party systems and indirectly to the stability of the state: 'That is what a stake is when partisanship fades away'. It is true that Daniel Bell wrote in 1968 about the decline of unifying values;[50] more recently, Inglehart has seen traditional party loyalties giving way to 'post-materialist' loyalties, to social movements, such as feminism, environmentalism and the like.[51] But it is also true that in the United Kingdom Seyd and Whiteley have urged upon politicians in both major parties the importance of a vibrant party organisation, and the importance of ideology to that vibrancy. Social movements may come and go, the argument seems to be, but the party remains central to the democratic structure of the state and that centrality implies partisanship.

In the present political climate however this is whistling down the wind. Our schoolboy who was so puzzled by non-representational art would surely be equally challenged by a party system dominated on the one hand by a party that is supposed to be conservative but is no longer confident even about what it wants to conserve and in its last incarnation as government was decidedly radical and not at all conservative, and on the other by a socialist party that has ceased to be socialist and in its present incarnation as government has proved to be essentially conservative. The organisational structure of both of these parties is geared towards increasingly lengthy electoral competition and more specifically to securing sufficient finance to sustain that competition. They increasingly fail to articulate the interests and aspirations of the social groups they once claimed to represent, and indeed those social groups have themselves changed beyond recognition. Those who represent the parties at Westminster tend more and more to come from a professional political background with correspondingly less contact with the 'real' life of the nation. To the general public they are almost indistinguishable and equally despised. The chief conclusion to be drawn from what we have discovered – the moral of our story – is that the British party system is not fit for purpose; it is no longer what it was 'supposed to be' and has yet to find a new identity with which it and we might be comfortable.

So why reform the electoral system? Because the politics so treasured by Hattersley are gone anyway; because the partisanship necessary for parliamentary politics to flourish does not imply adversarialism; because the parties that Schmitt and Holmberg, Klingemann and Fuchs, or even Seyd and Whiteley (now that they have studied the Liberal Democrats) champion are not locked in short-term adversarial combat: that is not the only form that competition takes. Since the mid-1980s British parties have undergone greater changes than at any time since the 1930s, but the adversarial spirit in which they operate has not. I suggested at the outset that Britain has only rarely been a genuinely two-party system and I went on to argue that in many respects the nation suffered the consequences (adversarial government) of operating as if it *were*, but without reaping the benefits (systematic accountability).

As Gordon Brown sets out his ambitions for government, apparently acknowledging some of the shortcomings of adversarial traditions, we can seriously doubt how successful his ideas of wider, more inclusive policy development can be within an adversarial context, or indeed how successful he expects them to be[52]. The most likely way to change that context for good, or at least for the foreseeable future would be through electoral reform. How can the Mother of Parliaments think proportional representation is the best method of election for the three new institutions it has created, and for elections to the European Parliament, but not for itself? In 1990 Kinnock established a working party under the eminent political philosopher Raymond Plant to consider electoral reform. The report supported reform and favoured a national referendum on the issue.[53] In 1997 Blair set up a commission under Lord Jenkins, which also reported in favour of reform.[54] Whether a government, having won an adversarial election, would ever commit itself to reforming the system that brought it to power is dubious, but there is wider support for reform than in the past, and if one of the major parties sought the support of the Liberal Democrats after an indecisive election, a commitment to a referendum could be demanded. The coalition (formal or informal) or minority government that might result from a more proportional election would signal the end of adversarialism in policy-making and bring British party politics, not kicking not screaming but liberated, into the modern world. It would bring an end to 'elective dictatorship' – governments elected by a minority of voters declaring that they had a mandate to do whatever they chose. It would prevent short-termism in policy-making and it would minimise the inflating of unreasonable expectations among voters before elections and the inevitable disillusion after. It would prevent the kind of macro and micro mismanagement of political institutions throughout the public sector, such as we discussed earlier this chapter in the field of health. It might do all of these things, though of course it might not. At least it would make them possible, whereas today they are not.

The public has lost faith in the party system, as voting statistics and levels of participation show.[55] Increasingly the major parties are faced with falling memberships. The parties react by trying to invent more inclusive forms of politics, the Conservatives with their 'listening campaign', Blair with his Great Conversation and now all the parties with their localism and their citizens' juries.[56] In July 2007 Prime Minister Brown broke precedent by announcing his government's forthcoming legislative programme and not waiting for the Queen's Speech at the state opening of parliament in November. Why? So that the British public could be consulted and have an input into legislative proposals. A month earlier David Cameron had pledged 'an unprecedented change in policy making by committing the party to giving the public a direct say in shaping the Tory election manifesto'.[57]

But for this involvement to work, politicians have to be prepared at least to engage with the opinions they hear. If either or both of the major parties seek genuinely to empower local communities, as they claim, it will be at the expense of their ability to control the nation through Westminster; their ability, that is, to act adversarially. As the debate over a referendum on the new European treaty that emerged from the 2007 Lisbon summit shows, the Labour government (which thinks it might lose) is anxious to avoid including the public, and the Conservative opposition (which thinks it might win) is anxious to ask the people. Strange that when it first took Britain into the European Economic Community a Conservative government did not think a referendum was necessary. The present system will not easily lend itself to government by consultation, but electoral reform would actually build consultation into the system.

Electoral reform would also be likely to allow the Liberal Democrats to sustain enough of their current strength nationally to create a three-party system, with the likelihood of some representation for smaller parties. This would transform British politics by introducing true majority government, by limiting the procedural excesses of adversarialism and yet retaining the invigoration of competition. British parties would need to walk the fine (but not *awfully* fine) line between adversarialism and 'post-ideological' politics. This task would be made the harder by the additional need to retain a sense of unity and national cohesion in the face of the constitutional complications that devolution has thrown up. Parties can accomplish these tasks only by retaining a strong sense of identity. That identity will probably continue to be expressed in some form of ideology, but in a three or more party system, identity politics will not result in adversarialism. Devolution will bring a greater degree of pluralism to the British party system anyway and a powerful third party at Westminster will change the way the whole system, or mix of systems operates. We still need our parties to fight each other even if – or perhaps precisely because (as Andrew Gamble tells us) – it's not a fight to the death. But adversarialism today has become a Madame Tussaud's waxwork representation of a kind of politics now gone that Shaw and Rose thought was a sham anyway. Of itself electoral reform will not solve the problems set out by Gerry Stoker in his sweeping analysis of democracy's failings,[58] but in my view – though not, I think, in Stoker's – it would be an essential first step.

Why is it then that not only Roy Hattersley and Matthew Parris but also the majority of party politicians at Westminster oppose electoral reform? Ignoring the obvious reason already alluded to – self interest – they could produce three apparently compelling arguments in favour of adversarialism. First it is capable of producing strong governments able to take tough decisions, as for example the Thatcher government did in the early 1980s when Britain, it seemed had become ungovernable. Let us examine this claim. MacDonald could not secure the support of his own party in 1931 for the tough economic package he believed to be necessary. Harold Wilson was unable to win the support of his own backbenchers in 1969 for the reform of the trade unions that he thought was vital, despite threatening to resign. So adversarialism does not necessarily produce strong governments taking tough decisions. But we can go further. The very problems that require tough decisions often represent the fruits of previous inappropriate partisan policies. Moreover if history offers any guide it suggests that in times of national crises the nation tends to turn not to adversarial but consensual government – to coalitions. This 'strong government' argument was deployed by opponents of electoral reform in New Zealand in the 1993 referendum campaign. Look, they said, at how the government was able to confront the grave economic crisis of the early 1980s. No government lacking the discipline induced by adversarialism could have managed this. But how did New Zealand get into this crisis if not as a consequence of a previous 'strong' government pursuing inappropriate policies with the help of their disciplined caucuses? Bizarrely these policies, collectively known as 'Big Government', were pursued by a right-wing conservative government, and the economic liberalism that 'saved' New Zealand was pursued by Labour. What might our schoolboy have made of that!

The second equally audacious argument holds that only adversarialism is capable of providing adequate scrutiny of government. But how often have oppositions been able to deflect or modify ill-judged government policies? The role of Her Majesty's loyal opposition has been summarised as to oppose everything, propose nothing and throw out the government. Is this effective scrutiny?

Thirdly they argue that the demise of adversarial parties will lead not to a new golden age of independently-minded backbenchers but to the sovereignty of powerful special interests. But as we have already observed, nobody has argued for the demise of parties, rather the demise of adversarialism. Scotland, Wales and New Zealand – not to mention most of the rest of the developed world – have effective if not vibrant party systems. In these polities it tends to be the majority of citizens who make governments, not, as in Britain, a tiny minority comprising floating voters in marginal constituencies – a number as small as 8,000 according to Polly Toynbee.[59]

Confrontational ideologies, the life's blood of adversarial politics, are history, but their baleful influence remains. They have bequeathed a rigidly confrontational style of policy-making and scrutiny to Britain that is belligerent, artificial and ineffectual.

From the 1980s onwards the government at Westminster has reformed every institution with which it comes into contact, more than once. Time it looked to itself. Our adversarial party system is no longer fit for purpose and needs to be changed. The internal and external problems facing the United Kingdom are as great as they have ever been and we look in vain for the proper way to address them through adversarialism. Writing over a century ago H.G. Wells fulminated against the short-termism of British adversarial democracy and concluded that asking a British government for a real change of policy was like asking a tramp for a change of linen.[60] Britain needs to follow New Zealand's lead of 1993 and hold a referendum on electoral reform. If New Zealand (or indeed Scotland and Wales) is any guide, it might take some time for party behaviour to adapt as a consequence of reform, but adapt it surely will. Although he might need some help from his father, the schoolboy who had such trouble with Picasso at the beginning of this book would still be able to make sense of our changed parties. But change they must or else Westminster politicians will continue to be like those earlier schoolboys in Thomas Gray's *Ode on a Distant Prospect of Eton College*:

> No sense have they of ills to come,
> Nor care beyond to-day.

Notes

1 Parties and the party system in Britain

1 Ware 1996.
2 G.B. Shaw, *Political Quarterly*, October–December 1935, quoted in Chappelow 1969: 312.
3 When asked by British communists in the 1920s whether they should support the British Labour for example, Lenin had replied in the affirmative – just as a rope supports a dying man.
4 Sara Laville, *Guardian*, 4 April 2005.
5 Ware 1996: 4–5.
6 Heywood 1977: 233–34.
7 Kirchheimer 1966: 177–200.
8 See, for example, Olson 1986: 165–89.
9 Madison 1941: 54.
10 J. Downs 1957: 25.
11 But there is a sting in the tail as far as Downs is concerned, for in his 'rational choice' theory of political behaviour, he argued famously that 'parties formulate policies in order to win elections, rather than win elections in order to formulate policies': J. Downs 1957: 28.
12 Maor 1997: 6.
13 Ware 1996: 5.
14 Ball 1981: 3.
15 Heywood 1977: 233–34.
16 Edmund Burke, *Thoughts on the Cause of the Present Discontents*, first published in 1770.
17 Epstein 1967: 5.
18 See, for example, Martin 1906: 655–707.
19 As, for example, Macaulay 1861 does, esp. vol. iv.
20 See Chrimes 1952.
21 Quoted in Williamson 1952.
22 Williamson 1952: 18.
23 Hume 1970: 532.
24 See Namier 1962.
25 Judge 1993: 70.
26 See O'Gorman 1975: 14–15.
27 Quoted in Hill 1976.
28 Hill 1976: 37–38.
29 Hill 1976: 227.
30 The term 'whipping-in' comes from hunting. When chasing the fox, the hounds would need to be 'whipped in' for the pack to retain its cohesion. As time wore on, all parties appointed teams of whippers in, or simply Whips, in order to maintain party discipline, especially in important parliamentary votes.

31 Plucknett 1946: 692.
32 See B. Harrison 1996: 33–35.
33 Feiling 1938: v.
34 See G.K. Roberts 1970: 18.
35 Ostrogorski 1902: 6.
36 Stephen 1867: 106–07.
37 Ostrogorski 1902: 22.
38 Chesterton 1917: 262.
39 Voltaire certainly thought so, and commended the British constitution, too, for its attitude towards individual liberty: see Voltaire 1931.
40 N. Baker 1973: 211.
41 This view is certainly accepted by modern historians, for example Cannon 1969; O'Gorman 1982.
42 Wiener 1981.
43 Gradual is as gradual does. As recently as 1963 the Conservative Party selected as its leader a member of the House of Lords and an aristocrat, the 14th Earl of Home, who was consequently obliged to renounce his peerage. It is reported that his mother, on hearing of his decision to accept the leadership of both party and nation, observed that it was 'very decent of Alec to do the Prime Minister thing'.
44 The Utilitarians were a group of early nineteenth-century radical politicians and political thinkers who argued that the purpose of government was, in their words, to provide 'the greatest happiness of the greatest number'.
45 See E. Barker 1967: 86.
46 Gilmour 1969: 24.
47 Katz and Mair 1994: 12.
48 Charles Dickens, *The Pickwick Papers*, first published in 1836.
49 Anthony Trollope, *Ralph the Heir*, originally published in 1871, concerns the by-election at the mythical Percycross. Trollope was to return to his Beverley experiences later, in *The Duke's Children*, 1880.
50 Ostrogorski 1902: 57.
51 Quoted in S.H. Beer 1969: 36.
52 Quoted in Thomas 1953: 14.
53 See Tether 1988.
54 Ostrogorski 1902: 142.
55 See, for example, Rae 1878; Tether 1990.
56 See Pugh 1982: 15–17.
57 J. Fisher 1996a: 7.
58 Feuchtwanger 1959: 199.
59 Pugh 1982: 50; see also Robb 1942.
60 See Marriott 1882.
61 Hanham 1959: 126.
62 The governing party received £10,000 annually, unaudited, from the Secret Service Fund until 1886. Additional funding, and funding for the opposition parties, for electoral purposes, was raised from peers, wealthy MPs and candidates. These efforts were augmented by the open bartering for honours. The sale of honours, including peerages, was begun by the Liberals in 1891: see Hanham 1959: 371.
63 Although some MPs vied for the votes of fewer than 2,000, others courted over 8,000: Hanham 1959, Appendix 2: 403.
64 Pinto-Duschinsky 1981: 49.
65 Hanham 1959: xvii.
66 Quoted in R. Barker 1971: 132.
67 Quoted in R. Barker 1971: 145.
68 Hanham 1959: xvii.
69 For example, Dangerfield 1966.

70 See James 1978: 320–55.
71 Single or divorced women had enjoyed votes in many local elections for several centuries. Famously the outcome of the election for the beadle in Charles Dickens' *Sketches of Boz* (1836) hung on the vote of one elderly female muffin maker! These women could vote in local Health and Education Board elections and in county and county borough elections (and the Scottish equivalents) from the 1880s.
72 Two were university seats, two were Northern Irish seats and five were in the pre-election year of 1958.
73 For an account of how this was accomplished, see R.A. Butler 1973: ch. 7.
74 In 1967, for example, of eight by-elections in constituencies held by Labour, no fewer than five were lost.
75 Had the seven Ulster Unionist MPs followed the usual pattern and taken the Conservative whip, Heath would have been returned to power.
76 For a discussion of this see Ingle 1986: 105–19.
77 Sartori 1976.
78 See Rasmussen 1979.
79 Seldon 1996.
80 Drucker 1979.
81 Until Hawke and then Keating won five consecutive elections for Labor between 1983 and 1996, the Right had been in office three times as long as the ALP.
82 Lijphart 1984.
83 McKenzie 1955.
84 Quoted in Gilmour 1969: 33.

2 Conservative Party ideology

1 Quinton 1978: 24.
2 Quoted in White 1950: 1.
3 See Hearnshaw 1932.
4 O'Sullivan 1976: 24.
5 See Gilmour 1977.
6 Brady 1968: 297.
7 Gissing 1886.
8 Quoted in Wagar 1965: 277.
9 Hogg 1969.
10 Hogg 1969: 99.
11 Leach 1996: 117.
12 O'Sullivan 1976: 12.
13 Blake 1972: 1.
14 Rose 1965: 143.
15 Iain Macleod (1913–70) was Leader of the House under Harold Macmillan and briefly Chancellor of the Exchequer under Edward Heath.
16 Julian Critchley (1930–2000) was a Conservative backbencher in the old Tory mould. A thorn in the flesh of the party leadership, he famously described Margaret Thatcher as 'the Great She-Elephant'.
17 S.H. Beer, 'Two kinds of Conservatism', *Observer*, 8 May 1955, quoted in Greenleaf 1983, vol. 2: 195.
18 Benjamin Disraeli, quoted in Smith 1967: 301.
19 Enoch Powell (1912–98) was a famous right-wing polemicist and orator, and a Conservative and then Ulster Unionist MP. He held Cabinet office but is primarily remembered for his outspoken views on race, immigration, patriotism and Europe.
20 E. Powell 1968: 8 (italics added).
21 Quoted in Norton and Aughey 1981: 27.

22 S.H. Beer 1965: 272.
23 Leach 1996: 124.
24 Uttley 1978: 51.
25 John Rawls argued in *A Theory of Justice* (1971) that social and economic inequalities were tolerable if they gave the greatest benefit to the least advantaged.
26 P. Walker 1977: 20.
27 Quoted in Norton and Aughey 1981: 37.
28 Norton and Aughey 1981: 47.
29 Quoted in Greenleaf 1983, vol. 1: 205.
30 Quoted in Dicey 1919: 225.
31 See Laski 1962: 130–32.
32 Herbert 1908: 5–6.
33 Hearnshaw 1933: 285–86.
34 Blake and Patten 1976: 12; see also Thatcher 1968.
35 Blake and Patten 1976: 10.
36 Norton and Aughey 1981: 92.
37 Maude 1963.
38 Thatcher's mentor, Sir Keith Joseph, had suggested that Macmillan's 'middle way' Conservatism represented the 'slippery slope to collectivism': Joseph 1975: 27.
39 Peel had been persuaded to support Catholic emancipation, for example, twenty years before. It is interesting to recall that in his political novels, Disraeli spoke of Peel's 'Conservatism' as a betrayal of what he termed 'true toryism'.
40 Gash 1977: 125.
41 Gilmour 1977: 86.
42 Feuchtwanger 1968: 10.
43 Ward 1974.
44 Norton and Aughey 1981: 107.
45 Disraeli 1980, book ii, ch. 5: 96.
46 Cornford 1963.
47 For a full account of this issue and its consequences, see James 1978.
48 Norton and Aughey 1981: 117.
49 Quoted in Norton and Aughey 1981: 128; for a full account of the work of these reformers, see R.A. Butler 1973, ch. 7.
50 See National Union of Conservative and Constitutional Associations 1941; Tory Reform Committee 1943.
51 Macmillan, in his younger days, had been MP for Stockton-on-Tees; he had witnessed first hand the poverty of unemployed people. Moreover his grandfather had been a Christian Socialist influenced by William Morris (see Chapter 3): Sampson 1968: 11–12.
52 Ramsden 1980: 226.
53 Schoen 1977.
54 Heath held an election in order to strengthen his hand to deal with a miners' strike. His platform was 'Who runs Britain?'
55 Gamble 1988: 231. For his analysis of the pre-Thatcher party, see Gamble 1974.
56 Gamble 1988: 232.
57 Gamble 1988: 85.
58 Milton Friedman, Nobel Prize winner in 1976 and author of, *inter alia*, *Capitalism and Freedom* (1962).
59 Gamble 1988: 50.
60 *The Independent*, 14 September 1987.
61 See Letwin 1992: chs 1, 2.
62 There are individual men and women, and there are families, said Mrs Thatcher in an interview with *Woman's Own* magazine on 31 October 1987, but there is no such thing as society.

63 *The Independent*, 21 July 1987.

64 See 'The politics of self', in Scruton 1988; see also Scruton 1980.

65 *Sunday Telegraph*, 6 March 1988.

66 *The Independent*, 19 July 1988.

67 *Daily Telegraph*, 10 October 1997.

68 *The Times*, 20 January 1999.

69 Much of the discussion on Cameron's politics is taken from an article by one of Cameron's special advisers: see Kruger 2006.

70 See Willetts 2003.

71 Conservative Party 2006.

72 See Schumann 1978: 807.

73 Hobsbawm 1990.

74 As Goschen pointed out: 'Government interference and protection have more attraction to those who find their class surrounded by evils and troubles', quoted in Greenleaf 1983, vol. 1: 215.

75 In G.B. Shaw's *Man and Superman* (1906) there is a memorable exchange between Jack Tanner and the bandit Mendoza in which the latter introduces himself as a brigand who lives by robbing the rich to which Tanner replies that he is a gentleman who lives by robbing the poor.

76 Gamble 1988: 192.

77 Hall 1980.

78 *Guardian*, 15 May 1995.

79 *The Times*, 5 October 1998.

80 Editorial, 'Cameron puts his faith in society', *Daily Telegraph*, 18 June 2007.

81 Polly Toynbee pointed out that Cameron's rhetoric about putting better provision of services before tax cuts was not being carried out by Conservative councils. She cited Hammersmith, which announced a tax cut of 3 per cent in 2007, and at the same time closed a mental health day centre, and Croydon, which announced a zero rate increase and cut 10 per cent investment in the voluntary sector (*Guardian*, 20 March 2007).

82 *The Week*, 619, 27 June 2007: 21.

83 Jo Revill and Nicholas Watt, 'Cameron faces split within Tory ranks', *Observer*, 1 July 2007.

84 This was the Europhile Quentin Davies, who joined Labour in June 2007 (*Daily Telegraph*, 17 June 2007).

85 *The Times*, 6 October 1998.

86 Watt, Nicholas, 'Cameron offers Deal to Liberal Democrats', *The Observer*, 16 December 2007.

3 Labour Party ideology

1 Robert Owen was a Welsh mill manager and owner whose New Lanark Mill, near Glasgow, was run on cooperative lines. Owen saw that the children of his workers were educated and that profits were shared. Although originally a follower of Jeremy Bentham, Owen became a committed and active cooperative socialist.

2 See M. Beer 1920.

3 Dennis and Halsey 1988:4.

4 *Matthew* 19:24.

5 *Luke* 12:33.

6 *Luke* 6:20.

7 *Acts of the Apostles* 4:4–5.

8 P. Jones 1968.

9 F.D. Maurice was author also of *Theological Essays* (1853), which so shocked the principal of King's College that he asked Maurice to resign from his post of Professor of Theology.

10   Charles Kingsley was author of the classic *The Water Babies* (1863).
11   Thomas Hughes was author of the classic *Tom Brown's School Days* (1857).
12   See Parsons 1988.
13   Dennis and Halsey 1988: 2.
14   Dennis and Halsey 1988: 4.
15   See Foote 1997: 33–39.
16   See, for example, Morton 1973.
17   Morris 1973b.
18   Morris 1973a.
19   In fact Trevor had been a Unitarian minister, though he later gave up his position to concentrate on his socialist activities.
20   After one visit the Webbs published a massive apologia for the USSR, *Soviet Communism: A New Civilisation?* (1935).
21   See Pelling 1987: ch. 6.
22   The LRC had contested the general election of 1900 with funds of only £33.
23   Hardie, it is reported, was carried shoulder high by his enthusiastic voters from West Ham to the Palace of Westminster.
24   Quoted in Saville 1973: 215.
25   D. Coates 1975: 12.
26   See Callaghan 1990: ch. 2.
27   *A Contribution to the Critique of Political Economy*, 1859, quoted in Berki 1975: 67.
28   Marx explores this idea in, for example, *German Ideology*, written in 1845.
29   Tressell 1965.
30   This is not a concept that Marx himself set out with any precision, though it has played a dominant part in Marxist theories since.
31   A series of extracts from representatives of each of these basic principles is included in Wright 1983.
32   See Crick 1994.
33   The SDF sought parliamentary representation to the extent even of fighting a by-election (unsuccessfully) against the Liberals in 1895 with clandestine financial support from the Conservative Party (the so-called Tory gold scandal).
34   G.B. Shaw 1932: 158.
35   From *Time and Tide*, 2 February 1945, quoted in Chappelow 1969: 321.
36   Margaret Cole (1961) has written a detailed history of the Fabians; see also Hugh 1984. For an account of the early years, see Mackenzie and Mackenzie 1977.
37   This form of democratic localism has remained at least at the level of aspiration: see Evan Luard, 'Socialism at the grass-roots', in Luard 1979: 145–60.
38   See Field 1970; see also R. Barker 1975.
39   See Wright 1987.
40   The circulation of *The Clarion*, which was pro-war, fell during this period from more than 80,000 to little more than 5,000.
41   Being unfit for military service, Orwell joined the Home Guard.
42   Berki 1975: 13.
43   H. Morrison, 'Consideration arising out of the General Election 1951', quoted in Fielding 1992.
44   L. Thompson, *Portrait of England: News from Somewhere* (1952), quoted in Fielding 1992: 148.
45   Orwell 1963: 157.
46   Wells 1970: 243.
47   See Ford 1989.
48   D. Coates 1975: 13.
49   Aldine 1929: 330.
50   Lyman 1957: 148.

51 For many syndicalists and fundamentalists, a general strike was the great catalyst for the overthrow of the capitalist state.
52 For a full analysis of these developments, see Berkeley 1978.
53 See Fyrth 1995.
54 Orwell 1963: 157.
55 Crosland 1956.
56 Crossman 1953.
57 Strachey 1953.
58 The aim of Clause Four was: 'To secure for the producers by hand and by brain the full fruits of their industry, and the most equitable distribution thereof that may be possible, upon the common ownership of the means of production.'
59 Ironically Prime Minister Wilson, who introduced the charges, had resigned from the Cabinet when charges were originally imposed in 1951.
60 See E. Shaw 1996: 82–88.
61 See Seyd 1987.
62 See Wickam-Jones 1996.
63 Schumpeter 1976.
64 Fukuyama 1993.
65 Gamble 1992; see also Kinnock 1986.
66 Marquand.
67 See E. Shaw 1994: 29–52.
68 Mandelson and Liddle 1996: 217.
69 Labour Party 1997.
70 J. Fisher 1996a: 83–85. B. Jones 1995, on the other hand, ascribes Blair's victory to astute tactics.
71 The term 'New Labour' was not in fact new. A party with this name had been formed by a group who had resigned in the mid 1980s from the New Zealand Labour Party. They, however, were rebelling against their party's move to the right. Confusingly New Labour in the Antipodes equated much more closely to Old Labour in the United Kingdom.
72 Callaghan and Tumey 2001; Diamond 2004.
73 E. Shaw 1998.
74 Wilks 1997: 692.
75 Radice and Pollard 1993: 16.
76 See Wilkinson 1998; see also Blair 1995. Here Blair refers to nationalisation as a 'wrong turn' and subscribes instead to the reformism of the New Liberals, which he associates with ethical rather than ideological socialism.
77 See, for example, Hutton et al. 1997.
78 See Will Hutton, *The State We're In* (1995).
79 See Ackernman and Alstott 1999.
80 Giddens 1998b.
81 Giddens 1998a.
82 See Studlar 2003. Note that an international forum was organised in 1999, involving Tony Blair, Bill and Hillary Clinton, Wim Kok, the Dutch Prime Minister, Gerhard Schroeder, the German Chancellor, and Massimo d'Alema, the Italian Prime Minister.
83 See 'About the Third Way', *Observer*, 1 June 1998; see also Giddens 2001.
84 Giddens 2001: 7.
85 Marquand 1998.
86 See Beach 2006 and, from a broader historical perspective, Plant et al. 2004.
87 S.H. Beer, *Modern British Politics* (first published in 1965), was titled *British Politics in the Collectivist Age* in the rest of the world.
88 See Hindness 1971.
89 Kellner 1998: 3.

90 Ingle 2002: 169.
91 Blair 1994: 4.

4 Conservative Party organisation

1   See Rose 1976a: 154–55.
2   McKenzie 1955: ch. 5.
3   Norton and Aughey1981: 242–43. Norton was happy enough with this model to retain it in his more recent *The Conservative Party* (1996: ch. 9).
4   Quoted in N. Fisher 1977: 3. The leader of any party can be axed by the poles (polls) but Churchill had in mind axing a leader to prevent him or her losing an election.
5   Writing in *The Independent* (14 May 1997), Anthony Bevins described his action as desertion, a 'gross abdication of responsibility, a dereliction of duty'.
6   Such a vote was to be triggered by 15 per cent of MPs writing to the chairman of The 1922.
7   'The party leader': Norton 1996: 147.
8   Norton and Aughey 1981: 250–52.
9   *Observer*, 16 December 1984.
10 The Prime Minister was intent on selling Westland to an American company whereas Heseltine preferred a European consortium.
11 The phrase 'poll tax' referred back to the tax imposed in the late fourteenth century by Richard II, which led indirectly to the Peasants' Revolt of 1381.
12 *Hansard*, HC 6 Ser, vol. 226, cols 284–85 (9 June 1993).
13 Richard Spring MP was the seventeenth Conservative to attract newspaper headlines of this general nature during Major's second administration (see *Guardian*, 11 April 1995).
14 Graham Riddick and David Treddinick were found by the House's Privilege Committee to have brought Parliament into disrepute (see *Guardian*, 5 April 1995).
15 As the 1997 election approached, three more Conservative MPs decided to stand down as a result of personal indiscretions (*The Independent on Sunday*, 30 March 1997).
16 Goodhart 1973: 15.
17 Norton 1996: 131.
18 *Guardian*, 21 May 1985. It is worth pointing out that the experienced Chief Whip, John (later Lord) Wakeham, was in hospital at this time. His restraining influence might otherwise have been crucial.
19 See Aspinall 1926.
20 Michael Brown, 'Confessions of a Tory rebel', *Guardian*, 2 August 1985.
21 Norton 1993: ch. 5.
22 Philip Cowley has contributed greatly to scholarship in this field. See, for example, Cowley 2005.
23 *Guardian*, 25 May 1995.
24 *The Independent*, 12 November 1996.
25 See Shell and Beamish 1993.
26 Norton and Aughey 1981: 258.
27 *The Times,* 9 October 1998.
28 Norton 1996: 152.
29 A-levels, she thundered in Cabinet, would be reformed 'over my dead body'.
30 *The Independent* 25 June 1997.
31 Pinto-Duschinsky 1972.
32 Hugo Young, *Guardian*, 7 March 1986.
33 In 1994, for example, John Major was obliged to appoint Jeremy Hanley, whose one claim to public recognition was that his father had been the famous wartime comedian Tommy Hanley.
34 *Sunday Telegraph*, 12 September 1993.
35 Norton 1996: 154.

36 In fact this is not entirely true: briefly, under the leadership of Lord Randolph Churchill, the Union did try unsuccessfully to assert itself against the parliamentary party and its leader Lord Salisbury.
37 McKenzie 1955: 151.
38 See Tether 1996b: 109–11.
39 *The Times*, 2 February 1998.
40 http://www.conservativewomen.org.uk/history.asp
41 *Guardian*, 5 April 1986.
42 *Daily Telegraph*, 14 December 1996.
43 *The Times*, 4 June 1998.
44 W. Woodward and T. Branigan, 'The A-list: New leader's drive for woman and minority candidates', *Guardian*, 19 April 2006.
45 A group has been established called Operation Black Vote and Cameron intends, through this group, actively to target wider ethnic participation at all levels in the party.
46 See Lynch 1998.
47 *The Scotsman*, 17 August 2006.
48 *The Herald*, 2 May 2005.
49 Norton and Aughey 1981: 218.
50 *Charter News*, Spring 1985.
51 McKenzie 1955: 24.
52 Gamble 1979: 40.
53 See Tether 1996a: 122.
54 Kelly 1989.
55 Gilmour 1971: 80.
56 Kelly 1989: 140.
57 Kelly 1989: 21.
58 Whiteley et al. 1994: 38–39.
59 Tether 1996b: 126.
60 This is an example that Florence Faucher-King gives in her excellent investigation of party conferences: Faucher-King 2005: 178.
61 Tether 1996b: 104.
62 Gamble 1979: 39.
63 *The Times*, 24 June 1998.
64 *The Times*, 9 June 1998.
65 *Daily Telegraph*, 15 August 1998.
66 *The Independent*, 26 March 2005.
67 Woodward, Will, 'Inside the Tory war room', *The Guardian*, 3 October 1967.
68 Pinto-Duschinsky 1981.
69 J. Fisher 1996b.
70 *Daily Telegraph*, 7 March 2007.
71 *The Times*, 13 February 1998. This article reveals that the donor's father, who had left Hong Kong in 1978 following police inquiries, had been hoping to return.
72 Grant 2005.
73 Tania Branigan, *Guardian*, 29 November 2006.
74 Cobain, Ian and Branigan, Tania 'Cameron pressed to reveal truth on Tory millionaire's tax', *The Guardian*, 10 November 1977.

5 Labour Party organisation

1 See McKenzie 1955: 426–31.
2 See P.M. Williams 1982.
3 Richard Cockerill, TV documentary *Blair: The Inside Story* (1), broadcast on BBC2, 18 February 2007.

4 See F. Williams 1961: 535.
5 For a full account of this period, see Young and Fielding 2003.
6 Plant 2004.
7 See K. Morgan 1999.
8 See Seldon and Hickson 2004 passim.
9 Even as he was preparing for electoral battle in 1997, Blair could 'talk the talk', as this extract from a pre-election conference speech shows:

> The next election is not a struggle for political power. It is a battle for the soul of our nation....We will take the excess profits of the new robber barons in Tory Britain in the privatised utilities and use it for the most radical programme of work and education ever put forward in Britain.

10 Tony Blair, in Cockerill, *Blair: The Inside Story* (1).
11 Cockerill, *Blair: The Inside Story* (1).
12 D. Coates and Lawler 2000.
13 Quoted in Cockerill, *Blair: The Inside Story* (3), broadcast on BB2, 6 March 2007.
14 *Guardian*, 17 February 2007.
15 For an account of this debate, see P.M. Williams 1979.
16 Brian Brivati is clear that, though a moderniser, Gaitskell was committed to the historical purposes of Labour in a way that Blair was not: see Brivati 1999.
17 Alan Watkins, *Observer*, 16 November 1980.
18 See Mitchell 1984: 51.
19 Shore 1993: 137.
20 *Guardian*, 4 June 1984.
21 E. Shaw 1999: 127.
22 See Ivor Crewe, *Guardian*, 30 September 1983.
23 Even Kinnock's position was under challenge. Shadow Cabinet colleagues made two attempts to replace him before the 1992 election with his deputy John Smith but the latter, who treated his leader with 'barely concealed hostility', refused to become involved (Nicolas Wapshott, *Observer*, 21 June 1992).
24 Butler and Kavanagh 1997: 49.
25 Brand 1992: 48.
26 Miliband 1972: 345.
27 See Hayter 2005.
28 Minkin 1991.
29 'The real Labour funding crisis', *The Economist*, 8 February 2007.
30 Minkin 1991: 262–67.
31 In 1981 four Co-operative-sponsored MPs left to join the SDP.
32 During one debate in Brussels, for example, Leslie Huckfield, who had exhausted his time and thus had his microphone cut off, produced a megaphone to continue his speech (*Guardian*, 23 November 1984).
33 Hilary Wainwright (editor of *Red Pepper*), *The Times*, 7 January 1998.
34 Russell and Sciara 2007.
35 M. Taylor 2001.
36 This is the phrase coined by the democratic left and referred to by Neil Lawson in Compass literature.
37 Smith 2000.
38 Patrick Wintour, *Guardian*, 10 November 2001.
39 Michael White, *Guardian*, 12 July 2005. The committee, for example, recommended that the PLP should not vote on the government's stated intention to replace Trident.
40 At the time Labour had an overall majority of 161.
41 Kelly et al. 2006.
42 *Labour Party Year Book 1984–85*, London, Walworth Road, 1985.

43 J. Fisher 1996a: 47.
44 E. Shaw 1990.
45 Kavanagh 1982a: 206.
46 Labour Party 1997: 8.
47 It was always Blair's intention to reform the NEC as a key to wider reforms (*Guardian*, 1 January 1995).
48 *The Times*, 30 September 1997.
49 *Daily Telegraph*, 26 September 1998.
50 *The Times*, 28 September 1998.
51 *Guardian*, 25 November 1985.
52 Blumler 1990: 103.
53 See McKibbins 1977, esp. ch. 7.
54 J. Torridge, *The Independent*, 6 October 1988.
55 Truth to tell, it remained a hindrance to left-wing attempts to take control of the party during the days of both Aneurin Bevan in the 1950s and Tony Benn in the early 1980s. Ian Aitken argued that a party controlled largely by the constituencies would be far more open to a 'disastrous Trotskyist take-over' (*Guardian*, June 22 1992); see also Lewis 1992.
56 K. Coates and Topham 1980: 319.
57 *The Independent*, 30 September 1988.
58 Leopold 1997.
59 Howell 1998.
60 *The Times*, 21 April 1997.
61 *Guardian*, 1 May 1995.
62 Quoted in McKenzie 1982.
63 *Guardian*, 19 June 1982.
64 *Sunday Times*, 31 January 1988.
65 See *Campaign Guide*, Conservative Research Department, London, 1983.
66 *Sunday Times*, 9 March 1986.
67 Seyd 1999.
68 Simon Jenkins described the process as 'evil, profoundly undemocratic' (*The Times*, 27 May 1995).
69 Hassan 2003.
70 Minkin 1987.
71 Attlee 1937: 93.
72 See McKenzie 1982.
73 See Faucher-King and Treille 2003.
74 *Guardian*, 1 October 1991.
75 Peter Jenkins, *Guardian*, 22 October 1980.
76 Faucher 1999.
77 J. Fisher 1996a: 80.
78 *Scotland on Sunday*, 16 November 1997. Eccleston was a major figure in Formula One racing. When Labour came to power, it banned tobacco advertising in all sports except Formula One racing.
79 Swraj Paul, the wealthy Indian-born industrialist, helped to pay for Blair's private office through a trust, the Industrial Research Trust, with a donation of £47,000 (*Observer*, 1 September 1996).
80 *The Times*, 22 April 1998.
81 *The Times*, 31 August 1998.
82 Butler and Kavanagh 1997: 55.
83 David Hencke and Will Woodward, *Guardian*, 16 March 2006.
84 Watt, Nicholas et al, 'Labour's Dangerous Donors', *The Observer*, 2 December 2007.
85 *Daily Telegraph*, 7 March 2007.

86 *Guardian*, 12 March 2007.
87 *Guardian*, 22 October 1980.
88 Mair 1997: 150.
89 *The Times*, 8 July 1998.
90 Tony Benn, *Tribune*, 3 April 1998.
91 *The Times*, 29 September 1997.
92 Minkin 1991: 291.
93 Mandelson and Liddle 1996: 215.
94 Mair 1997: 149.
95 Faucher-King 2005: 240.

6 Conservative politicians, activists and supporters

1 Burch and Moran 1985.
2 Mellors 1978.
3 Mellors 1978: 39.
4 Mellors 1978: 71.
5 Mellors 1978: 71.
6 Haxey 1939.
7 Quoted in Ross 1948: 236–38.
8 National Union of Conservative and Unionist Associations 1949: 13–14.
9 Butler and Pinto-Duschinsky 1980.
10 Burch and Moran 1985.
11 Burch and Moran 1985.
12 Rush 1986.
13 *The Independent*, 8 November 1988.
14 Thomas 1984.
15 D. Baker and Fountain 1996.
16 Critchley 1992.
17 Quoted in Thomas 1984.
18 *Observer*, 10 February 1985.
19 *Observer*, 22 May 1983.
20 Roth 1984.
21 *Observer*, 10 February 1985.
22 Crewe and Sarlvik 1980.
23 Butler and Pinto-Duschinsky 1980.
24 D. Baker and Fountain 1996.
25 Whiteley et al. 1994.
26 The following figures, like similar material in subsequent chapters, are extracted from data provided by Colin Mellors of the University of York, to whom I am most grateful.
27 All these figures are taken from Cracknell 2005.
28 *Today*, 14 August 1986.
29 *Guardian*, 9 February 1983.
30 Norton 1998.
31 The Maastricht Treaty, formally the Treaty of European Unity, signed on 2 February 1992, led to the creation of the European Union. Basically the Treaty created three pillars of European competence in foreign and security policy, justice and home affairs, and European Community matters (those for which the EC had been responsible). In the negotiations Major had fought successfully to retain opt-out clauses on membership of a common European currency and on the Social Contract, which bound states to common policies on, for example, employment. Moreover Major had striven to keep the 'f' word (federalism) off the Maastricht agenda. Nevertheless to his opponents, he had surrendered far too much.

32 Fresh Start became the title of a staunchly Eurosceptic group of about eighty MPs.
33 Norton 1998 gives a blow-by-blow account of the passage of the Maastricht legislation and points out how extraordinary a passage of events it constituted in the history of the Conservative parliamentary party.
34 According to *Guardian*, 25 April 1995, the 'Whipless Nine' were 'feted as heroes in their own constituencies and beyond' and were, regarded more generally as the tail that wagged the party dog.
35 *The Independent*, 9 October 1996.
36 Norton 1998: 104–06.
37 Holmes 1988.
38 Ramsden 1988: 470.
39 *Sunday Times*, 4 May 1997.
40 *Sunday Telegraph*, 2 November 1997.
41 Scott Report 1996.
42 Willetts 1998.
43 Ramsden 1988: 176.
44 *The Times*, 16 November 1996.
45 Quoted by Ronald Butt, *Sunday Times*, 16 October 1977.
46 *Sunday Telegraph*, 7 October 2007
47 See Guttsman 1963.
48 D. Baker and Fountain 1996: 86–97.
49 D. Baker and Fountain 1996: 97.
50 Ramsden 1988: 493.
51 Cowley 1997.
52 See Kavanagh and Butler 2005: 29–30.
53 Such was the opposition within the party leadership to Duncan Smith that Portillo, Maude and Hague, as well as Clarke, refused to serve under him.
54 Figures taken from the Sutton Trust 2005.
55 Whiteley et al. 1994.
56 Tether 1980.
57 Whiteley et al. 1994: 22.
58 See, for example, Crowson 2002.
59 For example, one campaign poster in 2005 declared: *It's not Racist to Impose Limits on Immigration.* However, since this was closely followed by the 2005 strap line *Are You Thinking What We're Thinking?* it took on a somewhat sinister flavour.
60 ICM Polls, for *Guardian*, November 2004.
61 Whiteley et al. 1994: 156–57.
62 Whiteley et al. 1994: 160.
63 Lynch 2003.
64 Cameron is qualified to play rugby for Scotland! His father is a Scot by birth and lineage.
65 ICM Polls, for *Guardian*, November 2004.
66 Rose 1976b: 208–09.
67 Butler and Stokes 1974: 181.
68 McKenzie and Silver 1968: 242.
69 See, for example, Abrams and Rose 1960.
70 Butler and Stokes 1974: 185.
71 In 1992, on a turnout of 77.7 per cent, the Conservative Party polled over 14 million votes, the largest popular vote polled by any British party and fully 7 per cent more than Labour.
72 See Jowell et al. 1988.
73 Butler and Kavanagh 1997.
74 Crewe et al. 1977.
75 Butler and Kavanagh 1983: appendix 2.

76 All these figures are taken from Kavanagh and Butler 2005: 197–98.
77 Kavanagh and Butler 2005: 235.
78 Norton and Aughey 1981: 175.
79 Brian Walden, *Sunday Times*, 8 November 1987.
80 Butler and Kavanagh 1983: 293.
81 Curtice and Stead 1997: 305.
82 Quoted in Ramsden 1988: 483.
83 Ingle 2007: 6–8.
84 ICM Polls for *Guardian*, November 2004.

7 Labour politicians, representatives, activists and supporters

1 See Kavanagh 1982b.
2 Cracknell 2005.
3 Mellors 1978: 50.
4 Quoted in Mellors 1978: 51.
5 Sutton Trust 2005: 5.
6 Mellors 1978: 74.
7 R.K. Kelsall et al., *Times Higher Educational Supplement*, 25 February 1972.
8 Kavanagh 1982b: 103.
9 Cracknell 2005: 4.
10 Cracknell 2005: 4.
11 *Sunday Times*, 4 May 1997.
12 Cracknell 2005: 4.
13 Simon 2006.
14 A useful general account of ideological developments within both parties, but especially Labour, is by Judge 1993.
15 See Finer et al. 1961: 104–14; Berrington 1963: 7–8.
16 Mellors 1978: 120.
17 Benn 1992: 70.
18 *The Independent*, 27 October 1987.
19 *Sunday Telegraph*, 20 July 1986.
20 A survey of 121 of the 130 marginal seats in the 1987 general election showed that a Labour government would have been younger, more middle class, better educated and almost certainly more radical than any of its predecessors: 70 per cent, for example, belonged to the Campaign for Nuclear Disarmament (*The Times*, 30 July 1986).
21 Cowley and Norton 1996.
22 Norris 1999.
23 Libby Purves, *The Times*, 2 December 1977.
24 *The Times*, 7 February 1998.
25 *The Independent*, 2 May 1997.
26 *The Times*, 12 December 1997.
27 Simon 2006: 26.
28 Simon 2006: 25.
29 Simon 2006: 25.
30 Kavanagh 1982b: 100.
31 The exceptions were Churchill, Callaghan and Major.
32 Burch and Moran 1985: 10.
33 Quoted in Mellors 1978: 78.
34 *Sunday Telegraph*, 11 January 1998.
35 Mary Ann Sieghart, *The Times*, 2 July 1998.
36 Libby Purves, *The Times*, 31 March 1998.
37 By Northern I mean England north of the Trent, Scotland and Wales.
38 Janosik 1968.

39 M. Harrison 1960: 238–39.
40 Turner 1978.
41 Turner 1978: 313.
42 Turner 1978: 314.
43 In the Bermondsey by-election of 1983, party leader Michael Foot had declared that one of those fighting for the candidacy, Peter Tatchell, would be selected over his dead body. Tatchell was duly selected and subsequently lost the seat, though Foot kept his head.
44 See Whiteley 1982; see also Kavanagh 1983, esp. ch. 3.
45 Whiteley 1982: 123.
46 Criddle 1984.
47 Criddle 1984: 123.
48 Criddle 1984: 123.
49 It was illegal to be politically active in an authority that employed you, so Militant activists got round this by becoming active in neighbouring districts.
50 *Sunday Times*, 22 November, 1987.
51 Seyd and Whiteley 1992.
52 Seyd and Whiteley 1992: 33.
53 Seyd and Whiteley 1992: 37, 202.
54 Mandelson and Liddle 1996: 216.
55 Mandelson and Liddle 1996: 218–20.
56 Mandelson and Liddle 1996: 220.
57 Mandelson and Liddle 1996: 229.
58 It is unfortunate that Seyd and Whiteley had not been able to differentiate between regions in their party membership analysis: there would have been some interesting comparisons.
59 *Daily Telegraph*, 2 August 1997.
60 *Sunday Telegraph*, 2 February 1998.
61 *The Times*, 11 March 1998.
62 *Sunday Telegraph*, 22 November 1998.
63 John Harris, *Guardian*, 7 April 2006.
64 BBC News, December 26 2006.
65 John Harris, *Guardian*, 7 April 2006.
66 John Harris, *Guardian*, 7 April 2006.
67 John Harris, *Guardian*, 7 April 2006.
68 Coulson 2005.
69 All the figures that follow are taken from this survey, which is available at the website www.YouGov.com
70 K. Roberts et al. 1977, esp. ch. 9.
71 Quoted in Butler and Kavanagh 1983: 278 (the original is in italics).
72 Peter Kellner, *New Statesman*, 23 June 1983.
73 Heath and MacDonald 1987.
74 Skidelsky 2002.
75 Butler and Kavanagh 1992: 62.
76 Butler and Kavanagh 1992: 279.
77 Butler and Kavanagh 1997: 251.
78 Figures calculated from Kavanagh and Butler 2005: 204.
79 Kavanagh and Butler 2005: 18.
80 Cowley 2002.
81 YouGov poll, quoted in Kavanagh and Butler 2005: 191.

8 Liberal Democrats – always the bridesmaid?

1 See T.A. Jenkins 2004.
2 Dangerfield 1966.
3 See Cooke 2002.

4 *The Times*, 27 January 1999.
5 McCallum and Readman 1947.
6 See Brack 2007.
7 Clarke 1978 is the main source for this account of events at the turn of the century. However, he was not concerned to make connections with the Alliance party of the 1980s; so these interpretations are my own.
8 It is interesting to note that a half-hearted attempt was made in 1984 to resurrect the Rainbow Circle by right-wing Labour MPs like Frank Field. This was a general debate on the desirability of arriving at some electoral arrangement between Labour and the Alliance with a view to forming an anti-Conservative coalition government.
9 Clarke 1983 sets out the principles of social democracy.
10 Meadowcroft 1981: 6.
11 Grimond 1959: 15.
12 Dodds 1957: 33.
13 Dodds 1957: 25.
14 In Greaves and Lishman 1981.
15 *Guardian*, 23 February 1979.
16 Roy Jenkins, a close friend of the Liberal leader David Steele, was the key figure in the development of the SDP and its alliance with the Liberals: see Adonis 2004.
17 R. Jenkins 1979.
18 R. Jenkins 1979.
19 Owen 1981.
20 Rodgers 1981.
21 S. Williams 1981.
22 See Studlar 1984.
23 Butler and Kavanagh 1984: appendix 1.
24 See Douglas 2005.
25 The voting was, by the Liberal party, 46,376 for, 6,325 against; by the SDP, 18,722 for, 9,929 against.
26 Hague became the only Conservative to win a parliamentary by-election in ten years.
27 The fullest account of the history of the SDP is by Crewe and King 1995.
28 See Stevenson 1996.
29 See Butler and Kavanagh 1988.
30 Holme 1997.
31 For a full account of the 'equidistance' debate, see Ingle 1995.
32 Quoted in Ingle 1995.
33 Marquand's vision for the Alliance was fully explored in Marquand 1989.
34 See Ingle 1987: 221.
35 Grimond 1959: 15.
36 This was accepted by a number of Labour activists. 'The Liberal Democrats', said one former Labour mayor after sixty years in that party, 'are now the only centre-left party and I am delighted to become a member'. He was one of four former Labour mayors to do so (*The Times*, 17 December 1997).
37 *The Independent*, 29 April 1997.
38 Most commentators agreed that the Liberal Democrat *Guarantee* was to the left of Labour's policy document, *New Labour: New Life for Britain*, in which the word 'socialist' was used only once.
39 As Joyce shows, the parties did indeed have much in common: see Joyce 1999.
40 Scottish and Welsh devolution had been advocated, along with Home Rule for Ireland, in 1894.
41 Not, as Alderman and Carter make clear, with the support of many within his party: see Alderman and Carter 2000.
42 See Seldon 2004: 273.

43 Ashdown 2000: 555.
44 Blair's own attitude to constitutional reform was nothing like as clearly formulated as that of the Liberal Democrats, or indeed as that of some of his own colleagues; see Seldon 2004.
45 Perhaps it was this reform, creating the fourth different electoral system, under which Scots vote (first past the post for Westminster, list system for Europe, additional member system for Holyrood and STV for local) that contributed most to the extraordinary – indeed scandalous – number of wasted votes in the Scottish elections of 2007.
46 Seldon and Kavanagh 2002: 126–27.
47 Although the joint committee established by Cook and Maclennan staggered on for two years after Ashdown's departure, it met only twice, to no significant purpose.
48 However, in 2007 at the party's Spring conference Campbell broached the subject of a possible future Lib-Lab coalition. Although he set a Brown government five tests (a deliberately high bar, his colleagues thought) a commitment to proportional representation was not one of them. It had always been a *sine qua non* for Ashdown.
49 Liberal Democrat Party, Policy Briefing no. 2, 1994.
50 Russell and Fieldhouse 2005: 43.
51 Clement Davies, who led the party in the 1950s, was set to effect the 'cushion style' of leadership; his aims for the party reflecting those of the last person to sit on him. For a fuller and kinder account of his leadership, see A.W. Powell 2003.
52 Marshall and Laws 2004 represent an attempt to introduce a more free-market approach into Liberal Democratic economic policy. Some regarded it as divisive.
53 This was particularly significant in Hughes' case because he had not prevented his constituency party from resorting to homophobic campaigning against his Labour opponent in the by-election that had originally brought him to parliament in 1983.
54 *Guardian*, 3 March 2007, referred to the whole episode judiciously as 'necessary but hurtful'.
55 Michael White, 'End of the Ming Dynasty?', *Guardian*, 4 May 2007.
56 Rawnsley, Andrew 'The Lib Dems must learn to tango with the style of Vince', *The Observer*, 16 December 2007.
57 *Daily Telegraph*, 3 August 1993.
58 See the Sutton Trust 2005.
59 The figures are taken from Cracknell 2005.
60 *Keesing's UK Record: 1994*.
61 Matthew Parris, *The Times*, 5 December 1997.
62 After the general election of 2005 and the various elections of 2007, Campbell claimed that, with their equal ability to contest with the Conservatives in the south and Labour in the North, the Liberal Democrats were, in fact, the only truly national party.
63 Liberal Democrats 1993.
64 This was a difficult decision for the party. The SNP and its supporters claimed that the SLD was following the UK party's lead in not being prepared even to discuss coalition (*Sunday Herald*, 6 May 2007). This is either naive or mischievous. During the election the SLD had made its opposition to a referendum on independence, to which the Nationalists were totally committed, abundantly clear. Should it then ignore those who had voted SLD on that understanding? However the way in which the party behaves in the coming parliament could make or break the novel idea (for Britain) of a minority government taking office with a view to serving a full term. Interestingly the New Zealand Labour Party did exactly this from 2004 to 2007.
65 See Laffin 2005, 2007.
66 W. Downs 1998.
67 Deshower 2003.
68 B. Taylor 2002.
69 See Brack 1996. For a fuller discussion of the policy making process, see Ingle 1996.

70 Brack 1996: 97.
71 Kavanagh and Butler 2005.
72 Criddle 1992: 219.
73 In 2004 the Liberal Democrats won the Leicester South by-election with an Asian candidate but he lost his seat at the 2005 election.
74 Criddle 1992: 120.
75 See Johnston 1986.
76 *The Economist*, 23 September 2004.
77 Bennie et al. 1996.
78 Whiteley et al. 2006.
79 Whiteley et al. 2006. 55. 43 per cent of the sample were ex-Liberals, only 14 per cent ex-SDP and the remaining 42 per cent had belonged to neither.
80 See Bennie et al. 1996.
81 Whiteley et al. 2006: 42.
82 Whiteley et al. 2006: 46.
83 Whiteley et al. 2006: 26–27.
84 Whiteley et al. 2006: 30–31.
85 Curtice 1996.
86 Kavanagh and Butler 2005: 236.
87 Kavanagh and Butler 2005: 45.
88 Russell and Fieldhouse paint a fuller picture of Liberal Democrat support that corroborates Curtice's earlier findings: see Russell and Fieldhouse 2005: 89–113.
89 Quoted in Kavanagh and Butler 2005: 191.
90 Toynbee, Polly, 'The Lib Dems face a clear choice', *The Guardian*, 16 November 2007.
91 Editorial, *The Times*, 21 January 1999.
92 Editorial, *The Times*, 21 January 1999.
93 Peter Riddell, *The Times*, 21 January 1999.
94 *Daily Telegraph*, 18 September 2007.
95 D. Walker 2003.
96 For example, at the Spring Conference in 2007, Campbell implicitly compared himself to a London centenarian, who had fought off a mugger. Later in the year, at the annual conference, he declared: 'When it comes to the next election I believe that there is some speculation the age will be a factor. You bet it will be, because I'll make it one'. (*The Guardian*, 21 September 2007).
97 *The Guardian*, 19 November 2007.

9 Britain's other parties

1 Strom1984.
2 Strom 1990.
3 Lorna Martin, 'Sheridan case leaves a party in splinters', *Observer*, 6 August 2006.
4 Lynch 2002: 55–58.
5 Thatcher had argued that her government's policies of privatisation constituted the only *real* devolution.
6 Lynch 2002: 161–90.
7 Lynch 2002: 236–37.
8 Lynch 2002: 253–57.
9 Salmond has always been perceived by some fundamentalists as too gradualist. When he came back to lead the party, there was talk of a new breakaway party being formed to provide more dynamism (Neil Rafferty, 'SNP rebels plan to form a new party', *Sunday Times*, 12 September 2004).
10 Lynch 2006.
11 This is why Lynch's book on the SNP tends to be structured around its electoral history: Lynch 2002.

12 Butt Phillip 1975.
13 Van Morgan 2006: 273.
14 K. Morgan 1981.
15 McAllister 2000.
16 Van Morgan 2006: 270.
17 Wyn Jones et al. 2001.
18 Key 2000.
19 P. Taylor 1997: 281–82.
20 Ingle 2006: 12.
21 The figures for the 2005 election, and all subsequent figures for that election, are taken from Kavanagh and Butler 2005.
22 www.greenparty.org.uk/news/3249
23 See Bennie 2004.
24 Kavanagh and Butler 2005: 246.
25 *Daily Telegraph*, 6 January 2007.
26 This was the outspoken Yorkshire millionaire, Paul Sykes.
27 *Guardian*, 29 July 2005.
28 *The Times*, 4 June 1983.
29 Paul Goodman, 'Why white hate won', *Sunday Telegraph*, 19 September 1993.
30 Shown by the BBC on 15 July 2004.
31 *Guardian*, 21 December 2006.
32 See Sykes 2005.
33 These policies are taken from the 2005 manifesto listed on the party's website in 2007.
34 Libby Purves, 'A BNP wolf stalks rural Britain, scenting victory', *The Times*, 3 February 2004.
35 BNP website: http://www. bnp.org.uk
36 Its two leaders have been Nick Wrack and now Linda Smith.
37 It was founded by George Monbiot, a Guardian journalist, and Salma Yaqoob, chair of the Birmingham Stop the War Coalition. Monbiot, however, resigned almost immediately.
38 For example, Nick Cohen wrote of Respect 'stoking the rage' of Muslims (*Observer*, 7 May 2006).
39 *Scotland on Sunday*, 4 June 2006.
40 Kavanagh and Butler 2005: 247.
41 Steve Brogan's 'Lies, myths and falsehoods: A day in the life of the BNP stronghold', *Guardian*, 8 July 2006, contains a number of quotations from actual and potential BNP voters along similar lines. One mother of a mixed-race daughter said that she would consider voting BNP precisely on the housing issue. Indeed the BNP campaign expressly linked the shortage of housing to the influx of immigrants and asylum seekers.
42 Kavanagh and Butler 2005: 204.
43 There are only a few occasions when the smaller parties have influenced Westminster politics decisively. However, Edward Heath tried to win the support of the Ulster Unionists when he was narrowly defeated in 1974. Had they agreed, he would presumably have returned to power. They did not. In 1995 the Major government narrowly won an EU fisheries vote on the strength of support from the Ulster Unionists. In 1979 the votes of the Ulster Unionists and the SNP, along with the Liberals, were decisive in unseating the Callaghan government.

Chapter 10 The British party system – fit for purpose?

1 Hayek 1979: 2–3.
2 It is strange that Home, like his colleague Lord Hailsham, who coined the phrase 'elective dictatorship', had Labour governments in mind when they criticised too powerful executives, when it was a Conservative Prime Minister, Margaret Thatcher, who was to explore the limits of executive power; see Douglas-Home 1976.

3 In Gamble and Walkland 1984.
4 G.B. Shaw 1960: 124; *Major Barbara* was first performed in 1905.
5 Rose 1984.
6 S.E. Finer advances this argument in *Adversary Politics and Electoral Reform* (1975).
7 Rose 1984: xxvii.
8 Lord McCarthy, the former trade union leader, for example, counted four changes in policy during the Labour government of 1964–70, four changes of policy during the 1970–74 Conservative government and five changes of policy during the 1974–79 Labour government in the field of incomes policy alone.
9 Rose 1984: 65.
10 What they represent is not so much parties contradicting each other as parties 'talking past' each other. He explains: 'A systematic analysis of the 1970 and 1974 manifestos shows that slightly more than half (57 per cent) of all manifesto pledges are nonpartisan' (Rose 1984: 65).
11 Norton 1975, 1980.
12 Hobson 1909.
13 Lenin 1999, first published in 1916.
14 Hennessy 1986.
15 Hugo Young, 'The strong-arm tactics that politicised Whitehall', *Guardian*, 17 July 1986.
16 Pliatsky 1980.
17 S.H. Beer 1965: 347.
18 S.H. Beer 1965: 347.
19 Gamble and Walkland 1984: 171.
20 Ashford 1981.
21 G.B. Shaw 1930: xiii.
22 Ingle and Tether 1981.
23 Ingle and Tether 1981: 143 (italics added).
24 Ingle and Tether 1981: 155.
25 For an account of the political career of Iain Macleod, who went on to become Chancellor of the Exchequer under Harold Macmillan, see Shepherd 1995.
26 See Roy Hattersley, *Guardian*, 18 June 2007. As Hattersley points out, the word 'feral' signifies not merely a savage state, but degeneration into a savage state. He argues that this is an accurate depiction of a process for which New Labour was substantially responsible.
27 *Guardian*, 18 June 2007.
28 Major 1999.
29 P. Morgan 2005.
30 Polly Toynbee, *Guardian*, 15 June 2007.
31 *The Times*, 7 July 1998.
32 Whiteley et al. 2006.
33 Kavanagh and Butler 2005: 245–46.
34 Mercer 1990.
35 Brown et al. 1997: 214.
36 It is nevertheless true that the Orange Order still flourishes in the west of Scotland and the rivalry between Scotland's two largest soccer clubs, Glasgow Rangers and Celtic, unequalled elsewhere in Britain for its intensity, is fuelled by religious animosity.
37 Scottish Election Survey 1977, quoted in Brown et al. 1997: 221.
38 Niethammer 1992: 36.
39 One of the best historical accounts of Scottish party politics is Hutchison 1986; see also Fry 1987.
40 Hutchison 1986: 207.
41 Fry 1987: 252.
42 *The Daily Telegraph*, 10 September 2007.

43 *The Guardian*, 7 December 2007.

44 At a notorious by-election in Hull North in 1966, the Labour Minister of Transport Barbara Castle suddenly announced the government's intention to build a bridge over the Humber. This beautiful construction has never managed even to service its debt. But Labour won the by-election!

45 Klingemann and Fuchs 1995: 429.

46 Klingemann and Fuchs 1995: 431.

47 *Scotland on Sunday*, 15 November 1998.

48 *The Times*, 23 January 1998.

49 Schmitt and Holmberg 1995: 123.

50 Bell 1968: 22–23.

51 Inglehart 1984.

52 Gordon Brown enlisted a number of advisers into his government who were not Labour supporters – a so-called government of all the talents. However this apparent exercise in consensus building was exposed as meaningless when Security Minister Lord West (a former Admiral of the Fleet) declared in an interview with the BBC that he had been unpersuaded of the need to extend the time in which a terrorist suspect could be held without being charged. He was promptly summoned to 10 Downing Street and in a subsequent interview two hours after the first admitted that he was indeed persuaded of the need to extend the period of detention. A perennial question in politics is: who guards the guardians – or in this case, who advises the advisers? The answer appears to be: the Prime Minister!

53 Stuart 2005: 295.

54 HM Government 1998.

55 A turnout in the mid to high 70s has been common since the Second World War. In 2001 and 2005 the turnout was 59.4% and 61.2% respectively.

56 *Daily Telegraph*, 21 May 2007.

57 *Daily Telegraph*, 16 June 2007.

58 Stoker 2006.

59 Polly Toynbee 'The Lib Dems face a clear choice', *The Guardian* 16 November 2007.

60 H.G. Wells, *Mr. Britling Sees It Through* (1916), quoted in Brown 1937: 88.

References

Abrams, M.A. and Rose, C.R. (1960) *Must Labour Lose?*, Harmondsworth: Penguin.

Ackerman, B. and Alstott, A. (1999) *The Stakeholder Society*, New Haven, CT: Yale University Press.

Adonis, A. (2004) *Roy Jenkins: A Retrospective*, Oxford: Oxford University Press.

Alderman, K. and Carter, N. (2000) 'The Liberal Democrat leadership election of 1999', *Parliamentary Affairs* 53: 311–27.

Aldine, R.B. (1929) *An Autobiography*, London: Hodder & Stoughton.

Ashdown, P. (2000) *The Ashdown Diaries*, vol. 1 (1997–99), Harmondsworth: Penguin.

Ashford, D. (1981) *Politics and Policy in Britain – The Limits of Consensus*, Oxford: Blackwell.

Aspinall, A. (1926) 'English party organisation in the early nineteenth century', *English Historical Review* 41: 389–411.

Attlee, C.R. (1937) *The Labour Party in Perspective*, London: Odhams Press.

Baker, D. and Fountain, I. (1996) 'Eton gent or Essex man?', in S. Ludlam and M.J. Smith (eds) *Contemporary British Conservatism*, London: Macmillan.

Baker, N. (1973) 'Changing attitudes towards government in eighteenth century Britain', in A. Whiteman (ed.) *Statesmen, Scholars and Merchants*, Oxford: Oxford University Press.

Ball, A.R. (1981) *British Political Parties*, London: Macmillan.

Barker, E. (1967) *Reflections on Government*, London: Oxford University Press.

Barker, R. (1971) *Studies in Opposition*, London: Macmillan.

Barker, R. (1975) 'Guild socialism revisited', *Political Quarterly* 46(3): 246–54.

Beach, M. (2006) *The Political Philosophy of New Labour*, Oxford: Blackwell.

Beer, M. (1920) *A History of British Socialism*, vol. 2, London: Bell and Sons.

Beer, S.H. (1965) *Modern British Politics*, London: Faber.

Beer, S.H. (1969) *Modern British Politics*, 2nd edn, London: Faber.

Bell, D. (1968) *The End of Ideology: On the Exhaustion of Political Ideas in the Fifties*, 2nd edn, New York: Free Press.

Benn, T. (1992) *Parliament, People and Power*, London: Verso.

Bennie, L. (2004) *Understanding Political Participation: Green Party Membership in Scotland*, Aldershot: Ashgate.

Bennie, L., Curtice, J. and Rudig, W. (1996) 'Party members', in D. MacIver (ed.) *The Liberal Democrats*, London: Prentice Hall.

Berkeley, H. (1978) *The Myth That Will Not Die*, London: Croom Helm.

Berki, R.N. (1975) *Socialism*, London: Dent.

Berrington, H.B. (1963) *Backbench Opinion in the House of Commons 1944–55*, London: Pergamon.

Blair, T. (1994) *Socialism: The Labour Party and the New Left*, Fabian Tract 565, London: Fabian Society.

Blair, T. (1995) *Let Us Face the Future*, Fabian Tract 571, London: Fabian Society.

Blake, R. (1972) *The Conservative Party from Peel to Churchill*, London: Eyre & Spottiswoode.

Blake, R. and Patten, J. (1976) *The Conservative Opportunity*, London: Macmillan.

Blumler, J. (1990) 'The modern publicity process', in M. Ferguson (ed.) *Public Communications: The New Imperatives*, London: Sage.

Brack, D. (1996) 'Liberal Democrat policy', in D. MacIver (ed.) *The Liberal Democrats*, London: Prentice Hall.

Brack, D. (2007) *Dictionary of Liberal Thought*, London: Politico's.

Brady, F. (ed.) (1968) *Boswell's Life of Johnson*, London: Signet Classics.

Brand, J. (1992) *The Power of Parliamentary Parties*, Oxford: Clarendon Press.

Brivati, B. (1999) 'Hugh Gaitskell', in K. Jefferys (ed.) *Leading Labour: From Keir Hardie to Tony Blair*, London: IB Taurus.

Brown, A., McCrone, D. and Paterson, L. (1997) *Politics and Society in Scotland*, 2nd edn, London:Macmillan.

Brown, I. (1937) *H.G. Wells*, London: Nisbett.

Burch, M. and Moran, M. (1985) 'The changing British elite', *Parliamentary Affairs*, 38(1): 1–15.

Burke, E. (1770) *Thoughts on the Cause of the Present Discontents*, London.

Butler, D. and Kavanagh, D. (1984) *The British General Election of 1983*, London: Macmillan.

Butler, D. and Kavanagh, D. (1988) *The British General Election of 1987*, London: Macmillan.

Butler, D. and Kavanagh, D. (1992) *The British General Election of 1992*, London: Macmillan.

Butler, D. and Kavanagh, D. (1997) *The British General Election of 1997*, London: Macmillan.

Butler, D. and Kavanagh, D. (2001) *The British General Election of 2001*, London: Macmillan.

Butler, D. and Pinto-Duschinsky, M. (1980) 'The Conservative elite 1918–78: Does unrepresentativeness matter?', in Z. Layton-Henry (ed.) *Conservative Party Politics*, London: Macmillan.

Butler, D. and Stokes, D. (1974) *Political Change in Britain*, 2nd edn, London: Macmillan.

Butler, R.A. (1973) *The Art of the Possible*, Harmondsworth: Penguin.

Butt Phillip, A. (1975) *The Welsh Question: Nationalism in Welsh Politics 1945–1970*, Cardiff: University of Wales Press.

Callaghan, J. (1990) *Socialism in Britain*, Oxford: Blackwell.

Callaghan, J. and Tumey, S. (2001) 'The end of social democracy?', *Politics* 21(1): 63–72.

Cannon, J. (1969) *The Fox/North Coalition*, London: Cambridge University Press.

Carroll, L. (1872) *Through the Looking Glass, and What Alice Found There*, London.

Chappelow, A. (1969) *Shaw: The Chucker Out*, London: Allen & Unwin.

Chesterton, G.K. (1917) *Return of Don Quixote*, London: Chatto & Windus.

Chrimes, S.B. (1952) 'Before 1600', in S.D. Bailey (ed.) *The British Party System*, London: Hansard Society.

Clarke, P. (1978) *Liberals and Social Democrats*, Cambridge: Cambridge University Press.

Clarke, P. (1983) 'Liberals and Social Democrats in historical perspective', in V. Bogdanor (ed.) *Liberal Party Politics*, Oxford: Oxford University Press.

Coates, D. (1975) *The Labour Party and the Struggle for Socialism*, Cambridge: Cambridge University Press.

Coates, D. and Lawler, P.A. (eds) (2000) *New Labour in Power*, Manchester: Manchester University Press.

Coates, K. and Topham, T. (1980) *Trade Unions in Britain*, Nottingham: Spokesman Press.

Cole, M. (1961) *The Story of Fabian Socialism*, London: Heinemann.

Conservative Party (2006) *Built to Last*, London: Conservative Party.

Cooke, C. (2002) *A Short History of the Liberal Party*, Basingstoke: Palgrave Macmillan.

Cornford, J. (1963) 'The transformation of Conservatism in the late nineteenth century', *Victorian Studies* 7(1): 35–66.

Coulson, A. (2005) 'The death of a mass membership party?', *Archive* 13(2–3).

Cowley, P. (1997) 'Just William? A supplementary analysis of the 1997 Conservative leadership contest', *Talking Politics* 10(1): 91–95.

Cowley, P. (2002) *Revolts and Rebellions: Parliamentary Voting under Blair*, London: Politico's.

Cowley, P. (2005) *The Rebels: How Blair Mislaid his Majority*, London: Politico's.

Cowley, P. and Norton, P. (1996) *Blair's Bastards: Discontent within the Parliamentary Labour Party*, Hull: Centre for Legislative Studies.

Cracknell, R. (2005) *Social Background of MPs*, Standard Note 1528, London: House of Commons Library.

Crewe, I. and King, A. (1995) *SDP: The Birth, Life and Death of the Social Democratic Party*, Oxford: Oxford University Press.

Crewe, I. and Sarlvik, B. (1985) 'Popular attitudes and electoral strategy', in Z. Layton-Henry (ed.) *Conservative Party Politics*, London: Macmillan.

Crewe, I., Barrington, B. and Alt, J. (1977) 'Partisan dealignment in Great Britain 1964–1974', *British Journal of Political Science* 7(2): 129–90.

Crick, M. (1994) *The History of the Social Democratic Federation*, Keele: Keele University Press.

Criddle, B. (1984) 'The election locally', in D. Butler and D. Kavanagh, *The British General Election of 1983*, London: Macmillan.

Criddle, B. and Waller, R. (1992) *Almanac of British Politics*, London: Routledge.

Critchley, J. (1992) *Some of Us: People Who Did Well under Thatcher*, London: John Murray.

Crosland, A. (1956) *The Future of Socialism*, London: Cape.

Crossman, R.H.S. (ed.) (1953) *New Fabian Essays*, London: Turnstile Press.

Crowson, N.J. (2002) 'Conservative Party activists and immigration policy from the late 1940s to the mid 1970s', in S. Ball and I. Holiday (eds) *Mass Conservatism:The Conservatives and the Public since the 1880s*, London: Frank Cass.

Curtice, J. (1996) 'Who votes for the centre now?', in D. MacIver (ed.) *The Liberal Democrats*, London: Prentice Hall.

Curtice, J. and Stead, M. (1997) 'The results analysed', in D. Butler and D. Kavanagh, *The British General Election of 1997*, London: Macmillan.

Dangerfield, G. (1966) *The Strange Death of Liberal England*, London: McGibbon & Key.

Dennis, N. and Halsey, A.H. (1988) *English Ethical Socialism*, Oxford: Oxford University Press.

Deshower, K. (2003) 'Political parties in multi-layered systems', *European Urban and Regional Studies* 10(3): 213–26.

Diamond, P. (2004) *New Labour's Old Roots*, Exeter: Imprint Academica.

Dicey, A.L. (1919) *Law and Public Opinion*, London: Macmillan.

Dickens, Charles (n.d.) The Pickwick Papers, London: Odhams Press.

Disraeli, B. (1980 [1845]) *Sybil*, Harmondsworth: Penguin.

Dodds, E. (1957) 'Liberty and welfare', in G. Watson (ed.) *The Unservile State*, London: Allen & Unwin.

Douglas, R. (2005) *Liberals: A History of the Liberal and Liberal Democratic Parties*, London: Hambledon & London.

Douglas-Home, A. (1976) *The Way the Wind Blows*, London: William Collins and Sons.

Downs, J. (1957) *An Economic Theory of Democracy*, New York: Harper.

Downs, W. (1998) *Coalition Politics, Subnational Style*, Columbus, OH: Ohio State University Press.

Drucker, H. (1979) *Multi-Party Britain*, London: Macmillan.

Epstein, L.D. (1967) *Political Parties in Western Democracies*, London: Pall Mall.

Faucher, F. (1999) 'Is there room for democratic debate at British Labour party conferences?', a paper presented to the Political Studies Association (PSA) annual conference.

Faucher-King, F. (2005) *Changing Parties: An Anthropology of British Political Party Conferences*, Basingstoke: Palgrave Macmillan.

Faucher-King, F. and Treille, E. (2003) 'Managing intra-party democracy: Comparing the French Socialist and British Labour Party conferences, *French Politics* 1(1): 61–82.

Feiling, K. (1938) *The Second Tory Party*, London: Macmillan.

Feuchtwanger, E.J. (1959) ' J.E. Gorst and the central organisation of the Conservative Party (1870–82)', *Bulletin of the Institute of Historical Research* 33.

Feuchtwanger, E.J. (1968) *Disraeli, Democracy and the Tory Party: Conservative Leadership and Organization after the Second Reform Bill*, Oxford: Clarendon Press.

Field, G.C. (1970) *Guild Socialism*, London: Well, Gardner, Dalton.

Fielding, S. (1992) 'Labourism in the 1940s', *Twentieth Century British History* 3(2): 138–53.

Finer, S.E. (1975) *Adversary Politics and Electoral Reform*, London: Wigram.

Finer, S.E., Berrington, H.B. and Bartholomew, D.J. (1961) *Backbench Opinion in the House of Commons 1955–59*, London: Pergamon.

Fisher, J. (1996a) *British Political Parties*, London: Prentice Hall.

Fisher, J. (1996b) 'Party finance', in P. Norton (ed.) *The Conservative Party*, London: Prentice Hall.

Fisher, N. (1977) *The Tory Leaders*, London: Weidenfeld & Nicolson.

Foote, G. (1997) *The Labour Party's Political Thought*, 3rd edn, London: Macmillan.

Ford, I. (1989) 'Women and Socialism', in E. Frow and R. Frow (eds) *The Politics of Hope*, Cambridge: Pluto.

Friedman, M. (1962) *Capitalism and Freedom*, Chicago, IL: University of Chicago Press.

Fry, M. (1987) *Patronage and Principle: A Political History of Modern Scotland*, Aberdeen: Aberdeen University Press.

Fukuyama, F. (1993) *The End of History and the Last Man*, London: Penguin.

Fyrth, J. (ed.) (1995) *Labour's Promised Land*, London: Lawrence & Wishart.

Gamble, A. (1974) *The Conservative Nation*, London: Routledge & Kegan Paul.

Gamble, A. (1979) 'The Conservative Party', in H.M. Drucker (ed.) *Multi-Party Britain*, London: Macmillan.

Gamble, A. (1988) *The Free Economy and the Strong State*, London: Macmillan.

Gamble, A. (1992) 'The Labour Party and economic management', in M. Smith and J. Spear (eds) *The Changing Labour Party*, London: Routledge.

Gamble, A. and Walkland, S. (1984) *The British Party System and Economic Policy 1945–83*, Oxford: Oxford University Press.

Gash, N. (1977) 'From the origins to Sir Robert Peel', in R.A. Butler (ed.) *The Conservatives*, London: Allen & Unwin.

Giddens, A. (1998a) 'The future of the welfare state', in M. Novak (ed.) *Is There a Third Way?*, London: Institute of Economic Affairs.

Giddens, A. (1998b) *The Third Way: The Renewal of Social Democracy*, Oxford: Polity Press.

Giddens, A. (ed.) (2001) *The Global Third Way Debate*, Cambridge: Polity Press.

Gilmour, I. (1969) *The Body Politic*, London: Hutchinson.

Gilmour, I. (1971) *The Body Politic*, revised edn, London: Hutchinson.

Gilmour, I. (1977) *Inside Right*, London: Hutchinson.

Gissing, G. (1886) *Demos: The Story of English Socialism*, London: Smith, Elder.

Goodhart, P. (1973) *The 1922*, London: Macmillan.

Grant, A. (2005) 'Party and election finance in Britain and America: A comparative analysis', *Parliamentary Affairs* 58(1): 71–88.

Greaves, B. and Lishman, G. (1981) *The Theory and Practice of Community Politics* (booklet), Hebden Bridge, West Yorkshire: Association of Liberal Councillors.

Greenleaf, W.H. (1983) *The British Political Tradition*, 2 volumes, London: Methuen.

Grimond, J. (1959) *The Liberal Future*, London: Faber.

Guttsman,W.J. (1963) *The British Political Elite*, London: MacGibbon & Kee.

Hall, S. (1980) 'Popular democratic versus authoritarian populism', in A. Hunt (ed.) *Marxism and Democracy*, London: Lawrence & Wishart.

Hanham, H.J. (1959) *Elections and Party Management*, London: Longmans Green.

Harrison, B. (1996) *The Transformation of British Politics 1860–1995*, Oxford: Oxford University Press.

Harrison, M. (1960) *Trade Unions and the Labour Party since 1945*, London: Allen & Unwin.

Hassan, G. (2003) *The Scottish Labour Party*, Edinburgh: Edinburgh University Press.

Haxey, S. (1939) *Tory MP*, London: Gollancz.

Hayek, F. (1979) *Law, Legislation and Liberty*, vol. 3, *The Political Order of a Free People*, London: Routledge & Kegan Paul.

Hayter, D. (2005) *Fightback!*, Manchester: Manchester University Press.

Hearnshaw, F.J.C. (ed.) (1932) *Social and Political Ideas in the Age of Reaction*, London: Harrap.

Hearnshaw, F.J.C. (1933) *Conservatism in England: An Analytical, Historical and Political Survey*, London: Macmillan.

Heath, A. and MacDonald, S. (1987) 'Socialist change and the future of the Left', *Political Quarterly* 58(4): 364–77.

Hennessy, P. (1986) *Cabinet*, Oxford: Blackwell.

Herbert, A. (1908) *The Voluntarist Creed*, London: W.J. Simpson.

Heywood, A. (1977) *Politics*, London: Macmillan.

Hill, B.W. (1976) *The Growth of Parliamentary Parties 1689–1742*, London: Allen & Unwin.

Hindness, B. (1971) *The Decline of Working Class Politics*, London: Paladin.

HM Government (1998) *The Report of the Independent Commission on the Voting System*, Cmnd 4090, London: The Stationery Office.

Hobsbawm, E. (1990) *Nations and Nationalism since 1780*, Cambridge: Cambridge University Press.

Hobson, J.A. (1909) *The Crisis of Liberalism: New Issues of Democracy*, London: King.

Hogg, Q. (1969) *The Conservative Case*, Harmondsworth: Penguin.

Holme, R. (1997) 'Sausages or policemen? The role of the Liberal Democrats in the 1997 campaign', paper to the Elections, Public Opinion and Parties (EPOP) annual conference.

Holmes, M. (1988) 'The Conservative Party and Europe: From Major to Hague', *Political Quarterly* 69(2): 133–47.

Howell, C. (1998) 'From New Labour to no Labour? The Blair government in Britain', a paper delivered to the American Political Science Association (APSA) conference, Boston, MA.

Hugh, P. (1984) *Educate, Agitate, Organise: 100 Years of Fabian Socialism*, London: Methuen.

Hughes, Thomas (1999) *Tom Brown's Schooldays*, Harmondsworth: Penguin Popular Classics.

Hume, D. (1970 [1824]) *History of Great Britain*, vol. II, Harmondsworth: Penguin.

Hunt, A. (ed.) (1980) *Marxism and Democracy*, London: Lawrence & Wishart.

Hutchison, I.G.C. (1986) *A Political History of Scotland; Parties, Elections and Issues*, Edinburgh: John Donald.

Hutton, W. (1995) *The State We're In*, London: Jonathan Cape.

Hutton, W. and Congdon, Tim (1997) *Stakeholding and its Critics*, London: Institute of Economic Affairs.

Ingle, S. (1986) 'The emergence of multi-party politics', in J. Hayward and P. Norton (eds) *The Political Science of British Politics*, Brighton: Wheatsheaf.

Ingle, S. (1987) *The British Party System*, Oxford: Basil Blackwell.

Ingle, S. (1995) 'The Liberal Democrats and equidistance', *Parliamentary Brief* 4(2).

Ingle, S. (1996) 'Party organisation', in D. MacIver (ed.) *The Liberal Democrats*, London: Prentice Hall.

Ingle, S. (2002) *Narratives of British Socialism*, Basingstoke: Palgrave Macmillan.

Ingle, S. (2006) 'The green shoots of a Conservative revival?', in M. Rush and P. Giddings (eds) *Palgrave Review of British Politics 2005*, Basingstoke: Palgrave Macmillan.

Ingle, S. (2007) 'Labour's Love Lost', in M. Rush and P. Giddings (eds) *Palgrave Review of British Politics 2006*, Basingstoke: Palgrave Macmillan.

Ingle, S. and Tether, P. (1981) *Parliament and Health Policy: The Role of the MPs 1970–75*, Farnborough: Gower.

Inglehart, R. (1984) 'The changing structure of political cleavages in western society', in R.J. Dalton, S. Flanagan and P.A. Beck (eds) *Electoral Change in Advanced Industrial Democracies: Realignment or Dealignment?*, Princeton, NJ: Princeton University Press.

James, R.R. (1978) *The British Revolution 1886–1939*, London: Methuen.

Janosik, E.G. (1968) *Constituency Labour Parties in Britain*, London: Pall Mall Press.

Jenkins, R. (1979) *Homethoughts from Abroad*, The 1979 Dimbleby Lecture, London: BFL Film and TV Database.

Jenkins, T.A. (2004) *The Liberal Ascendancy*, Basingstoke: Palgrave Macmillan.

Johnston, R.J. (1986) 'A further look at British political finance', *Political Studies* 34(3): 466–73.

Jones, B. (1995) 'Clause Four and Blair's brilliant campaign', *Talking Politics* 8(1).

Jones, P.d'A. (1968) *The Christian Socialist Revival, 1877–1914: Religion, Class, and Social Conscience in Late-Victorian England*, Princeton, NJ: Princeton University Press.

Joseph, K. (1975) *Freedom under the Law*, CPC 569, London: Conservative Political Centre.

Jowell, R., Witherspoon, S. and Brooks, L. (eds) (1988) *British Social Attitudes*, Aldershot: Gower.

Joyce, P. (1999) *Realignment of the Left? A History of the Relationship between the Liberal Democrat and Labour Parties*, London: Macmillan.

Judge, D. (1993) *The Parliamentary State*, London: Sage.

Kandinsky, W. (2006 [1911]) *Concerning the Spiritual in Art*, trans. M.T.H. Sadler, London: Tate.

Katz, R.S. and Mair, P. (1994) *How Parties Organise: Change and Adaptation in Party Organisations in Western Democracies*, London: Sage.

Kavanagh, D. (1982a) 'Representation to the Labour Party', in D. Kavanagh (ed.) *The Politics of the Labour Party*, London: Allen & Unwin.

Kavanagh, D. (1982b) 'Still the workers' party? Changing social trends in elite recruitment and electoral support', in D. Kavanagh (ed.) *The Politics of the Labour Party*, London: Allen & Unwin.

Kavanagh, D. (1983) *The Labour Party in Crisis*, London: Methuen.

Kavanagh, D. and Butler, D. (2005) *The British General Election of 2005*, Basingstoke: Palgrave Macmillan.

Keesing's UK Record: 1994 (1994) Cambridge: Circa Publications.

Kellner, P. (1998) *New Mutualism: The Third Way*, London: Co-operative Party.

Kelly, R. (1989) *Conservative Party Conferences: The Hidden System*, Manchester: Manchester University Press.

Kelly, R., Gay, O. and White, I. (2006) 'The House of Commons in 2005: Turbulence ahead?', in M. Rush and P. Giddings (eds) *Palgrave Review of British Politics 2005*, Basingstoke: Palgrave Macmillan.

Key, R. (2000) *The Green Flag: A History of Irish Nationalism*, Harmondsworth: Penguin.

Kingsley, Charles (1994) *The Water Babies*, London: Wordsworth Children's Classics.

Kinnock, N. (1986) *Making Our W*ay, Oxford: Blackwell.

Kirchheimer, O. (1966) 'The transformation of the Western party systems', in J. la Palombara and M. Weiner (eds) *Political Parties and Political Development*, Princeton, NJ: Princeton University Press.

Klingemann, H.-D. and Fuchs, D. (eds) (1995) *Citizens and the State*, Oxford: Oxford University Press.

Kruger, D. (2006) 'The right dialectic', *Prospect* September: 32–37.

Labour Party (1985) Labour Party Yearbook 1984–85, London: Wallworth Road.

Labour Party (1997) *Labour into Power: A Framework for Partnership*, London: Labour Party.

Laffin, M. (2005) *Coalition Formation and Centre–Periphery Relations in a National Political Party: The Liberal Democrats in a Devolved Britain*, London: Economic and Social Research Council.

Laffin, M. (2007) 'Comparative British central–local relations', *Public Policy and Administration* 22: 74–91.

Laski, H. (1962) *The Rise of European Liberalism*, London: Allen & Unwin.

Leach, R. (1996) *British Political Ideologies*, London: Prentice Hall.

Lenin, V.I. (1999 [1916]) *Imperialism: The Highest Stage of Capitalism*, London: Resistance Books.

Leopold, J. (1997) 'Trade unions, political fund ballots and the Labour party', *British Journal of Industrial Relations* 35(1): 23–38.

Letwin, S.R. (1992) *The Anatomy of Thatcherism*, London: Fontana.

Lewis, J. (1992) *Labour's Constitutional Crisis*, London: Conservative Political Centre.

Liberal Democrats (1993) *The Constitution of the Liberal Democrats: The Federal Party*, Dorchester: Liberal Democrat Publications.

Lijphart, A. (1984) *Democracies, Patterns of Majoritarian and Consensus Government in Twenty-One Countries*, New Haven, CT: Yale University Press.

Luard, E. (1979) *Socialism without the State*, London: Macmillan.

Lyman, R.W. (1957) *The First Labour Government, 1924*, London: Chapman and Hall.

Lynch, P. (1998) 'Preparing for devolution: The Scottish Conservatives after the 1997 electoral wipeout', *Regional Studies* 32(2): 1–14.

Lynch, P. (2002) *The History of the Scottish National Party*, Cardiff: Welsh Academic Press.

Lynch, P. (2003) 'The Scottish Conservatives, 1997–2001: From disaster to devolution and beyond', in M. Garnett and P. Lynch (eds) *The Conservatives in Crisis*, Manchester: Manchester University Press.

Lynch, P. (2006) 'The Scottish National Party: The long road from marginality to blackmail and coalition potential', in L. De Winter, M. Gómez-Reino and P. Lynch (eds) *Autonomist Parties in Europe: Identity Politics and the Revival of the Territorial Cleavage*, Barcelona: Institut de Ciènces Politiques i Socials.

McAllister, L. (2000) 'The new politics in Wales: Rhetoric or reality?', *Parliamentary Affairs* 53(3): 591–604.

Macaulay, T.B. (1861) *History of England*, New York: Harper and Brothers.

McCallum, R.B. and Readman, A. (1947) *The British General Election of 1945*, London: Macmillan.

Mackenzie, N. and Mackenzie, J. (1977) *The First Fabians*, London: Weidenfeld & Nicolson.

McKenzie, R.T. (1955) *British Political Parties*, London: Heinemann.

McKenzie, R.T. (1982) 'Power in the party: Intra party democracy', in D. Kavanagh (ed.) *The Politics of the Labour Party*, London: Allen & Unwin.

McKenzie, R.T. and Silver, A. (1968) *Angels in Marble*, London: Heinemann.

McKibbins, R. (1977) *The Evolution of the Labour Party 1916–24*, London: Oxford University Press.

Madison, J. (1941) *The Federalist*, New York: Modern Library.

Mair, P. (1997) *Party Systems Change: Approaches and Interpretations*, Oxford: Oxford University Press.

Major, J. (1999) *Autobiography*, London: HarperCollins.

Mandelson, P. and Liddle, R. (1996) *The Blair Revolution*, London: Faber & Faber.

Maor, M. (1997) *Political Parties and Party Systems*, London: Routledge.

Marquand, D. (1989) *Our Different Vision*, Federal Green Paper 17, Hebden Bridge, West Yorkshire: Hebden Royd Publications.

Marquand, D. (1998) 'The Blair paradox', *Prospect* May: 19–24.

Marriott, W.T. (1882) 'The Birmingham Caucus', *Nineteenth Century* 11: 946–63.

Marshall, P. and Laws, D. (eds) (2004) *The Orange Book: Reclaiming Liberalism*, London: Profile Books.

Martin, R.B. (1906) 'The electoral "Swing of the pendulum"', *Journal of the Royal Statistical Society* 69(4): 655–707.

Marx, Karl (1964) *The German Ideology*, Moscow: Progress Publishers.

Maude, A. (1963) 'Party palaeontology', *Spectator*, 15 March.

Maurice, F.D. (1988) *The Kingdom of Heaven*, London: Macmillan.

Meadowcroft, M. (1981) *Liberal Values for a New Decade*, Manchester: North West Community Papers.

Mellors, C. (1978) *The British M.P.*, Farnborough: Saxon House.

Mercer, K. (1990) '"Welcome to the jungle": Identity and diversity in post-modern politics', in J. Rutherford (ed.) *Identity, Community, Culture and Difference*, London: Lawrence & Wishart.

Miliband, R. (1972) *Parliamentary Socialism*, London: Merlin.

Minkin, L. (1987) *The Labour Party Conference*, London: Allen Lane.

Minkin, L. (1991) *The Contentious Alliance*, Edinburgh: Edinburgh University Press.

Mitchell, A. (1984) *Four Years in the Death of the Labour Party*, London: Methuen.

Morgan, K. (1981) *Rebirth of a Nation: A History of Modern Wales*, Oxford: Oxford University Press.

Morgan, K. (1999) 'James Callaghan', in K. Jefferys (ed.) *Leading Labour: From Keir Hardie to Tony Blair*, London: IB Taurus.

Morgan, P. (2005) *The Insider*, London: Ebury Press.

Morris, W. (1973a) *A Dream of John Ball*, in A.L. Morton (ed.) *Three Works by William Morris*, London: Lawrence & Wishart.

Morris, W. (1973b) *News from Nowhere*, in A.L. Morton (ed.) *Three Works by William Morris*, London: Lawrence & Wishart.

Morton, A.L. (ed.) (1973) *The Political Writings of William Morris*, London: Lawrence & Wishart.

Namier, L. (1962) *Crossroads of Power: Essays on Eighteenth Century England*, London: Hamilton.

National Union of Conservative and Constitutional Associations (1941) *Report of the Central Committee on Post-war Reconstruction*, London: Conservative Party.

National Union of Conservative and Unionist Associations (1949) *Interim and Final Report of the Committee on Party Organisation*, London: Conservative Party.

Niethammer, L. (1992) *Has History Come to an End?*, London: Verso.

Norris, P. (1999) 'New Labour, new politicians?', in G. Evans and P. Norris (eds) *A Critical Election: British Parties and Voters in Long-Term Perspective*, London: Sage.

Norton, P. (1975) *Dissension in the House of Commons 1945–74*, London: Macmillan.

Norton, P. (1980) *Dissension in the House of Commons 1974–79*, Oxford: Oxford University Press.

Norton, P. (1993) *Does Parliament Matter?*, Brighton: Harvester Wheatsheaf.

Norton, P. (ed.) (1996) *The Conservative Party*, London: Prentice Hall.

Norton, P. (1998) 'The Conservative Party: "In office but not in power"', in A. King et al., *New Labour Triumphs: Britain at the Polls*, Chatham, NJ: Chatham House.

Norton, P. and Aughey, A. (1981) *Conservatives and Conservatism*, London: Temple Smith.

O'Gorman, F. (1975) *The Rise of Party in England 1760–82*, London: Allen & Unwin.

O'Gorman, F. (1982) *The Emergence of the British Two-Party System*, London: Edward Arnold.

Olson, M. (1986) 'A theory of the incentives facing political organizations: Neo-corporatism and the hegemonist state', *International Political Science Review* 7(2): 165–89.

Orwell, G. (1963) *The Road to Wigan Pier*, Harmondsworth: Penguin.

Ostrogorski, M. (1902) *Democracy and the Organization of Political Parties*, London: Macmillan.

O'Sullivan, N.K. (1976) *Conservatism*, London: Dent.

Owen, D. (1981) *Face the Future*, London: Cape.

Parsons, G. (1988) *Religion in Victorian England*, Manchester: Manchester University Press.

Pelling, H. (1987) *A History of British Trade Unionism*, Harmondsworth: Penguin.

Pinto-Duschinsky, M. (1972) 'Central Office and "power" in the Conservative Party', *Political Studies* 20(1): 1–16.

Pinto-Duschinsky, M. (1981) *British Political Finance 1830–1980*, London: American Enterprise Institute.

Plant, R. (2004) 'Political thought: Socialism in a cold climate', in A. Seldon and K. Hickson (eds) *New Labour, Old Labour: The Wilson and Callaghan Governments 1974–1979*, London: Routledge.

Plant, R., Beach, M. and Hickson, K. (2004) *The Struggle for Labour's Soul; Understanding Labour's Political Thought since 1945*, London: Routledge.

Pliatsky, L. (1980) 'Ministers and officials', *London Review of Books* 10 (July).

Plucknett, T.F.T. (1946) *Taswell Langmead's Constitutional History*, 10th edn, London: Sweet & Maxwell.

Powell, A.W. (2003) *Clement Davies: A Liberal Leader*, London: Methuen.

Powell, E. (1968) 'Conservatism and social problems', *Swinton Journal*, Autumn.

Pugh, M.J. (1982) *The Making of Modern British Politics 1879–1939*, Oxford: Blackwell.

Quinton, A. (1978) *The Politics of Imperfection*, London: Faber & Faber.

Radice, G. and Pollard, S. (1993) *More Southern Discomfort*, London: Fabian Society.

Rae, W.F. (1878) 'Political clubs and party organisation', *Nineteenth Century* 3: 908–32.

Ramsden, J. (1980) *The Making of Conservative Party Policy*, London: Longman.

Ramsden, J. (1988) *An Appetite for Power*, London: HarperCollins.

Rasmussen, J. (1979) 'Was Guy Fawkes right?', in I. Kramnick (ed.) *Is Britain Dying?*, London: Cornell University Press.

Rawls, J. (1971) *A Theory of Justice*, Cambridge, MA: Belknap Press.

Robb, J.H. (1942) *Primrose League, 1883–1906*, New York: Columbia University Press.

Roberts, G.K. (1970) *Political Parties and Pressure Groups in Britain*, London: Weidenfeld & Nicolson.

Roberts, K., Cook, F. and Semeonoff, P. (1977) *The Fragmentary Class Structure*, London: Heinemann.

Rodgers, W. (1981) *The Politics of Change*, London: Secker & Warburg.

Rose, R. (1965) *Politics in England*, London: Faber.

Rose, R. (1976a) *The Problem of Party Government*, London: Pelican.

Rose, R. (1976b) 'Voting behaviour in Britain 1945–74', in R. Rose (ed.) *Studies in British Politics*, 3rd edn, London: Macmillan.

Rose, R. (1984) *Do Parties Make a Difference?*, 2nd edn, London: Macmillan.

Ross, J.F.S. (1948) *Parliamentary Representation*, London: Eyre & Spottiswood.

Roth, A. (1984) *Parliamentary Profiles*, London: Parliamentary Profile Services.

Rush, M. (1986) 'The selectorate revisited: Selecting party candidates in the 1980s', *Teaching Politics* 15(1): 99–114.

Russell, A.T. and Fieldhouse, E. (2005) *Neither Left nor Right? The Liberal Democrats and the Electorate*, Manchester: Manchester University Press.

Russell, M. and Sciara, M. (2007) 'Parliament: The House of Lords – Negotiating a strong second chamber', in M. Rush and P. Giddings (eds) *The Palgrave Review of British Politics 2006*, Basingstoke: Palgrave Macmillan.

Sampson, A. (1968) *Macmillan: A Study in Ambiguity*, Harmondsworth: Penguin.

Sartori, G. (1976) *Parties and Party Systems: A Framework for Analysis*, Cambridge: Cambridge University Press.

Saville, J. (1973) 'The ideology of labourism', in R. Benewick, R.N. Berki and B. Parekh (eds) *Knowledge and Belief in Politics*, London: Allen & Unwin.

Schmitt, H. and Holmberg, S. (1995) 'Political parties in decline?', in H.-D. Klingemann and D. Fuchs (eds) *Citizens and the State*, Oxford: Oxford University Press.

Schoen, D.E. (1977) *Enoch Powell and the Powellites*, London: Macmillan.

Schumann, H.G. (1978) 'The problem of Conservatism', *Journal of Contemporary History* 13(4): 803–17.

Schumpeter, J. (1976) *Capitalism, Socialism and Democracy*, London: Allen & Unwin.

Scott, R. (1996) *Report of the Inquiry into the Export of Defence Equipment and Dual-Use Goods to Iraq and Related Questions*, Scott Report, HC 15, London: HMSO.

Scruton, R. (1980) *The Meaning of Conservatism*, Harmondsworth: Penguin.

Scruton, R. (ed.) (1988) *Conservative Thinkers*, London: Claridge Press.

Seldon, A. (1996) *How Tory Governments Fall*, London: Fontana.

Seldon, A. (2004) *Blair*, London: Free Press.

Seldon, A. and Hickson, K. (eds) (2004) *New Labour, Old Labour: The Wilson and Callaghan Governments 1974–1979*, London: Routledge.

Seldon, A. and Kavanagh, D. (2002) *The Blair Effect 2001–5*, Cambridge: Cambridge University Press.

Seyd, P. (1987) *The Rise and Fall of the Labour Left*, London: Macmillan.

Seyd, P. (1999) 'New parties, new politics? A case study of the British Labour Party', *Party Politics* 5(3): 383–405.

Seyd, P. and Whiteley, P. (1992) *Labour's Grass Roots*, Oxford: Oxford University Press.

Shaw, E. (1990) 'A better way to make policy', *New Socialist*, December 1989-January 1990: 30–33.

Shaw, E. (1994) *The Labour Party since 1979*, London: Routledge.

Shaw, E. (1996) *The Labour Party since 1945*, Oxford: Blackwell.

Shaw, E. (1998) 'The determinants of the programmatic transformation of the British Labour Party', a paper given at the American Political Science Association (APSA) conference in Boston, MA.

Shaw, E. (1999) 'Michael Foot', in K. Jefferys (ed.) *Leading Labour: From Keir Hardie to Tony Blair*, London: IB Taurus.

Shaw, G.B. (1906) *Man and Superman: A Comedy and a Philosophy*, London: Constable.

Shaw, G.B. (1930) Preface to *The Apple Cart*, London: Constable.

Shaw, G.B. (1932) *Essays in Fabian Socialism*, London: Constable.

Shaw, G.B. (1960) *Major Barbara*, Harmondsworth: Penguin.

Shell, D. and Beamish, D. (1993) *The House of Lords at Work*, Oxford: Oxford University Press.

Shepherd, R. (1995) *Iain Macleod: A Biography*, London: Pimlico.

Shore, P. (1993) *Leading the Left*, London: Weidenfeld & Nicolson.

Simon, S. (2006) 'New Labour odysssey', *Prospect* October: 22–26.

Skidelsky, R. (2002) 'Five years Labour', *Prospect* May: 22–26.

Smith, P. (1967) *Disraelian Conservatism and Social Reform*, London: Routledge & Kegan Paul.

Smith, P. (2000) 'The iron law of malarkey', *Representation* 37(1): 60–64.

Stephen, L. (1867) 'On the choice of representatives by popular constituencies', in *Essays on Reform*, London: Classics.

Stevenson, J. (1996) 'Liberals to Liberal Democrats', in D. MacIver (ed.) *The Liberal Democrats*, London: Prentice Hall.

Stoker, G. (2006) *Why Politics Matters: Making Democracy Work*, Basingstoke: Palgrave Macmillan.

Strachey, J. (1953) 'Tasks and achievements of British Labour', in R.H.S. Crossman (ed.) *New Fabian Essays*, London: Turnstile Press.

Strom, K. (1984) 'Minority governments in parliamentary democracies', *Comparative Political Studies* 17(2): 199–227.

Strom, K. (1990) *Minority Governments and Majority Rule*, Cambridge: Cambridge University Press.

Stuart, M. (2005) *John Smith: A Life*, London: Politico's.

Studlar, D.T. (1984) 'By-elections and the Liberal/SDP Alliance', *Teaching Politics* 13(1): 84–95.

Studlar, D.T. (2003) 'The Anglo-American origin and international diffusion of the "Third Way"', *Parties and Policy* 31(1): 26–52.

Sutton Trust (2005) *The Educational Background of Members of the House of Commons and House of Lords*, London: The Sutton Trust.

Sykes, A. (2005) *The Radical Right in Britain: From Social Imperialism to the British National Party*, Basingstoke: Palgrave Macmillan.

Taylor, B. (2002) *Scotland's Parliament: Triumph and Disaster*, Edinburgh: Edinburgh University Press.

Taylor, M. (2001) 'Party democracy and civic renewal', *Political Quarterly*, special issue.

Taylor, P. (1997) *Provos: The IRA and Sinn Féin*, London: Bloomsbury.

Tether, P. (1980) 'Kingston upon Hull Conservative party: A case study of a Tory party in decline', *Hull Papers in Politics* 19, Politics Department, University of Hull.

Tether, P. (1988) 'Conservative clubs: A neglected aspect in Conservative organisation', *Hull Papers in Politics* 42, Politics Department, University of Hull.

Tether, P. (1990) 'Conservative Clubs', PhD thesis, University of Hull.

Tether, P. (1996a) 'Members and organisation', in P. Norton (ed.) *The Conservative Party*, London: Prentice Hall.

Tether, P. (1996b) 'The Party in the country: Development and influence', in P. Norton (ed.) *The Conservative Party*, London: Prentice Hall.

Thatcher, M. (1968) *What's Wrong with Politics?*, CPC 419, London: Conservative Political Centre.

Thomas, D. (1984) 'The New Tories', *New Society*, 2 February.

Thomas, I.B. (1953) *The Party System in Great Britain*, London: Phoenix House.

Thompson, L. (1952) *Portrait of England: News from Somewhere*, London: Gollancz.

Tory Reform Committee (1943) *Forward – By the Right*, London: Conservative Party.

Tressell, R. (1965) *The Ragged Trousered Philanthropists*, St Albans: Panther.

Trollope, Anthony (1996) London: The Folio Society.

Turner, J.E. (1978) *Labour's Doorstop Politics in London*, London: Macmillan.

Uttley, T.E. (1978) 'The significance of Mrs Thatcher', in M. Cowling (ed.) *Conservative Essays*, London: Cassell.

Van Morgan, S.A. (2006) 'Plaid Cymru – The party of Wales: The new politics of Welsh Nationalism at the dawn of the 21st century', in L. De Winter, M. Gómez-Reino and P. Lynch (eds) *Autonomist Parties in Europe: Identity Politics and the Revival of the Territorial Cleavage*, Barcelona: Institut de Ciènces Politiques i Socials.

Voltaire (1931) *Lettres sur les Anglais*, New York: Macmillan.

Wagar,W. (ed.) (1965) *H.G. Wells: Journalism and Prophecy*, London: Bodley Head.

Walker, D. (2003) *The Strange Rebirth of Liberal England*, London: Methuen.

Walker, P. (1977) *Ascent of Britain*, London: Sidgwick & Jackson.

Ward, J.T. (1974) 'Derby and Disraeli', in D. Southgate (ed.) *Conservative Leadership 1832–1932*, London: Macmillan.

Ware, A. (1996) *Political Parties and Party Systems*, Oxford: Oxford University Press.

Webb, S. and Webb, B. (1935) *Soviet Communism: A New Civilisation?*, London: Longman Green.

Wells, H.G. (1916) *Mr. Britling Sees It Through*, London: Cassell.

Wells, H.G. (1970) *The New Machiavelli*, Harmondsworth: Penguin.

White, R.J. (1950) *The Conservative Tradition*, London: Nicholas Kaye.

Whiteley, P. (1982) 'Declining local membership and electoral support', in D. Kavanagh (ed.) *The Politics of the Labour Party*, London: Allen & Unwin.

Whiteley, P., Seyd, P. and Richardson, J. (1994) *True Blues: The Politics of Conservative Party Membership*, Oxford: Oxford University Press.

Whiteley, P., Seyd, P. and Billinghurst, A. (2006) *Third Force Politics: Liberal Democrats at the Grassroots*, Oxford: Oxford University Press.

Wickam-Jones, M. (1996) *Economic Strategy and the Labour Party*, London: Macmillan.

Wiener, M. (1981) *English Culture and the Decline of the Industrial Spirit: 1850–1980*, Cambridge: Cambridge University Press.

Wilkinson, A. (1998) *Christian Socialism: Scott Holland to Tony Blair*, London: SCP Press.

Wilks, S. (1997) 'Conservative governments and the economy', *Political Studies* 45(4): 689–703.

Willetts, D. (1998) 'Conservative renewal', *Political Quarterly* 69(2): 110–18.

Willetts, D. (2003) 'The Conservatives in Opposition', *Conservative History Journal* 1(1): 21–24.

Williams, F. (1961) *A Prime Minister Remembers*, London: Heinemann.

Williams, P.M. (1979) *Hugh Gaitskell: A Political Biography*, London: Cape.

Williams, P.M. (1982) 'Changing styles of Labour leadership', in D. Kavanagh (ed.) *The Politics of the Labour Party*, London: Allen & Unwin.

Williams, S. (1981) *Politics is for People*, Harmondsworth: Penguin.

Williamson, H.R. (1952) 'The seventeenth century', in S.D. Bailey (ed.) *The British Party System*, London: Hansard Society.

Wright, A. (1983) *British Socialism*, London: Longman.

Wright, A. (1987) *R.H. Tawney*, Manchester: Manchester University Press.

Wyn Jones, R., Tristan, D. and Heath, A. (2001) 'Welsh election study', in Wyn Jones, R. and Heath, A. *Wales Life and Times Study*, London: National Centre for Social Research.

Young, J.W. and Fielding, S. (2003) *The Labour Governments 1964–70*, Manchester: Manchester University Press.

Index